PRAISE FOR

ICE TIME

"A nifty hat trick. [Atkinson] not only chronicles his old team's return to semi-glory, he also forges a three-generation link among his dead father, himself, and his five-year-old son who's just learning to skate, and he proves that you can go home again—if you bring along your goalie pads." —*Boston Globe*

"It's a memorable journey, part reportage, part memoir, all heart. It's also a book about hockey culture, everything from the early morning skates, to the bus rides, to the cramped locker rooms, to the bonds that last a lifetime. Atkinson knows it all."

—Bill Reynolds, *Providence Journal*

"Atkinson offers affecting elegies to small-town life. Admirably modest, blue-collar, and Northern to the core, *Ice Time* may make you long for snow before Thanksgiving, and ice on the lakes."

—*New York Times Book Review*

"H. G. Bissinger wrote the definitive high school football retrospective with 1990's *Friday Night Lights*. Bill Reynolds chronicled Chris Herron's high school basketball career in the critically acclaimed *Fall River Dreams*. That leaves high school baseball and hockey as sports waiting to be immortalized in the literary canon. It's time to cross hockey off the list." —*Eagle Tribune*

"Until now, *The Game* by Ken Dryden pretty much stood alone in the annals of great hockey writing. Finally, stiff competition comes from New England author Atkinson, whose yearlong study of the high school hockey squad from his alma mater is a bona-fide masterstroke." —*Publishers Weekly* (starred review)

"Anyone who has played a high-school sport will appreciate Atkinson's portrayal of the Rangers' cabalistic world. . . . A sensitive and beautiful book." —*Boston Phoenix*

"The more I read of *Ice Time*, the more I was hooked. Far more than just a chronicle of a high school hockey season, Jay Atkinson's book is an evocative, bittersweet, poetic journey of a grown man trying, as we all try, not to recapture youth but to remember the splendor of it." —H. G. Bissinger, author of *Friday Night Lights*

"Atkinson is an unabashed proponent of the way life is lived and hockey is played in the small towns of New England."
—*Capital Times* (Madison, WI)

"With a style at turns wistful and profound, Atkinson observes the timeless passion of the players and the game." —*Boston* magazine

"This is definitely a 'guy' book, one that any would-be or any weekend warrior will appreciate, especially hockey players. But it also would make a good gift for the woman who lives with such a man, and has trouble understanding what force compels a 45-year-old man to leave his warm house at 11:30 on a winter night and drive twenty miles to skate in some smelly rink." —*Buffalo News*

"[Atkinson] seamlessly weaves his past with current events, detailing the team's fortunes while lovingly recalling his own at that time of life." —*Virginian-Pilot*

"*Ice Time* is a great read for anyone who savors emotionally charged writing, descriptive detail, and compelling, behind-the-scenes stories."
—*Lowell* (Massachusetts) *Sun*

"Following a young team's single season, [*Ice Time*] is an emotionally charged, heart-warming tale of personal triumphs, both on and off the ice, of friendship, loyalty, perseverance, and dedicated parents."
—*Library Journal*

"An artful class portrait of a town seen through the lens of a game, a tight-throated personal journey back into youth and a keen description of the life force that hockey can be."
—*Kirkus Reviews*

"In this affecting memoir, [Atkinson] recalls his own hockey-playing experiences (especially his late father's 'Attaboy, Jay' cheers, which echoed through nearly empty rinks) and attempts to evaluate the father he's been and will be for his young son."
—*Booklist*

"Jay Atkinson, in only his second book, has taken himself over the top. For those who have played a sport, and—curiously—for those who never have, this ice-smooth prose will resonate in memory for a long time. About the prose: For the most part, it is quiet, but there is a subtext that renders father–son love and the hard price of victory, as well as the equally hard price of defeat. Somewhere in this book, you will find your heart joyously broken."
—Harry Crews, author of *A Childhood: The Biography of a Place*

A Tale of Fathers, Sons, and Hometown Heroes

•JAY ATKINSON•

THREE RIVERS PRESS

NEW YORK

Published by Three Rivers Press, New York, New York.
Member of the Crown Publishing Group, a division of Random House, Inc.
www.randomhouse.com

Originally published in slightly different form in hardcover by Crown Publishers in 2001.

Printed in the United States of America

Design by Susan Maksuta

Library of Congress Cataloging-in-Publication Data
Atkinson, Jay, 1957–
Ice time / by Jay Atkinson.
1. Hockey—Massachusetts—Methuen. 2. School sports—Massachusetts—Methuen.
3. Atkinson, Jay, 1957– 4. Methuen High School (Methuen, Mass.)—Hockey.
I. Title.
GV848.4.U6 A85 2001
796.962'62'097445—dc21 00-065968

ISBN 0-609-80994-6

10 9 8 7 6 5 4

First Paperback Edition

For the friends of my youth

"You don't have to be a seasoned tactician
to realize that your ass is cold."

—Michael Herr, *Dispatches*

Contents

ICE TIME

FOREWORD

"1968"

I HAD TWO UPBRINGINGS. Coming of age in Methuen, Massachusetts, a small, bowtie-shaped community on the New Hampshire border, my buddies and I went to public school, attended Mass on Sundays, and joined a benign paramilitary organization known as the Cub Scouts. For fun, sometimes we threw rocks at cars or rode around on our Stingray bicycles, singing "Hey, hey, we're the Monkees!" Among the densely packed three deckers, in a neighborhood bounded by asphalt, we played football and baseball on the street, sewer cap to sewer cap. As far as we knew, this was life.

In the summer of 1968 just after I turned 11, my father got a new job and we moved across town to Central Street: larger, more well-appointed homes, vast lawns that doubled as playing fields, and within a half-mile radius, two small ponds and a tree-lined swamp. When the leaves fell off the trees and November passed into December, the swamp froze over, and I was introduced to a different world from the one I had known. Here the sport of choice was ice hockey (and when the ponds melted, street hockey). Dad bought me a pair of skates and a straight-bladed Victoriaville stick. I was in business.

But what sets hockey apart from sports like football and baseball is that you can't simply go out there and play. Of course you're welcome to try, in the sense that, theoretically, you can climb into the family jalopy and enter the Indy 500. It's just that your chances of being competitive are pretty slim. To excel at hockey—to sail over the ice throwing body checks, dodging your opponents, and blasting the puck into the net—you have to first master the rudiments of skating. An odd and esoteric skill, perhaps, but one that's completely necessary.

Most of the kids in my new neighborhood had been skating for two or three years, and some had been lacing up the blades even longer than that. They swooped across Lynch's swamp in graceful arcs, like they had a special dispensation to reduce gravity. Eventually I gained the courage to join them, wobbling around in a little half-circle as players from both teams whizzed past on either side. But there was something strangely invigorating about all that cold clear air, and the echo of sticks and pucks against the snow-padded hillside.

One night a certain kid failed to show up, and they asked me to play goalie. At the end of the swamp closest to the streetlight, there was a "net" that someone had knocked together from two-by-fours and rusty chicken wire. I was handed a pair of battered sofa cushions for leg pads and an old catcher's mask and first baseman's mitt, and directed into the crease. The game began and one of the players on the other team streaked toward me. He rifled a shot on goal, and I came sliding out and knocked it aside. My teammates cheered, as the loose puck was gathered up and they all went zooming the other way. Using the blade of my stick, I cleared ice shavings from in front of the net, like an old pro. In that instant, I discovered my passion for the sport.

As I worked on my skating and played hockey for hours at a time, I found my knack for the game increasing. We played every day after school and I would clomp home from the swamp wearing rubber guards over my blades, and my mother would spread newspapers under the kitchen table so I could have dinner without untying my skates. Then afterward, I would go back out and play another game in the moonlight. Once you get the hang of it, hockey is a fantastic, leg-burning workout, the puck zinging up and down like a giant game of pinball. You receive a special kind of thrill from making a velvety pass, or blasting an accurate shot on the fly. And there's nothing like the quick geometry of a carom that goes from the blade of your stick into the back of the net.

From Lynch's swamp we moved on to the dank, cavernous rinks of the North Shore, huge, corrugated-metal sheds that resembled airplane hangars. By the age of 13, I was one of the goalies for a team called the Methuen Flyers, in a men's league where most of the players drove cars spray-painted "Colt-45" and drank beer and smoked cigarettes in the locker room. There were bloody fights on the ice, in the stands, and outside in the parking lot. The games were usually played after midnight and I was scared to death, but my pals and I were hockey fanatics. Several nights a week, we'd gather in someone's living room to watch the Boston Bruins slug it out with other NHL teams on Channel 38. Urged along by the Bruins' popularity, we became the first generation of Methuen rink rats.

Unlikely as it may sound, the explosion of hockey in towns like Methuen can be traced to a particular moment. In what has been called the most famous hockey photograph ever taken, 22-year-old Bruins' sensation Bobby Orr is depicted scoring the winning goal against St. Louis in the 1970 Stanley Cup Finals. Half a second after being tripped by St. Louis Blues defenseman Noel Picard, Orr was captured flying through the air, his stick raised, mouth curved into an exultant ovoid. Many New Englanders remember that image the way they recall where they were the day Jack Kennedy was assassinated. More than any other single moment in the history of sport, Bobby Orr's goal led the way into hockey for a massive army of players and fans. If Helen of Troy's face launched a thousand ships, Orr's feat gave birth to half a million shin pads and twice as many bumps and bruises.

In November 1974, I was a senior when Methuen High School announced the formation of its very first varsity hockey squad. Coach Bruce Parker's tryouts, which were grueling and lasted a week, attracted twice the number of players who would make the team. (There were ten goalies vying for what turned out to be four spots—including my childhood rival, Mike Lebel, an agile six-footer with blazing red hair.) During the initial practice, I finished last in a long, lung-searing drill and while I leaned against the boards, gasping and sputtering, Coach Parker, a noted disciplinarian, boomed out, "Welcome to high school hockey, Mr. Atkinson." Being singled out was embarrassing, but it also gave me hope: the coach knew my name and was charting my progress, however meager.

On Friday afternoon, the roster was posted on the door to the Athletic Department office. Running up to examine it, some kids whooped and cheered, and others turned away with drooping faces or kicked at the wall in disgust. When I finally approached and saw my name next to the number 28 that I had been assigned to wear, it was one of the happiest moments of my life. (Almost a third of the varsity came from our little neighborhood; Mike Lebel and some of the rest came from the west end of town, and Hank Marrone and Ronnie DiCenso and the other Italian kids lived in the east end.) Twenty hockey players would wear Ranger jerseys for the first time—and I was one of them.

My memories of that season are indelible. Methuen's new high school and rink were still under construction, and that first year—my only year, since I was a senior—training was held before school in the morning. In darkness we rode a silent, chilly bus from our locker room beside the football stadium to the rink at Brooks School in North Andover. By 5 A.M., we were on the ice for practices that turned some kids' stomachs inside out. (The basketball and wrestling teams practiced at 2:30 P.M. in the high school gym, a comparatively luxurious arrangement.) But these sacrifices made the hockey team an elite group, and the envy of many of our classmates.

We only won five games out of twenty-one in 1974–75 and my ice time was limited, since I wouldn't be returning the next year. But I can't think of that season without thinking of my father, Jim Atkinson. Over the course of my career, he spent as much time in rinks as I did, although he never played hockey and didn't have an athletic bone in his body. My dad was a big, bearded man with a funny, toe-stabbing way of walking, flat-footed as a duck, the kind of guy who wore linen suits and drank vodka-cranberry year-round. A little too short for his weight, too loud on the telephone; nearsighted, flatulent in the evenings, but calm, principled, punctual, and true. Rushing in the dark to various rinks and back home again, we used to talk about hockey, about how I was doing in school, my girlfriend, a little bit of everything. In fact, when I started to get into trouble as a teenager and my father nearly kicked me out of the house, riding to hockey games together was about the only time we did talk. I understand now that Jim Atkinson came to love those crummy old rinks because they allowed him to stay close to me. He was a pretty smart guy that way.

I picture my dad in the bleachers, wearing the blue-plaid Nova Scotia tam he always brought to my games. It's the very early hours of the morning—there's nobody in the rink except the players and a few parents—and he's sitting there blowing on the hot edge of his tea and watching us limber up. The referee floats out from the timekeeper's box, the game starts, and the players go charging back and forth. Suddenly the other team races into our zone and somebody cranks up a shot. I jab at the air, the puck goes *thwack* into my catching glove and from the shadowy region beyond the glass, I hear, "Way to go, Jay." It was always good to have him there: my witness.

My old man died in the summer of 1983. He was buried on the Fourth of July, a bright, temperate, almost iridescent day, the kind of day when we were young my father would pile us all into the car for a drive to the beach. I got home just as the afternoon began to lose its hard currency and the stubbled lawns were diffused into particles with the passing of daylight into dusk. The bigger houses along the street, set back and framed with hedges, were still. On either side, giant shade trees doubled in the shadows and left the substance of everything in doubt except the single white line that ran down the center of the road. Somewhere over the housetops a band was playing, drumbeats rattling over the shingles and dormers. Less than a mile away, at Nicholson Stadium, the fireworks began as small, shivering lines of red, whistling up into the night sky.

The windowpanes shook all along the porchfront. Then there was a long sputtering trail of sparks and boom—*See ya, Dad.* See you after midnight, loading up our old station wagon with my goalie stick and pads. See you outside the locker room, winking at me as the players clack over the rubber mats and dart onto the ice. See you in the lobby of all those seedy rinks, jangling your car keys and stamping your feet, no good reason to be freezing your ass off at 2:30 in the morning. No reason at all, except for me.

Today, I have a 5-year-old son named Liam who's been playing hockey since before he could walk, with an upturned laundry basket as the net and a spatula for a stick. Liam is a little over three feet tall, with hair a dirty gold color and earnest brown eyes, a snub nose, and full lips. His closet is already packed with various hockey jerseys, and he sleeps beneath a framed photograph of Bobby Orr, in the home whites of the Boston Bruins, his hair a-flutter as he soars up ice. Around here, Orr is the alpha and the omega as far as hockey players go. And although he hasn't played in more than twenty years, the former Bruins' defenseman is my son's hero. An apparition on grainy old videotape, Bobby Orr is just the sort of mythic figure a boy should look up to. He was a superior presence on the ice, no scandal ever tainted his career, and my mother loved him—in that maternal way that icons should be loved.

Once or twice a week, Liam and I turn up for public skating at Methuen High School, cruising in a giant circle while kids of all ages go waltzing past. Three years ago, Liam started out on double-runners, pushing a milk crate around the ice, and soon could glide around the rink unassisted. But his skating prowess aside, it's in the breezeway at home where my son's immersion in the sport has really taken place. After supper most evenings, we carry out the net and plastic sticks and Liam dons an array of miniature equipment. Each game begins with the lights turned down and the singing of the national anthem. I'm the goalie, the referee, and the play-by-play announcer, but Liam's the star.

Lately I notice that my son's technique is improving, and it won't be long until I have to make an effort to compete with him—first a small one, then more and more, until soon enough, no amount of whirling and scrambling on my part will be sufficient. Because, of course, as Liam discovers his game, I'll lose mine. I still play hockey a few times a week during the winter and stay in pretty good shape year-round, but I'm 42 years old and feel my love of hockey being threatened by life's responsibilities as much as the creaking in my knees. Liam's growing interest in the sport makes me realize that it's time to give something back: to my hometown, my old team, and the local kids. So a quarter century after I took off my varsity jersey for the last time, I'm returning this year as a volunteer assistant with the Methuen Rangers and enrolling Liam in the youth hockey program.

As a community, Methuen is split between old habits and loyalties, and the dubious promise of something better. Pull off the highway into Mamma Mary's restaurant and you'll find Charlie Bonanno at the grill, serving up his famous omelet-on-a-toasted-heel. The place looks like a Sicilian funeral home with its blood-red wallpaper and carpets, faux Tiffany lamps, and a smattering of bad oil paintings. Ranged along the counter, slack-bellied tradesmen discuss the upcoming mayoral race and which of two Italian-American candidates they will vote for. One of the regulars seated there announces that his son will play for the varsity hockey team this season, the others murmur and nod, and Charlie throws another heel onto the grill.

With a population of 40,000, this is small-town America, where everyone not only knows your name but they knew your father's and your grandfather's name and what they did for a living and who they chummed around with. Hockey is part of Methuen's culture, where fathers and mothers work extra shifts to afford their kid's ice time and frayed hockey pants and tattered gloves get passed down from sister to brother. And though hardly anyone learns the game outdoors these days, the districts that produce the best players remain intact: the Italian east end, the west side with its town forest and lake, and the area around Central Street.

But like a lot of New England towns with open space, Methuen is growing and gentrifying; three-hundred-thousand-dollar homes are popping up like mushrooms, and the character of its blue-collar neighborhoods is disappearing. While Charlie Bonanno serves up homemade sausage to his clientele of plumbers and roofers and stonemasons, a fleet of Volvos and BMWs sail past on Merrimack Street, their occupants scarfing down bagels and yakking on their cell phones. At the local grocery store, these young Rockefellers stalk around like whippets with their bony jaws and high-haired, slender wives. All they care about is money and golf.

Methuen still draws most of its hockey players from among the sons and daughters of the firefighters, electricians, postal workers, and schoolteachers who live in modest one- and two-family homes and have traditionally made up the largest segment of the town's population. Oddly enough, a significant number of Methuen's best athletes don't even play sports in high school. Instead, they get after-school jobs, not because their families are poor, but simply because they have grown up with the habit of work. Like their parents, they see regular employment (certainly not basketball or football, and sometimes not even college) as the way to get ahead.

Underneath all this, hockey is ingrained into Methuen's collective identity. Alone among the major sports, it often requires the commitment of an entire family for an individual player to excel. The equipment and ice time are expensive, the hours at the rink are long and late, and it takes many years for a kid to master the elements of skating and team play.

Because of the requisite dedication, it tends to be a sport that people stick with. In my heart, I believe my son will become a hockey player and that he probably already is one. After all, I learned the benefits of teamwork and hustle and persistence and made most of my deepest friendships at the rink. If Liam does decide to play, I'll be there to lug his equipment, offer a few tips, and provide him with encouragement, just as my father did for me.

The pinnacle for most local kids is to finish his or her career playing for Methuen High. Over the years, the Rangers have produced a handful of prospects who've gone on to play for colleges like Plymouth State and Babson and St. Michael's. But mostly they graduate to the industrial leagues around Boston, or to Sunday night pickup games with their old buddies, where the goalies are suspect and the players end up reminiscing and drinking beer in the high school parking lot. However, the current Ranger hockey team is loaded with experience at just about every position: an all-star goalie, tons of speed, and a handful of dangerous goal scorers. After twelve years of playing together and the rising expectation that this will be a benchmark season, these kids have something to prove.

I have often fantasized about going back to high school, to take one more shot at that defining period in my life. This book details my return to Methuen High after twenty-five years, in order to discover what it was about my experiences there and on the ice that shaped me and my future. At the same time, I examine a group of teenagers and their parents and coaches, revealing in their quest the struggles that kids and parents everywhere must contend with. My intention is to usher readers back to a galvanizing experience, when dreams were born and life was a vague corridor that waited mostly up ahead.

So as the Methuen Rangers set out on their quest, I'm poised on the brink of middle age, my hometown is filling up with strangers, and my young son is just catching on to the sport that will help determine his identity. As an assistant coach, I'll be there to see the most talented Ranger team in over a decade go through the crucible of tryouts and cuts, the big games, the bus rides, and to relive that one year that helped make me who I am today.

PROLOGUE

"DRIVING TO LOWELL"

THE FIRST GAME OF THE SEASON comes on the road in mid-December, against the Dracut Middies. Parked behind Methuen High, the big, dirty school bus is sending up plumes of exhaust as the kids file out of the building. Senior tri-captain Chris Cagliuso is silhouetted against the horizon, a slant of hips to balance the weight of his equipment bag, stick held upward like a lance. In many ways, he's the standard bearer for this year's team, following his brother Brett, who played for the Rangers and went on to star at Holy Cross. All the young players look up to Cagliuso.

Bus driver Chuck Trudel hands each of the varsity coaches a lollipop as we climb the battered metal stairs. "Ol' Leadfoot Chuck," says assistant coach Dave Martin. "Control yourself now. It's almost Christmas."

Trudel plays a classic rock station over his radio as the players jostle one another and settle into their seats. Dressed in shirts and ties covered with their white game jerseys, the Rangers fill the aisle on both sides, their bags stuffed into the last four rows. In the dim space of the bus, it's like a time warp as I swivel my head around and survey the team, just as Creedence Clearwater Revival wades into their 1972 hit "Proud Mary."

And I never lost one minute of sleepin',
Worryin' 'bout the way things might have been.

Some players are sprawled across two seats, looking as if they're asleep. Others listen to music on their headsets, or talk in semiloud voices about the anatomical properties of certain young women and which electronic games really kick ass. The coaches sit up front, and assistant Jon Morin is the last to get on. "Let's roll, Chuck," he says.

"Where we goin'? The Janas?" asks Trudel, as the bus lurches into gear. Morin nods and takes his seat.

Our driver is a hockey fanatic; his daughter Becky is the Rangers' starting jayvee goalie and the obvious choice for the varsity job next year. Chuck Trudel is wearing a blue corduroy jacket emblazoned with *Methuen Youth Hockey* and a matching baseball cap. "You gonna be good this year?" he asks the coaches.

Morin glances over at Dave Martin and head coach Joe Robillard and they all laugh. "We'll let you know as soon as they drop the puck," Morin says.

My seat on the bus reflects my role with the team, especially at this point of the season. I'm in no-man's-land, with Robillard and his assistants sitting two rows in front of me and all the players behind. Since I have no experience as a coach and am more than two decades removed as a player, nobody knows quite what I'll be doing this year, myself included. As we emerge from Ranger Road and turn onto Pleasant View Street, I'm wondering if I'll be on the bench or in the stands for the game and whether I can do or say anything that any single player will find useful. After competing in various sports for many years, this is my first real experience watching from the sidelines and I'm not sure how it's going to work out.

Most of all, I'm thinking about my dad, and whether I have the patience and humility to become the sort of man he was. As I grow older, and my son begins a life of school and sports and other activities, I often find myself saying the same things my father once said to me. It makes me think of how many people, as they ascend to the skinny end of the pole, suffer the gravity of years pulling them back to the ground they came from—the notions and predilections of their parents.

Lacing up his skates one day, I asked Liam if he was going to play for the Rangers when he got older. We were both looking down at his miniature feet. "I'm going to play for the little-kid Rangers," he said. Liam can't imagine himself as a young man and strangely enough, neither can I—the only difference being that I'm still certain he will become one.

It occurs to me that I have to forge my ties with Liam day by day, and that if I'm going to teach him anything it has to be in the present. Right now I'm still at my playing weight, with a resting heart rate under sixty beats per minute, but sometimes I sit listening to the faint and distant echo of something—whatever malady is coming to knock me off my pins and send my heart rate up and down the roller coaster. I'm at the age where all it takes is a couple of funky nodes under my arm, a few lab tests, and it's all over. I've seen it happen.

Most days I get up before dawn, run four or five miles, write for a few hours, go skating with Liam or play hockey in the driveway, and take a long walk through the woods with a miniature tape recorder and pad of paper. So far I've avoided a host of middle-aged complaints and I'm still keen-eyed enough to read a newspaper in the dark, all of that the result of an athletic life, and that life a dividend from the long cold winter of 1975. And if it ended tonight, with an infarction that could stop a train or some kind of grand mal seizure, it was a life worth living because I squeezed everything from it that I possibly could.

Seated in the back of the bus, star forward Chris Cagliuso is regaling his teammates with a story about waiting in line for Bruce

Springsteen tickets. Being around the hockey players reminds me that I wish I had my youth back—not to do it differently, just to do it again. Kids have a willingness to move on to the next fascination when the moment expires, a rare quality in most grown-ups, who seem to enjoy hanging on to things too long. And that's what I'm asking myself as we head for the Janas rink: by helping out with the Rangers this year, am I moving forward, or simply living in the past?

We're driving down Route 113 toward Dracut when we find ourselves behind a large green van, one of those bulky vehicles favored by suburban moms. It's nearing dusk and as we approach Elmwood Cemetery, where my parents and grandparents are buried, I realize that an inversion of the landscape is occurring inside the deep, glossy finish of the van's rear end. The world behind us, and out to either side—the gaunt image of trees, high-tension wires riding their buttresses, even the crypts and crosses of Elmwood—is passing into the sheen of the van, all of it reflected into a reverse image of itself, collapsing inward as our vehicles travel along. After a moment, it becomes clear that the vanishing point of this horizon is the last little arrowhead of the past, not the pointed future one expects as one goes forward.

Each of the oak trees lining the road gets thrown on screen and inflated to its full height, with every branch and knot represented in intricate detail; just as quickly the trees become blurred, are reduced by increments and whipped back to the outer edges of the vista. In rapid succession, the telephone poles loom up, strung with six or eight wires, then each pole shrinks to the size of a tiny bristle and is whisked away.

I'm mesmerized. The whole of time, its array of moving shapes, all in relation to one another in a finite space, is forever rising, presenting itself as one object, and then disappearing both forward and backward into a farther space that no longer moves, no longer coexists with time's arrow but is still *somewhere,* out of ken. It dawns on me that nothing ever changes; it's only our changing relationship to the things we see and experience that fixes us inside our particular journeys. We're always moving and, just as surely, always leaving ourselves behind. So as I move forward this year, into the 1999–2000 Ranger hockey season, I'll be just as surely going back to 1974–75 and my old friends and memories.

The old world collapses, and the new world continues on. And so goes the past, and so go the shapes from the past that are no longer with us, and so we all go, the players and coaches and me, rolling along Route 113 toward Dracut.

1

SEE YOU IN SEPTEMBER

LOCATED ON A SLOPING WOODED LOT near the town center, Methuen High School is a large, scored concrete bunker with a 125-foot smokestack. The main building, which resembles a graham cracker factory, is a two-level rectangular structure divided into north and south "houses" and containing the main office, guidance department, cafeteria, and academic offices and classrooms. Connected by an enclosed promenade are a full-sized ice rink, adjoining locker rooms, and a 2,000-seat assembly hall.

At the end of this ramped concourse is the 17,000-square-foot field house, which includes three regulation basketball courts, an eighth-of-a-mile running track, weight lifting and fitness area, volleyball courts, batting cage, and boys and girls locker rooms. The Athletic Director's office, Physical Education Department, Athletic Trainer, Music Department, and ROTC program are also located in or adjacent to the field house.

Dressed in a blue and gold polo shirt, dark blue chinos, and running shoes, phys ed teacher and hockey coach Joe Robillard confesses to a little nervousness as he looks over his class rosters at quarter to seven in the morning. Popular among students for his laid-back manner and dry wit, "Mr. Robes" has been an amiable presence at Methuen High for twenty-five years. Beneath his soft-spoken demeanor, however, Robillard is a determined, competitive man, a former goalie on the 1972 National Championship Boston University hockey team. During gym classes, where the energetic Robillard cavorts among varsity athletes and other kids, one of his favorite refrains is "I thought you guys were supposed to be good."

Robillard and his best friend and office partner, Fran Molesso, have been teaching and coaching since 1975, but they still get a few butterflies when the 1,700 kids come pouring through the orange doors of Methuen High for the first day of the 1999–2000 school year. At this hour the field house is empty, except for the over 100 royal blue championship banners draped on the walls, heralding past Ranger achievements in everything from baseball to wrestling.

In the boys' phys ed office there's a row of full-size lockers and tacked to the wall, hand-printed posters that read "Eliminate the Possibility of an Excuse" and "Do the Right Thing." While competing in one of the toughest leagues in the state, Joe Robillard's career record as a head hockey coach is 180-156-44. (He has coached 1,200 Ranger competitions over the past twenty-five years, in ice hockey, baseball, soccer, track and field, cross-country, and field hockey.) Inside his locker, Robillard keeps a tiny "W" with adhesive on the back that he awards to the biggest whiner in each class. At 48, he's trim and fit, a loose-limbed fellow with hazel eyes and a thick "cookie duster" mustache.

"Shame on me if I don't stay in shape," says Robillard, explaining how he participates in nearly every class while keeping a running commentary on the action. "On the football field, I'm Joe 'Willy' Namath. At tennis, I'm Ivan Lendl. Larry Bird on the basketball court—until I pull a hamstring."

My "job" at Methuen High is a loose mixture of substitute teacher, volunteer hockey coach, and self-appointed hall monitor. This particular building, with its ice rink and field house, opened in the fall of 1976, when I was a freshman at Acadia University in

Nova Scotia. But watching an undersized Asian boy with cerebral palsy and bad skin totter to his gym locker, I'm reminded how tough high school is for some kids. Just trying to fit in can be a full-time job for someone who falls outside the norm. As a hockey player and above-average student, I had it pretty easy, dating cheerleaders and editing the school newspaper, and still thought I was in hell.

There's a controlled chaos in the main hallway leading "upstairs" to the academic half of the school, a huge chattering mass of teenagers in baggy jeans, faded baseball hats, long clingy skirts and wool sweaters. The office resembles an ant colony, with a line of teachers, students, and staff coming from one direction to drop off various bits of paperwork and another coming the other way, picking it up. Mimi Hyde breezes in, a petite, sandy-haired woman who coaches girls' basketball, and announces in her loud-speaker voice, "Everybody's having a good time."

Hyde, 48, personifies the athletic success enjoyed at Methuen High. A member of the Massachusetts high school basketball hall of fame and former Ranger herself, Hyde's overall record as varsity coach at Methuen is 393-83. Her teams captured state championships in 1985–86 and 1998–99, joining football and boys' track coach Larry Klimas, girls' head track coach Brenda Clarke-Warne, and wrestling coach Bob Fitzgerald at the highest level of interscholastic athletics. Methuen also produces a significant number of individual state champs, like senior Sean Furey, currently the top-ranked high school javelin thrower in the nation with a personal best of 227' 3". (The varsity hockey team reached the state semifinals in 1992–93 but has never won a championship.)

At center court in the field house is a six-foot caricature of a man in buckskins, waving a flintlock rifle. Methuen High's athletic teams are named for Robert Rogers and his celebrated band of guerrilla fighters, Rogers' Rangers. Major Rogers was born on November

18, 1731, near the intersection of Hampshire Road and Cross Street in Methuen. Although believed by many locals to have served in the Revolutionary War, Rogers' Rangers actually fought on the British side in the French and Indian War of the late 1750s. According to contemporary accounts, Rogers was "six feet in stature . . . and well known in feats of strength," and his daring winter raids against French emplacements on Lake Champlain and what is now Quebec are the stuff of legend. The Rangers sometimes fought in snowshoes and on ice skates and terrified their enemies by hatcheting and scalping prisoners.

A generation ago, kids who had struggled up from the sandlots and backyard rinks of Methuen considered it a privilege to wear that cartoon Ranger on their jerseys. But in this era of sophisticated youth sports, where the inflated expectations of some parents can ruin the experience for the child and the coach, becoming a Methuen Ranger is a different business. After greeting me in the office, Mimi Hyde asks, tongue-in-cheek: "How come you're not writing about *my* team? We won the state championship, you know." Then she relates a story about a woman who called her a few years ago, lobbying for a guaranteed college scholarship for her basketball-playing eighth-grade daughter. Mimi told the woman she couldn't promise her daughter anything, but if the youngster worked hard and earned good grades, she might get to play varsity ball at Methuen. Instead the girl enrolled at archrival Central Catholic and now, as a junior, sits on the bench.

Methuen High principal Ellen Parker also starts her work day early, buttonholing students as they pour through the main hallway at 7:15, telling them to clip on their ID badges and take off their hats. She's forceful and direct but pleasant, a small woman with a booming voice she honed during ten years as a varsity coach.

This is Parker's second year of what she calls her "ten-year plan" for improving Methuen High. Trying to get a grip on what sort of kid grows up in Methuen, I'm reminded of the mild inferiority complex that seems to run through all of the town's doings. In a box somewhere I have a photograph of my father wearing a lacquered cowboy hat and a corny red, white, and blue golf shirt emblazoned with "I LIKE METHUEN." He's manning the grill at some sort of municipal barbecue circa 1977, and every time I see that old picture it strikes me funny that the motto isn't "I'M CRAZY ABOUT METHUEN" or "DON'T YOU JUST LOVE IT HERE?" It's as if living in Methuen is an endurable necessity, like taking your pretty cousin to the prom. But then I recall that love for a town or an old hockey rink or a set of playing fields is like the sun shining in the sky. You never look at it. Hardly do you remark upon it. But you always know it's there.

After twenty-five years as a teacher and administrator in the region's poorest and its most affluent communities, Mrs. Parker says the issues for all teenagers are the same: "Hazing, discipline, drugs, boy-girl relationships, and things that happened at the mall that are brought into the school." Still, she believes there's a tremendous amount of work to do as principal of Methuen High. Although the school is bright and cheerful and bustling with chatty teenagers, a tour through the building illustrates the wear and tear of twenty-five years: missing ceiling tiles, torn carpets patched with duct tape, and unkempt stacks of papers and boxes littering the teacher's area.

"We need more pride," says Parker. "Look around. We're average. In every way, we need to be better."

Comparing MHS to other local schools, Parker says that some systems are better than others at hiding their problems from parents and the media, that's all. Methuen High is an open building—there are no metal detectors, routine locker searches, or heavy police presence. "This is not a prison," says Parker. "The kids are my best lifeline to the street." A single police officer is assigned to the school, Methuen High graduate Jim Mellor. "I use Jim if I need to enforce 'the law.' Other than that, he's a presence in the school."

While wandering through the north house, a number of things I learned in high school come drifting back. Like *osmosis,* the tendency of fluid to pass through a semipermeable membrane. How the circumference of a circle equals its diameter times pi. And how to unhook a girl's bra with the index finger and thumb of my left hand. When I attended Methuen High, there was one black kid in the school and a handful of Latinos. Today students from twenty-four countries fill the hallways, bringing with them an equally diverse constellation of academic preparation, family background, and cultural expectations. But the experience of high school, for better or worse, remains pretty much the same.

During our rounds, Parker and I stop into the "Behavioral Resource Room," a barren, graffiti-scarred area off the cafeteria that houses a dozen sullen, listless kids who are staring at the wall, and a bored middle-aged woman who's staring back at the kids. These individuals cannot get along in the school's general population and sit here in a kind of purgatory, measuring off their adolescence with curses and sighs. Parker tells me of a dangerous, profane encounter she had with one of these "students"—a showdown reminiscent of her hardscrabble childhood in Springfield, Massachusetts.

"I'm a firm believer that all kids can learn—but not always in my building," says Parker. "We're not supposed to be in this business."

Near lunchtime Fran Molesso and I stand in the hallway outside the main office watching the stragglers and con-artists ducking in and out of class. The ex-college gymnast is trim and muscular, with shining olive skin, dark hair, and a well-kept mustache. Molesso reminds me that the overwhelming majority of students are where they're supposed to be, doing what they're supposed to be doing. Although disgusted at how grubby the school looks on the first day, after twenty-five years Molesso says he's still impressed by how polite and easygoing Methuen adolescents are in general.

"They're fun to be around," says the gym teacher, who grew up in Northport, New York. "Maybe it's because they're brought up mostly blue collar, so the parents have to work hard. But they're always respectful."

Half a mile from the high school, Pleasant Valley Street divides Methuen into the old and the new. Heading east, you'll pass through a complicated set of traffic lights and then an apple orchard will start running on your right, forty-five acres farmed for well over a hundred years by Charles Mann and his descendants. On the left, construction gangs are building a new shopping and entertainment complex known as "The Loop." It looks like an archaeological dig at Cheops: great misty mountains of dirt, men with pry bars heaving slabs of granite, and here and there across the vast dusty plain, tumbled piles of Mesozoic rock and huge sections of drainage pipe standing on end like cisterns.

Built on the same site in 1973 was the doomed edifice of the Methuen Mall; before that it was all cow pasture and apple orchard. I remember when Pleasant Valley Street was a country road and my cousins the Leonharts and I would cross the meadow to steal apples and douse each other in the brook. When the mall went up, a cheap, low-rise structure that contained a hundred stores, hockey pal Gary Ruffen and I applied for set-up jobs and worked at places like General Nutrition Center and So-Fro Fabrics. Over the years, I bought clinging polyester shirts at Chess King, science fiction novels at Lauriat's, and ate inexpensive T-bones at York Steak House—notions that I no longer ascribe to, and stores that are no longer in business. So when the mall closed a few years ago, I didn't lose any sleep over it.

The Loop will include a Super Stop & Shop, several chain stores and restaurants, and my favorite feature: an eighteen-screen cinema multiplex. Across the street from the main entrance is Mann Orchards, owned by Donald and Ruth (Mann) Fitzgerald, and their son Bill and his wife, Kathy. The Mann family acquired the land around 1850, and Bill Fitzgerald's great-grandfather, Charles W. Mann, first sold eggs and tomatoes produced here in 1877. In his long lifetime, Charles W. Mann was an orchard keeper and farmer, dowser, pomologist, prodigious diarist and writer, and adviser to renowned local millionaire Edward F. Searles.

Like his ancestor, Bill Fitzgerald, 45, has a green thumb and a thousand ideas for improving his business and the town in general. At this time of year, Fitzgerald is finishing up the harvest, preparing his lands for winter, and greeting some of Methuen's most prominent citizens in his store. A perusal of his great-grandfather's diary illustrates that things haven't changed much in this part of town. One hundred years ago today, Charles W. Mann wrote, "Finished tearing down the barn and teamed away most of it. Cleaning up weeds etc round the hill and pond. . . . Mr. Searles over in P. M. Filled and covered stone silo and finished the corn cutting."

Methuen has a long and varied history. Created in 1726 from a large parcel of land annexed mostly from Haverhill, the town was named by Massachusetts Governor William Dummer for his friend Sir Paul Methuen of England. The first public building was erected in 1728 on Meeting House Hill, opposite where Holy Family Hospital now stands, and its lot included the town's first cemetery, known as Ye Old Burying Ground. During the Revolutionary War, a company of local men under Captain John Davis fought at the Battle of Bunker Hill, which could be heard in Methuen, nearly thirty miles distant. Three of Davis's men were killed that day—Ebenezer Herrick, Joseph Hibbard, and James Ingalls, surnames that can still be found in Methuen's telephone listings.

In many ways, the juxtaposition of Mann Orchard and the Loop symbolizes my hometown and what it's now becoming. Like Peter Miville at the 1859 House, Ken Greenwood at Thwaite's Market, and Bob Sr. and Bob Jr. at Sheehan's gas station, Bill Fitzgerald and Mann's are part of that last line of family businesses that stretches across Methuen. Back in 1971, the Fitzgeralds sold twenty-two acres of their orchard to developers of the Methuen Mall. Today, the family operates a large, well-equipped farm store and grows more than twenty varieties of apples—the picking starts the first week in July and finishes at the end of September, due to the varying growth cycles.

"In this business, you can't change your production quickly in order to keep up with demand," says Bill Fitzgerald, a hearty, bespectacled man dressed in overalls. He notes that a dry cleaning chain at the Loop will progress from cellar hole to full-blown retailer in three months. "I planted some new apple trees three months ago and there's been two inches of growth on them," Fitzgerald says.

Fitzgerald, who also grows peaches, pears, nectarines, tomatoes, cucumbers, and butternut squash, says that it's difficult to maintain a family business in the age of the super store. "I tell my two boys, if you want to do this, it's a whole ton of work," he says. "Right now, they're not sure what they're going to do."

When Bill was a kid, the farm store was open from mid-August until mid-April—basically as long as their apple stock held out. Now they're open year-round, 8 A.M. to 6 P.M., seven days a week. Their signature item is homemade apple pie, baked with their own fruit—just as Thwaite's specialty is the individual pork pie and Peter Miville's 1859 House makes the best local fish and chips.

"There's no question you get tired," Fitzgerald says. "Ask Kenny Greenwood at Thwaite's. That business is Kenny and Kenny is that business. The most important thing is your health, whether it's physical or psychological. But the real reason we're still here is family."

Standing on the porch of the farm store, while bulldozers crank over piles of gravel across Pleasant View Street, Fitzgerald tells me that developers have approached him, fishing for the price he would need to sell the entire orchard. For now, he's not going anywhere.

But Bill Fitzgerald is curious about the Loop. "I take them over a peach, and get some information," he says.

As I pull away from Mann's with a dozen things racing through my mind—pick up my dry cleaning, stop at the bakery, drop off my mail—a dented blue van is coming the other way and I look over and there's my old hockey teammate Ronnie DiCenso behind the wheel. He has the same heavy-browed look that I must be wearing, the same middle-aged preoccupations, but we spot each other and immediately brighten up. As we draw parallel, I speak his name in a clear voice that fades to a whisper and Ronnie does the same for me. And in an instant a hundred forgotten episodes come roaring back, all the laughs I shared with the young Ronnie DiCenso, and then we pass through the intersection and drive off in separate directions.

By the time I get home, Liam is ready for bed and I take him in and we say our prayers and then, as I do just about every night, I tell him a story about how he's playing for the Boston Bruins against this or that NHL team and scores the winning goal. The story doesn't take long; it never does. Within five minutes Liam is asleep, one arm flung across my chest, the palm of his hand no bigger than a silver dollar. I stare into the soft gray darkness, listening to my son's breath running in and out, and think about how swiftly time passes. It's like you've got all the time in the world and then suddenly, it's gone.

2

THE ICE SKATE TAO

On Thursdays Liam and I go over to the municipal rink in Haverhill after he gets out of kindergarten, for an hour or so of unstructured skating. For just $3 we usually have the ice to ourselves, but one morning a young figure skater and her mother join us. The girl is just a wisp of a thing, like a Popsicle stick with a mop of thick brown hair. She flies around the rink with incredible speed, executing double toe-loops and axels and long graceful jumps.

Dressed in a pink nylon running suit and sipping coffee, her mother watches from the bench, armed with a box of tissues for her sniffling daughter. Liam and I skate past and the woman says, "He's *so* cute. How old is he?"

Like any parent, I love to talk about my kid, so I dig in my edges and stop short. "He's five. Just getting a little extra practice in."

"He skates very well. Great posture. He keeps a nice straight toe line for his age."

I feel a dangerous surge of pride. "He's been on the ice for three years," I tell the woman. "Is that your daughter? She's quite a little skater."

The trap has been sprung. Leaning over the bench, the woman drops her voice to a conspiratorial tone, like I'm about to hear a wonderful secret. Her face is covered in makeup and framed with dyed black hair. "My daughter is just getting over the flu. She didn't even want to skate today, but we have the regionals next Wednesday and then the New England's and she has two workouts scheduled for this afternoon at the Colonial and I said, 'Why not try it, dear? And if you don't feel well, we'll just go home.' But look at her. She's a trouper."

On the ice, the tiny 11-year-old attempts a difficult maneuver and falls, sliding quite a ways on her rear end. Caught in midsentence, the woman frowns at her daughter and the girl springs up, wearing one of those painful false smiles that professional skaters use when they ruin a routine. I look out there and wonder why she isn't in school.

"—and all this came after her big ankle injury in May, when the customized boots we ordered from California were bothering her and the designer kept saying 'Don't worry. It'll take five days to break them in,' and on the fifth day, sure enough, her ankle blew out and she was off the ice for five weeks. Five whole weeks. Can you imagine it?"

As the woman blathers on about ruptured growth plates and defective soles and the Merrimack Valley's most pernicious case of influenza, I decide that no, I could never imagine such a thing. Looking into her fanatical eyes and listening to the drone of her voice, I'm reminded that passions are born, not made, and swear I'll never do that to my kid. Just then Liam waddles by the bench, saying that he's tired and wants to go home.

"Let's go," I say, taking him by the hand. "I'll buy you a bag of pretzels."

A few days later, Liam and I arrive at the rink for his first youth hockey practice and Methuen's peewees are playing Saugus in the earlier hour. I hoist Liam up on the boards and we watch the game for a few minutes. The goalie makes a save and curls over, snow from the shavings in the crease freckling his back, and his defensemen standing over him with their sticks across their chests. It's been a long time since I've been down there cradling the puck, relieved to spot it beneath my glove or pad, feeling protected by the legs marking me off from the other team. Behind me, a lot of the parents are yelling instructions and criticism. But just because you're a kid doing something and maybe not doing it very well by someone's else's standard, doesn't mean it isn't important to you and won't stay with you when you're not doing it anymore.

As I arrange Liam's equipment on the bench, I find myself facing a double row of screaming hockey moms, their coffee cups stained with lipstick, hair sprayed into fantastic shapes. Calling out their sons' names, they screech like banshees at every shift in Methuen's fortune, imploring the Lord Himself to intervene on their behalf. One of the women catches me staring and smiles. "Pretty soon this'll be you," she says.

The three years Liam has already spent inside rinks and his slow but gradual improvement as a skater pay off immediately, as I hoped they would. Right at 9:30 A.M. the forty or fifty kids in the "Learn to Skate" program are either on the ice or queuing up at the gate, in their caged helmets, miniature gloves, skates, and dark blue Methuen Jr. Rangers' jerseys. The grandstand is overflowing with proud and anxious mothers, fathers, and grandparents, dressed in wool and fleece and nylon construction-company jackets. Half of those assembled have cameras or video recorders, and as more kids climb over the boards, the popping flashbulbs make it seem like a Hollywood star is in the building.

As I tie Liam's skates and buckle on his helmet, he says little, except that one of his shin guards is pinching him. I fix it, and then we stand in line to go on the ice. There is chaos and a "lifeboat" mentality at the rink door: kids being turned away for improper or missing equipment, experienced players squeezing in and out, and several children on skates for the first time, crying to go home. Two coaches are charged with leading the disconsolate and terrified novices back to the bench, where mothers take the children in their arms and shower them with kisses, and a few stern fathers urge their little offspring to "get out there and try, goddamnit."

Liam waits his turn, has his equipment checked, and glides onto the ice with a broad smile on his face. Since we neglected to stop in the lobby for the Jr. Rangers' shirt, I run back to get one while the head coach puts Liam through a quick skating assessment. When I return with the jersey, there's a stout woman in an alpaca coat blocking the door. Her daughter is splayed over the ice, moaning that she wants to quit. The woman says they'll go home if the child tries once more to cross the rink.

"And no noodle legs. Keep your legs straight," says the woman.

I flag Liam down and take off his helmet and gloves and roll on his brand-new mesh jersey. "Wow," he says. "The Rangers." Then he notices I'm not wearing my skates. "You have to get off the ice, Dad."

Twice the coaches direct Liam to the novice group occupying center ice and both times he wheels around and joins in with the more advanced kids. Finally one of the coaches relents and Liam proves that he can execute all the drills: striding out to a traffic cone, circling it, and returning; and jumping over a hockey stick that's lying on the ice. He has a big smile on his face the whole time, even when he says something to another kid and they have a shoving match and Liam falls down. Liam has already spent more than a hundred hours on this ice surface and over the next twenty-eight Saturdays, he'll meet new friends, learn some skills, and his determination and endurance will be tested to the limit.

At one point, Liam is resting along the boards with the other kids and I'm standing behind the glass there and call out to him. Liam smiles but he can't hear me and then the kid beside him—"Devin" is scrawled on his helmet—says something and they both laugh and the coach blows his whistle and they skate away. It's like witnessing my son being born into another world.

Just the other day Liam and I were at Nicholson Stadium watching the football team play against Andover on a beautiful fall evening. The Methuen Ranger's Marching Band lined up by twos outside the chainlink fence and marched onto the field, through the "Players' Only" gate and along the paved path, one hundred and thirty strong, the drummers tapping out the "street beat." In their long blue capes and plumed hats, they poured by for half a minute or so, and it was plain that they had a sense of belonging. They all shared a heartbeat, and together they walked the line.

We were sitting with an old friend of mine who lives across the street from the stadium. He told me that his 11-year-old son played noseguard for the "C" team in Methuen Youth Football. "That's my dream," he said, between puffs on his cigarette. "To see my kid play on this field for the varsity."

When I think about that, and of the woman in the alpaca coat warning her daughter about "noodle legs," it's a reminder to teach Liam that he should have dreams and work hard at fulfilling them. But they have to be his own dreams, not mine.

A short distance away there's a kid with ginger hair and freckles who's refusing to take part in the workout, and for almost the entire hour his redheaded dad squats beside the door, refusing to let him quit the practice. At times, as I wander down that way, following my own son's progress, I hear the boy pleading with his father and sobbing. Finally the horn blows and the Zamboni drives out and the kids file off the ice. The man looks out at the rink, a disgusted expression on his face, and then takes his son's hand and leads him away.

"You screamed like you were being murdered out there," he says.

On a cold clear weekday afternoon, I hop in the car for the drive to Zwicker's Hockey Shop in Bedford, Massachusetts. At my age, going to Zwicker's is the closest I get to feeling like a kid in a toy store. It doesn't look like much from the street: a low whitewashed building with hand-lettered signs telling customers to USE OTHER DOOR. When I was a teenager, they used to sell lawnmowers and snowblowers, the latest models lined up on the tarmac outside like new sports cars, but now they're all hockey, year-round.

Homer Zwicker once sharpened skates for the Boston Bruins, and most days you'll catch a glimpse of him in the raised area where they keep the machine, an old, sparse-haired gent in work-clothes and safety glasses, bent over the sharpening wheel, which grinds and whirs and throws off tiny white sparks.

Inside, Zwicker's is like a crowded warren, used equipment piled in various cardboard boxes to your left as you enter, and to the right, cubbyholes stuffed with shiny plastic helmets, goalie gear, figure skating costumes, and yard after yard of hockey sticks, sorted by brand: KoHo, Sherwood, Victoriaville, Christian Brothers, Northland, and the rest, all classified by length and curve and the "lie" of the blade. Behind the cash register a small white plaque hangs on the wall:

THE ICE SKATE TAO

It isn't time that dulls the
edge of the blade, it's things.
My ice skates haven't been used
since they were sharpened in 1938.
They're still sharp, no ice has
rubbed the edges. He who ignores
things has made time disappear.

Jack Kerouac—
Some of the Dharma

While I wait to have my skates sharpened, I tell the grandmotherly Mrs. Zwicker, with her bun of gray hair and spectacles hanging on a beaded chain, that I need a new stick. "What do you want?" she asks.

I have my heart set on a Sherwood P.M.P. 5030, the feather-lam with right-hand curve, style 44. With a tiny nod, Mrs. Zwicker leads me down the threadbare runner to where all the sticks are kept in deep horizontal racks, blades turned out. In black marker on the narrow width of the blade is the legend "5030" and Mrs. Zwicker draws the stick out.

"This is the 'SC' with the tapered grip," I say to her. "I want the 44."

Mrs. Zwicker sends me out to the car for my old stick so I can compare the two directly. The curves are identical, but the shaft of the new model is half an inch longer. "They replaced the old 44 with the 'Ray Bourque,'" she says, naming the 39-year-old NHL defenseman. "The lie is the same, and so is the curve."

I hoist the stick by the shaft like I'm shaking hands, feeling the warp and weight of it. "It's a little longer than the 44," I say. "And a little heavier maybe."

"Shave it," says Mrs. Zwicker, turning to assist another customer.

Like a lot of my favorite businesses, straight talk is what keeps me coming to Zwicker's, as well as the fact that old Homer is a virtuoso of the blades. I wear Bauer Supreme Composites, the shells remounted at a slight inward angle to compensate for my flat feet. I get the blades ground deep at least four or five times a month, with a radius that places my weight over the middle third of the skate. When I mention in passing that I occasionally lose my balance while striding forward, almost like I'm being pulled backward by an invisible force, 38-year-old Zwicker skate man Jim Psareas asks if I tie my skates tightly and wrap my tendon guards with tape. I reply that I do.

"You're locking your feet in," says Psareas, a short, stocky fellow with dark hair. He demonstrates with my skate held between us. "So you can't point your toe at the end of your stride, like you're supposed to." He suggests that I leave off the tape and gives me a handful of wafer-thin cardboard shims to build up the heels a fraction of an inch on either side. When I achieve just the right "downhill" feeling, they'll measure the shims and build tiny orthotics for me.

I'm impressed with how quickly Psareas has divined my problem. "Everything here orginated with Homer (Zwicker)," he says. "I knew nothing when I started. I don't even ice-skate."

3

SKATE IN LEBANESE

WORKING AS PHYS ED TEACHERS at Methuen High allows Joe Robillard and his office partner, Fran Molesso, the best of the adult and adolescent worlds. They're both husbands and fathers and work long days that often stretch from 6 A.M. until 10 or 11 at night. But they spend a good part of that time cutting each other up and laughing. As Joe and I are passing by the main office one afternoon, another teacher is putting up photographs of the girls nominated for homecoming queen, and Robillard immediately goes over and joins in the kibitzing with a group of four or five teenagers. Each has a vigorous opinion and overruling them all for a moment, Robillard wants to know why a member of the field hockey team named Emily isn't listed.

"She's a smart kid, and a good kid and good athlete and a real knockout," says Robillard, who coaches field hockey in the fall, ice hockey in the winter, and jayvee baseball. "She's got my vote."

One of the young women gathered there reminds Robillard that, as a teacher, he doesn't have a vote.

"Oh yeah, right. Well, I should," says Robillard, laughing along with the kids.

When Mr. Robillard announces to his class that he will retire at the end of the semester and that I'll be taking his place, the kids are shocked by the put-on, until Mr. Molesso says that the nursing home on the corner has a bed available and Robillard feels compelled to take advantage of it.

"I'll take advantage of you, Mr. Mo," Robillard says, displaying his fist.

Later, in the office, Molesso pulls a hideous rubber mask from his locker and he and Robillard conspire to scare a couple of freshmen with it. Strategically placing a mesh bag filled with playground balls inside a dark closet, Molesso dons the mask and hides among the shadows. Then Robillard hollers into the locker room for a particular kid. In walks a pint-sized boy with large brown eyes and spectacles, eager to please his instructor.

"Grab the footballs for me, will you please?" asks Robillard, intent on his plan book.

The boy walks past the desk. Reaching into the closet for the footballs, he's blown back by the concussion of Molesso's loud "Ooo-arghh." The boy leaps in the air with a shriek, then grabs the footballs and tears across the office, depositing them at Robillard's feet. Molesso comes out of the closet, and he and Robillard double over with laughter. Then Molesso takes off his mask.

"You have to give the kid credit," says Fran Molesso, inspecting the bag of footballs. "He completed his mission."

A tall, slender boy named Drew Soley drops by the office with his athletic permission slip and when he departs, Molesso asks if he's a hockey player. "He's not a hockey player yet, he's only a freshman," Robillard says. Even highly touted kids have to prove themselves, and they can't do that until November when tryouts start.

During a rare quiet moment in the office, Robillard tells me that his two sons have played football and basketball and participated in gymnastics, but never played hockey—he was always coaching on

Saturdays during the Learn to Skate program. "Sometimes I feel like I'm coaching everybody's kid but my own," he says. "They've never said they regretted it, and I hope they never do."

Robillard informs me that fifty-four students have signed up for hockey this year, several more than the recent average. (He's allowed to keep thirty-six players, varsity and junior varsity combined.) During a meeting in the assembly hall to explain that I'll be writing a book about the team, approximately twenty of the players, in baggy pants and baseball caps, occupy two rows off to my left. The book is going to be about them—they know that much—but they're closed in tight because they don't know me. With the principal and school superintendent and all the coaches in attendance, I can tell that the kids are surprised by the administrative weight behind the whole deal, even a little flattered and ready to get excited about it, but as teenagers and athletes they're waiting to see how cool it's going to be. Studying their faces is like gazing at twenty plaster masks. If I'm going to get inside their heads—inside their team—what I did twenty-five years ago doesn't matter anymore. I will have to prove I belong.

Sixteen-year-old Albert Soucy is a quick little winger who skims over the ice like a waterbug. Although he was born in Lawrence, Massachusetts, Soucy spends every summer in his parents' hometown of St. Basil, New Brunswick, where he attends a hockey school. Described by Coach Robillard as a "great little kid" from a French-speaking family, last year Soucy neglected to seek tutoring in English literature and flunked the subject during second term. He was therefore declared academically ineligible near the end of the 1998–99 season and the team struggled without his offensive spark. His teammates are counting on him to remain eligible this year.

In his gym class, the friendly, pie-faced Soucy and I choose the blue sticks for a game of floor hockey, and Joe Robillard grabs one of the yellow sticks and plays for the other team. During the game Soucy and I hardly say anything to each other, but running back and forth, passing the little orange ball and trying to avoid Robillard's nimble-footed defense, we communicate in a language without words. Albert uses his stick like a scalpel, making sharp little passes into the gap and weaving easily among the other kids. Twice he and I attempt a simple give-and-go and the second time it works: my pass arrives at the goalmouth just as he does and Albert bangs it in. Now I have a little credibility.

When class ends, Soucy comes over and shakes my hand and asks if I want to skate with him and a couple of other players this afternoon. Supervised practices aren't scheduled to begin for another few weeks, but one of the perquisites of having a rink in the high school is the abundance of ice time. Always a hound for free ice, I quickly accept the offer.

Right after school I meet Albert Soucy and another hockey player inside the rink. Sophomore Dan Gradzewicz, with his shock of yellow hair and fighter's jaw, resembles an athlete from the 1920s. They're both shy kids, very polite, and for a few minutes nothing much happens out there because they keep passing me the puck as soon as they get it. Finally we get into a rhythm of skating and passing, taking shots at the shallow end of an overturned net.

Gradzewicz is a solid kid, thick through the shoulders, and a good skater. He's a candidate for varsity and plans on playing defense under Coach Jon Morin. But his game looks soft. I'm nowhere near any of these kids as a skater or puckhandler, but whenever I approach Gradzewicz, the yellow-haired sophomore maintains a large gap between us and backs up until he nearly crashes into the net.

"Hey, Dan," I call out to him. "Show a little aggression once in a while."

When we're resting against the boards, I ask Soucy to demonstrate this nifty little "drag" move I've seen him use. Grinning proudly, he cradles the puck with the blade of his stick, dragging it behind him as he skates along. Just as the puck reaches a point almost directly behind him—when an opponent would surely lunge for it—Soucy slides the puck between his own skates and kicks it ahead to his forehand. Executed properly, the move will leave a defender clutching at thin air.

"Pretty nice," I say. "But if you're at center ice and it doesn't work, you're giving up a rush going the other way. Use it in their end of the rink."

"Okay, Mr. Atkinson," Soucy says. He practices the move down low in the corner. When they think I'm not looking, Soucy and Gradzewicz glance at each other and smile.

Every Monday night I play hockey at Methuen High with a bunch of rink rats, including my former teammate Gary Ruffen and Ranger assistant coach Dave Martin and an old high school classmate named Mike Alianiello. Gary Ruffen and I have known each other since we were 12, and I was the goalie and he was a defenseman on several hockey clubs together, including the Ranger varsity. Six-two and lanky, Ruffen is a natural athlete, an expert golfer, skier, and fly fisherman. While the younger guys turn the air blue with raunch, or discuss the availability of overtime at the machine shop where most of them work, Ruffen and I'll put on our equipment and talk about some game we played in a rink that burned down twenty years ago.

Five minutes before we're scheduled to go on the ice, Dave Martin enters the room carrying a bag of equipment and wearing his ancient leather helmet. Mike Alianiello wiggles his eyebrows and says, "Look at that old relic."

Martin doffs his headgear and bows.

"Not the helmet," says Alianiello. "You."

"Hey, do you have clearance from your cardiologist?" Dennis Dube asks Martin.

Dube is standing on the bench in a pair of gym shorts, attaching the green fiberglass brace that runs from his midshin to his thigh and holds his right knee together. His hockey equipment is prehistoric and his body is a wreck: the bulging hairy stomach, a torn hamstring, two fists filled with mangled knuckles. The only thing he's wearing that's less than ten years old is the shiny black garter belt used to hold up his hockey socks. Someone hollers that Dube's new garter is a sexy addition to his wardrobe and the balding 45-year-old performs a grind on top of the bench that's obscene in every sense of the word.

But if I were having lunch with the top literary editors in New York, all of them vying for my next book, and Dennis Dube wandered in—gimpy kneed, thin on top, missing tooth—I would excuse myself from the table and join Monsieur Dube at the bar. I've known him since we were 15 and played together on a talent-laden youth hockey team called the Methuen Blues, along with Dave Martin and lifelong friend John Kiessling and several other characters. Dube was—and is—a fierce, hard-skating defenseman with an unpredictable slap shot and a reckless style that clears half the ice surface when he cranks it up.

When I was in tenth grade and playing on the Blues, the coaches selected the league all-star team and I was passed over. The night of the game I was hanging out at Dan's Sub Shop in Methuen Square when my father burst in to say that one of the goalies was sick and I'd been chosen to take his place. We hustled out to the car where my gear was waiting and my father drove straight to the Frost Arena in Lawrence and I hurried onto the ice. During the warm-up I got into a nasty argument when one of the players from our team, a big tough French kid, blasted a shot just as I took my mask off. The puck came within inches of my head and the two of us started yelling at each other and I threw a punch at him. He knocked me over and in all that goalie equipment I was like a turtle on its back, absorbing punches while I spit into the kid's face.

The other players, the coaches, and the referees were stunned. Here the game hadn't even started and there's a fistfight—between two guys from the same team, no less. Just then word of the fracas reached Dennis Dube in the locker room. Charging out with only one skate on and his other foot bare, Dennis paddled across the rink and smashed into my assailant, his momentum carrying them to the boards where Dube did some serious whaling on the kid.

"Don't you ever touch my fucking goalie," he said.

I played the greatest game of my life that night. The other team was loaded with top players and they charged at us in waves, firing shots from every angle and following hard to the net. But powered by adrenaline and my strangely heightened senses, I anticipated their movements and through some trick of the mind slowed and enlarged the puck until even their hardest shots floated up to me like balloons. Time after time, I'd cover up and Dennis Dube would race back to stand over me, spraying ice chips and fighting like a gladiator. I'll never forget it.

During tonight's game, I'm sitting on the bench next to Dube and notice a black splotch on his face. "What the hell is that?" I ask.

He reaches up, opens his face mask, and peels it off. "An old piece of leather," Dube says. "My skin must be flaking."

Suddenly he leans over the boards and screams at this Lebanese kid to get moving. Then Dube plops back down on the bench, wipes the sweat from his face, and snaps his mask back in place. "I don't know why I'm yelling," he says. "There's no word for 'skate' in Lebanese."

Paul Trussell, who works at the rink, glides past the bench and laughs at us. "I'll give a hundred bucks to anyone who can knock me down," he says.

"Go knock Trussell on his ass," Dube says to me.

"He's on our team."

"So what?"

On the ice I usually know what Gary Ruffen will do and where he'll go and that makes the game a lot of fun. On our first shift, Ruffen and I are skating with big Kevin Bell, and we fling the puck back and forth, scoring two goals within a minute. A couple of shifts later I head straight for the net while Ruffen and Bell, both graceful skaters, weave in and out with the puck, dazzling our opponents. Bell fakes one defenseman and throws a slick pass over to Ruffen, cutting through the slot. The goalie sticks out a padded leg and stops Ruffen's deflection, but the puck bounces up and I zoom in and pick the puck out of the air and hammer it into the net.

Leaning over our sticks, we glide back through center ice, trying to catch a breather. A little eye movement and three quick smiles and here they come again. But that moment makes balancing my checkbook and going to the dentist and all the other bullshit that comes along during the week fade far into the distance.

Gary Ruffen and I played on the Methuen Bengals in Pop Warner football when we were eighth graders. One of my earliest memories of our friendship is of a game we played against Lexington in the fall of 1970. Gary was our punter and I was playing left tackle on the kicking team when Gary really got a hold of one. It must have traveled more than thirty yards in the air and then hit a puddle, skipping past their deep man, and rolling and rolling toward the goal line. We ran downfield and I looked at Gary through the bars of my helmet and we started laughing. We were only 13 and it was a fifty-yard punt.

Gary was always a funny guy on the bench and the bus. After the Lexington game, which we lost, our coach was fuming. "You guys are playing Mickey Mouse football," he said.

Leaning over to me, Ruff whispered, "Then he must be Walt Disney."

On Monday nights, we play in front of an empty grandstand, except for an occasional wife or girlfriend. The rink is practically deserted, magnifying our shouts and the boom of the pucks resounding off the glass. This evening, one guy's dad is in attendance. He's a frail man wearing an old car coat, attached to a portable oxygen tank with the clear plastic line and cannula looped over his ears. The player's name is Dan and I don't know him very well; he's a pleasant fellow who lives in New Hampshire and has never played organized hockey. His dad, obviously in poor health, is here to watch his son skate, perhaps for the last time.

Dan has a career night. In one sequence, he scoops the puck along the boards, shimmies between two defenders, and tucks his shot beneath the slow-moving goaltender and into the net. Dan sinks to one knee and glides into the corner, pumping one arm with his stick held aloft. His skate catches in a rut and he topples over; the other guys all laugh.

Up in the bleachers, a thin man with his face made puffy by steroids is on his feet and applauding. The sound of his hands, like two dry sheaves, echoes weakly across the arena. Dan gets up, dusts himself off, and salutes his father, all alone in the empty grandstand at the far end of the rink.

After our game, Dennis Dube is holding his stomach and looking a little green. "That lo mein I had for supper is right here," he says, holding a rigid hand across his neck. "It's high mein."

This strikes me funny and Mike Alianiello says, "What are you laughing at?"

"You."

I trade a dollop of shampoo for the use of Dube's soap. Opening the box, I ask him, "Hey, do these hairs come with it, or are they extra?"

Dube walks past in a faded green towel, rubbing his bald head. "Those are all numbered, and after I shower I put them back in," he says. Everyone in the locker room starts laughing, and Dube adds, "The only place I don't have hair is the top of my head and the bottom of my feet."

I leave the rink close to midnight and drive across the tough part of town and stop at a convenience store. A couple of wise guys in satin warm-ups are lounging against the plate glass window and inside, the scaly clerk waits on customers without pausing in her harangue against the deadbeats who pump gas and then take off. She never bothers calling the cops, she says, because they obscure their license plates with mud and duct tape.

The clerk signals me with her hand. "You just missed it," she says. "A couple minutes ago, there was a female solicitor outside, selling it for ten bucks a pop."

I hand over the money for my bottled water. "She can't be much of a lawyer if she only charges ten dollars," I say.

I walk back outside and open the water in my car. Little maple trees line the sidewalk, part of some beautification project that has failed, and their leaves hang limp and black like shrouds. I take a long drink of the water and it passes into my stomach with a rush, bringing life back into me. After two hours of skating and swearing and laughing, water is the most powerful beverage on earth.

4

TRIALS AND TRYOUTS

It's an overcast Friday morning in November, with the wind from the north and no sound except for wrinkled leaves scratching over the pavement. The interior of the high school seems as empty and silent as a cathedral, absent all the usual chatter and door slamming. As I head past the ice rink and downstairs to phys ed, three Latino boys in baggy jeans are rising toward me, heads lowered, just the squeak of their rubber soles on the treads.

Just then Ellen Parker's voice breaks over the PA, apologizing for the bad news she's about to deliver. Announcements are commonplace in a high school, but there's something about the hush in Mrs. Parker's tone that freezes the Latino youths in place, one boy ahead of me now and two behind.

I'm looking straight into the oldest kid's face; he's about 17 years old, with a high and tight haircut and two gold earrings. Her voice ringing through the deserted corridors, Mrs. Parker says that a member of the junior class named Claire Krupica died at home yesterday. Although little information is available at this time, the principal of Methuen High promises to keep the school community informed. Additionally, grief counselors will be available to talk to students and staff about the tragedy.

The two younger boys look at the oldest one and he shakes his head: he didn't know the girl. But they wait in respectful silence until the announcement ends, and then they move on.

In the next instant, a heartrending shriek fills the air. On the lower stairwell, a girl begins sobbing in a loud, tremulous voice and then asks a piercing question: "Why do I keep losing my friends?" The three Latino boys shudder as they climb the ramp toward the academic houses. By the time I run down the stairs, someone has collected the distraught girl into an office and the corridor has grown still.

In the winter of 1970 I used to walk home from Lynch's swamp with Bill Tinney, a tall, good-looking kid with dark hair who lived on Pleasant Street. He was in the eighth grade, a year ahead of me, so we didn't have much in common except our love of the bumpy swamp and the hockey games we used to play there. One cold starless night Bill and I walked to the corner of Central Street and said good-bye beneath the streetlight. Hunched inside an old army fatigue jacket with his skates dangling over his shoulder, Bill saluted me and turned toward home. Not long after that the ice was buried in snow and then it grew warm and Lynch's was ruined for the year. I never saw Bill Tinney again.

The story we all heard was that he died of an aneurysm on the first day of spring. An energetic kid with a big field behind his house, Bill decided to mow this huge expanse of sawgrass and goldenrod in order to construct a one-hole golf course for himself and all his buddies. He went out early and worked at it for several hours, mowing and chopping and raking. At some point in the afternoon he turned on the outside spigot for a drink of water and it was the sound of the hose running that was said to have drawn his mother out of the house finally. He must have been lying there in a soggy heap, the water pouring over him just like the blood vessel that had ruptured in his brain. The older kids said that's what happened when you got an aneurysm. The word sounded strange to me, like a solemn ritual I was hearing about for the first time.

They waked him at Pollard's Funeral Home, and I was allowed to leave school early so I could attend with all the other hockey players. Even though I was dressed in my Sunday clothes, I ran all the way to Pollard's, dodging hydrants, jumping over fences. When I arrived the other kids were in one of the smoking rooms, filling their suit pockets with the free cigarettes. Then the funeral director came in and said it was time to view the body.

Bill Tinney was lying there with his hair combed and he looked young and waxy and dead. We gathered around the bier while one of our guys wrapped Bill's hockey stick in white tape from toe to shaft. Then we all signed it and the funeral director slid it down alongside Bill in the coffin and drew up the satin cover and closed the lid. That night I couldn't sleep, thinking about my signature on that stick lying next to Bill Tinney under the ground.

In the phys ed office I learn that the dead girl was bubbly and well liked and had given Coach Robillard the "No Whining" sticker he displays on his clipboard. As the first class of the day sits bunched up and whispering on the field house floor, Joe Robillard and Fran Molesso stand to one side with their rosters, wondering whether to proceed with normal activities.

"My daughter's a year younger than Claire," Robillard says. "When I got the call, I started to well up."

It's that sort of day at Methuen High, a strange mixture of normalcy and grief, some of the kids crying and painting murals along the main corridor and others taking tests and eating their lunches as if nothing unusual has happened.

"We have to walk a tricky line on a day like this," says Ellen

Parker. In just her second year at Methuen High, she has seen four kids buried from a population of 1,700. "There's a group of kids who are sincerely grief-stricken and distraught, and then there are the nose pickers of the world who are looking to take advantage of the situation."

Over the course of the morning, Kurt Walsh, one of last year's hockey captains, visits Joe Robillard in his office. Walsh is spending a year at Robillard's alma mater, Brewster Academy in New Hampshire, and in the eight months since I've seen him, the blond-haired defenseman has put on fifteen pounds of muscle and grown an inch. Prepatory schools like Brewster offer an extra year of education to kids who need to grow physically and academically before entering college. Walsh and Robillard smile at each other and shake hands.

Just then a voice comes over the PA, asking students to recite the Pledge of Allegiance. And even though the phys ed office lacks an American flag and is empty, 18-year-old Walsh and 48-year-old Robillard immediately break off their conversation and stand at attention with their right hands over their hearts. In the bowels of the field house, there is no one to witness this gesture of discipline and respect, but it's just the sort of thing Robillard believes is his most important job at Methuen High. There's a hand-lettered sign above his desk that reads: "The Best Kind Of Pride Is That Which Compels A Man To Do His Best When No One Is Watching."

At noon a young reporter from the *Eagle-Tribune* arrives to conduct an interview with Mrs. Parker on the impact of the Claire Krupica tragedy on Methuen High. They sit beside each other in the principal's office like two uneasy diplomats, the reporter staring at his pad of paper, Parker looking off somewhere at the wallpaper. In subdued tones, the reporter asks for details about Claire's academic history and reputation as a "good kid," receives mostly perfunctory answers and scribbles down a phrase here and there. After a few minutes of this, he tries to dig deeper, fishing for something scandalous in the day's events. But Mrs. Parker is like stone. When the reporter asks to "take a lap around the school," she denies his request. A short time later, the reporter is ushered out of the building.

"My job is to protect these kids," says Parker, watching through the window as the reporter drives off. "This school is a community and our community is entitled to grieve in private."

She's had more practice at this activity than a public school official could reasonably expect. Last year three popular teenage girls died in an automobile crash less than two months into Parker's tenure as principal. "That was a real trial by fire," she says. "The people here wanted to see my emotion, but they also wanted me to demonstrate leadership."

At the end of this long school day, the students and staff witness a little bit of both once again, as Parker makes another announcement in the presence of Claire Krupica's grief-stricken mother. Her voice breaking, Ellen Parker itemizes the details of wake and burial and expresses her confidence that the student body will acquit itself well under very difficult circumstances.

A short while later, I meet her in the deserted main corridor near the murals, which smell of fresh paint. "Hoo. I almost lost it there," says Parker. "I mean, I'm a mom, too."

At 7:30 A.M. on the first day of hockey tryouts, freshman Dan Martin pops out of his mother's van and heads for the main doors of Methuen High. He's small and slight, with short dark hair parted in the middle and gelled into bristles on top of his head.

"It's just another practice to me," says Martin, shrugging off any notion of pressure. He adds that he quit the fall youth hockey program because "the coach was getting on my nerves. He doesn't know anything about hockey."

Martin wears an ensemble of loose-fitting khaki and a wispy moustache. His father, Dave Martin, has been one of Me High's assistant hockey coaches for fifteen years and is a form teammate of mine. His mother, Cathy, graduated with me from the high school. Dan Martin's parents are divorcing. He's 14 years old.

Martin goes straight into first period math class, where his teacher begins laying out problems on the blackboard amid the great rumble of voices that surrounds us. Methuen High exemplifies the "open concept" at its worst—a building style popular in the 1970s that features portable dividers instead of floor-to-ceiling walls—an "energy efficient" but windowless cavern filled with stale air.

Dan Martin's math class is engulfed by white noise; students pass incessantly in the gaps between the dividers and there's an overwhelming sense that everything here is temporary, although the school has been this way for twenty-five years. When called on, Dan rattles off the answers, but seated in the last row, he's also free to keep up a running dialogue with his friends. His mind wanders from the blackboard instruction and occasionally he meanders around the room: to the pencil sharpener, over to another table, and up to the teacher's desk for a piece of paper. Even with only fifteen kids and an earnest instructor, Martin founders. From his perspective, being a freshman at Methuen High is all about killing time.

In history class, the soundtrack of a video on World War II blares from the next classroom area while Martin's teacher declaims from a handout on the early medieval church, alternating paragraphs with various students who read aloud in timid, halting voices and stumble over multisyllabic words. The collapse of the Roman Empire doesn't seem to interest Dan Martin very much. When his teacher asks him to define literacy, he shakes his head. "Huh. You just told me that yesterday," Martin says, in an appeasing tone.

Soon the class is asked to write a brief essay on the handout. Outlining a strategy compliant with statewide standardized testing,

ïes the assignment to a ridiculous degree. Yet the
n like they've been asked to prove God's exis-
They are expert reductionists: the teacher dic-
ers and working in little groups, the kids
ıon to the meekest of their peers.

year's tenth graders—the class of 2003, which includes Dan Martin—will be the first to face a mandatory graduation test, the Massachusetts Comprehensive Assessment System. The outlook is bleak, even at suburban schools like Methuen High. In a sample round of testing last year, 32 percent of Massachusetts' tenth graders failed English language arts, and 53 percent failed math. Methuen students performed slightly better than average; 28 percent failed the English portion and 50 percent flunked the math test.

In a state where legislators are quick to ram through their own pay raises, it's shocking to learn that the starting salary for a public school teacher in Methuen is only $26,083. During a conversation in the main office, my tenth-grade algebra II and trigonometry teacher, Judy Hiller, offers her instruction: "You don't do this for the money. It's a vocation."

For some teachers at Methuen High, it's a vocation under siege. "This place is going to hell in a handbasket," says Lynne Cheney, an old friend who teaches home economics. "I don't need some maladjusted 17-year-old telling me to fuck off."

Unfortunately, as Cheney develops and promotes Methuen High's online, in-house restaurant, Eatdotcom, she feels that "students who can't pass Applied Math are being dumped in here where there's fire and knives."

The only sound is the deep loud crunch of skate blades as the varsity candidates warm up by circling the rink. After five minutes, Coach Robillard calls the players to center ice and instructs them to "take a knee." There are a few anxious faces inside the caged helmets, but for the most part the core players have been together for years and there's every indication they will remain together on the varsity.

Robillard tells his players to "be competitors and bust ass" and then assigns them into groups, where they'll remain for the first half of the practice. Assistant Coach Jon Morin dumps a milk crate filled with pucks over the boards, and each player carves one from the mass of black disks and skates at top speed through a configuration of six traffic cones known as the "peanut drill."

"I don't want to see anybody coasting out here," yells Robillard. "I want you to go nuts."

After the first set of skating drills, the two goalies, all-star Dan Bonfiglio and last year's backup Dave Gray, work together at center ice: skating backward and forward in their goaltending stance, running the width of the rink on their knees, and chatting like it's the social hour. They've already made the team.

Athletic trainer Kevin MacLennan arrives in the rink and leans over the boards to tell me that Dan Bonfiglio has a rare nervous condition. One day last spring he passed out in the nurse's office at Methuen High and had his heart tested and was fitted for a pacemaker. "It kicks in when his heart rate drops," says the 24-year-old MacLennan, indicating that the paperwork clearing Bonfiglio to play is tied up with the school nurse.

Robillard skates over and asks his trainer for an update on Bonfiglio's condition, which is called neurocardiogenic syncope. Essentially, it's an abnormal nerve reflex that causes blood vessels to dilate rather than constrict, limiting blood flow to the heart and brain. Instead of speeding up to compensate, the heart slows down, which can lead to unconsciousness and seizures.

After being reassured that the kid is all right, Robillard asks Bonfiglio if he's made an extra pad for the left side of his chest and the goalie says no. "You've had all fall," Robillard says. "Take a hard shot there and that's your career."

Lined up in an arc surrounding the goalies at each end, the players execute a rapid fire drill, shooting a barrage of pucks at the nets. Amid the clap of wood on vulcanized rubber, Robillard says that he knows in thirty minutes who'll make his team. "But I give 'em a couple days, give 'em the benefit of the doubt."

Weak skaters certainly stand out—Assistant Coach Jon Morin calls them "chibbers." Dave Martin, who coaches in blue jeans and an old hooded sweatshirt, works alongside me as the players in the second group line up and we slap a piece of athletic tape on their helmets and scribble their names across it. A short, loud, keg of a man with a mashed nose and thinning hair, Martin, 44, was once a fiery competitor in hockey and soccer and just as well known as a hell-raiser. He's the main taskmaster during tryouts and describes his coaching method as "the one who kicks them in the ass if they need it." To earn his living, Martin climbs telephone poles as a lineman for the Massachusetts Electric Company.

Always uncensored, Martin asks one of his returning jayvees if he saw a former teammate who was home for Thanksgiving from the Marine Corps. "He looks great," Martin says. "Too bad he didn't lose all that weight last year—he would've been a force in hockey instead of a short fat dumb Frenchman."

Somehow a bird has gained access to the rink and it swoops above the heads of the nervous freshmen and sophomores kneeling at center ice. Coach Robillard repeats his speech from the varsity tryout, adding that playing hockey is a privilege and that he expects all of the candidates to be good citizens. Right before practice begins, he tells one player he's not invited to try out upon hearing a report that the student swore at a teacher.

"Don't embarrass yourself and certainly don't embarrass me," Robillard tells his charges.

Perhaps the most nervous of all the jayvee candidates is junior Nicole Pienta, an all-star field hockey goalie who has cobbled together a patchwork of borrowed equipment and is trying out on a whim. Pienta, 16, is a fine-boned, attractive girl with a kewpie doll face and straight brown hair. But she's very competitive, has a warrior's mentality, and is not afraid of the puck. I decide right there to make Nicole my project.

In the first drill, the goalies lie facedown on the ice and spring to their feet as Jon Morin fires pucks at them. While Dan Bonfiglio demonstrates almost perfect technique, I glide over to Nicole and talk in her ear. "A goalie has to take every advantage she can. See how Dan keeps his eyes on the puck even when he's lying flat? And you should cheat out of the crease until Coach Morin sends you back. Cut down the angle. Give him less to shoot at."

Nicole nods her head up and down. Her turn comes after Dave Gray. She succeeds in stopping one shot out of ten and skates back over to me. "Good job," I say. "You got one. We'll get out here early tomorrow and work on getting up and down."

Little shell-shocked Pienta grins at me through the bars of her cage. "Okay," she says.

That night, I'm getting dressed in the locker room for my usual Monday night game and hear a youth hockey coach in the corridor outside, screaming at one of his 13-year-old players for having "no fucking heart." His profane tirade grows ridiculous and I stand up at the same time as another guy who is half-dressed and we storm out to the corridor. But the kid is already gone when we get there, and the "coach" is back on the ice. He's a chibber himself, his shaved head glowing crimson from his tantrum. The other player and I look at each other and spit on the mats and go back into the locker room.

In the phys ed office the next morning I report the incident to Joe Robillard and Fran Molesso. I'm surprised how common that sort of abuse is in youth hockey, now that I'm spending extra time at the rink.

"It's not just youth hockey, it's all sports," says Molesso. "It's too many parents living through their kids."

Robillard listens to my description of the episode and nods his head. "I think you coach the way you were coached—if you ever were," he says, noting that his coaches at Burlington High School, Brewster Academy, and Boston University were all graduates of Boston University.

During the next gym class I meet jayvee hopeful Nicole Pienta on the ice for an extra workout. Dressed in a gray sweatsuit and goalie skates, Nicole admits that she's a long shot to make the team but "has no quit in her." We take a few laps to warm up and then I put her through some agility drills: skating back and forth the width of the ice in her goalie's stance, lateral movement in the goal crease, and a quick geometry lesson on maintaining a proper angle to the shooter.

We stop for a breather after twenty minutes, leaning on our sticks at the north end of the rink. "It's fun, but I'll probably be back out for track by next week," says Pienta. "They're not gonna keep a junior with no experience."

"Don't give up," I tell her. "Volunteer to go first in all the drills. Ask for extra ice. Make it hard for them to cut you."

Every time I change the exercise, Nicole bobs her ponytail and executes the repetitions. At one point I lay my stick down in the goal crease and she moves east to west, jumping over the shaft with a little crow hop. Robillard comes to the rink door and watches her work out. "She's a good little athlete," he says, shaking his head.

Before the afternoon tryout, star forward Chris Cagliuso holds court with coaches Robillard, Martin, and big Joe Harb outside the varsity locker room. According to Robillard, Cagliuso, who along with seniors Dan Bonfiglio and Thom DeZenzo is a tri-captain for the 1999–2000 season, puts extra pressure on himself because of his brother Brett's exploits. (After a stellar career at Methuen High, Brett Cagliuso played for Holy Cross and last year scored the Crusaders' winning goal in overtime of the league championship semifinal.) Chris is not the dominant high school player his brother was, notes Robillard, but he's pretty darned good.

Fresh from his prep school interview at Phillips Exeter, Cagliuso is dressed like an Ivy Leaguer in a blue blazer, khaki pants, and club tie. "I've been working on my game all summer," he says. "And I'm gonna unveil it during the scrimmage on Saturday."

Martin leaps up and pinches both of Cagliuso's cheeks. "I can't wait to see the brand-new Chris Cagliuso," he says. "God knows, I'm sick of the old one."

Just then sophomore Dan Gradzewicz passes by and asks Coach Martin if he's seen Albert Soucy. "Why, you lookin' for advice? He'll tell you to stay home and quit playing hockey. You want advice, pick someone smarter. Although from a frog to a polack, that's an improvement, I guess."

Dan Bonfiglio appears to tell Coach Robillard that he has to sit out until the paperwork comes through for his heart ailment. A quiet, sleepy-eyed kid who plans to attend a top college where hockey will no longer be "a priority," Bonfiglio doesn't seem fazed by his condition. His doctor simply has to fill out a "return-to-participation" form and is busy today with surgeries, the goalie says.

Trainer Kevin MacLennan drops by and listens to Bonfiglio, then says, "This is a very unusual case. We have to play it by the rules."

The Rangers' all-star goalie can be dominant one night, invisible the next. I'm told he has a tendency to sulk, and at other times, to showboat. In last year's heartbreaking 5-4 loss to Beverly in the state tournament, the pivotal event was Bonfiglio's ten-minute misconduct penalty for slashing an opposing player. Since he's a senior, this is his last chance to prove he can win the big game.

The players emerge from their locker room and cluster around the rink door in full gear, as the Zamboni makes a final pass over the ice. "Ssshh. Don't say anything," says Dave Martin when he sees a notebook sticking out of my pocket. "The words you say may come back to haunt you."

"Yours certainly will," I tell him.

Coach Robillard blows his whistle and gathers the candidates around the bench. "Not all of you are going to make this team," he says. "You're being evaluated at all times—before, during, and after practice. They say you get soft when you get older, but I don't think I'm getting soft. I'm getting aggravated. I want to see you DO THIS STUFF RIGHT."

Immediately after his chalk talk, Robillard introduces a new drill that includes a sliding "Chicago turn" at center ice by all three players in each group. Robillard doesn't like the first run-through and singles out a returning defenseman. "Step up! Step up! Jeesh. Another dumb hockey player. No wonder you get lousy grades."

With toots from Coach Robillard's whistle echoing in the background, Jon Morin calls over hulking defenseman Paul St. Louis. "What did I tell you yesterday?" he asks, bopping St. Louis in the face mask with the heel of his stick. "Stay in the middle of the ice."

Jon Morin and I are the only two people in the rink who played for legendary high school coach Bruce Parker. Morin graduated four years after I did, in 1979, and went on to prep at Deerfield Academy and captained a Division III national championship team at Babson College. Today he's the business manager for a health care company and, at 38, a muscular, hard-nosed guy who can still skate and shoot better than the average high school player. The most tactical of the Ranger coaches, Jon Morin organizes the defense and demonstrates many of the drills. When Morin goes flying down the ice, it reminds me of Mr. Parker scrimmaging against our team without wearing any equipment. He used to say that he'd put on the gear when he felt one of us could touch him.

Bruce Parker, a complex man with the erudition of a college professor and the bearing of a Marine Corps drill instructor, coached the Rangers from 1974 until 1978 and his continuing influence on the program can be seen in the meticulous habits of Jon Morin. ("I still remember things Coach Parker taught me better than twenty years ago," Morin says.) In the mid-1970s, Parker had won a state hockey championship in Acton-Boxborough and insisted on the very best facilities and equipment while coaching in Methuen—a situation that led to criticism when he failed to produce instant champions. Mr. Parker moved on to state championships with other programs, in New Jersey, on Cape Cod, and in Framingham, Massachusetts. Since his departure, more than one observer has noted how infighting among Methuen politicians and parents and school administrators often transforms those most dedicated to the town into their own worst enemies.

Many former players remember Bruce Parker with fondness and warmth and others with a lingering bitterness over his rigid system and what they considered a martinet's disposition. One of my old teammates recalls the time he scored a power play goal against Dracut only to be reprimanded for not passing to the centerman, as we had practiced. Mr. Parker also has abundant self-confidence, a quality that irritates some people and delights the rest. While Mike Lebel was coaching Wentworth Institute in the late eighties, he came into their deserted rink one day and there was Bruce Parker, sitting all alone. Our former coach held up a piece of the skate-sharpening machine and said, "Michael. This broke down, and I'm the only guy on the East Coast who can fix it." Lebel thought this was hilarious: after not seeing each other for ten years, there was no hello, no how do you do, just a statement of hard, cold fact.

Despite his eccentricities, Mr. Parker treated his players with consideration and respect. When I was editor of the high school newspaper and we were holding a fund-raiser, I went to Mr. Parker's classroom to see if he wanted his car washed. Our coach drove a brand-new Ford Toronado, maroon with cream-colored leather seats, and a burnished steering wheel that was like the wheel of a ship. He handed me his keys, saying, "Remember, Jay. Nobody drives my car but you," and I walked out to the parking lot like I had received a commission from God himself.

I owe a lot to Bruce Parker. He taught me how to get the most out of my abilities and about striving for excellence in all things. After graduating from Methuen High, I earned a total of six varsity letters at Acadia University and have played on four championship rugby teams over the years. I even scored a try in the Mexico City stadium where Bob Beamon set a world record in the long jump. Bruce Parker may have produced better, more high-achieving members of society than me. He certainly coached better hockey players. But one thing's for sure: when Mr. Parker talked, I listened as well as anybody.

5

ANTRONIG-PARSHA

IN HISTORY CLASS, DAN MARTIN answers three questions in a row about the Catholic Church in medieval times, competing with the sharpest girl in the class for their teacher's approbation. When he's also the first to recognize an illuminated manuscript in his textbook, a wiseass in the rear of the classroom asks Martin if he has "one of them fuckin' computer chips" planted in his brain. "You used to be stupid," the kid says.

"I know," says Martin, surprising even himself.

In his Norwegian print stocking hat and wispy moustache, Dan Martin looks like a sinister elf. For the rest of the hour, he slouches deeper in his chair and chats with his neighbors, shamed into mediocrity. The teacher in the space next door calls former Russian president Boris Yeltsin "a raging alcoholic" and Martin repeats it and starts laughing with his buddies.

"Certain things you take on faith," says Martin's teacher, his voice rising over the din. "When the church says that God is three persons in one—the Father, the Son, and the Holy Spirit—you're required to accept it."

"Do you believe that?" Dan Martin asks.

"I do," the teacher says. Martin is pensive.

Half of the students in the class lack pens, paper, and textbooks;

and most have attention spans of only a few seconds. Near the end of the hour, the teacher attempts to make a point about the Benedictine Order. "The monks had enormous discipline," he says, looking straight at young Martin. "Athletes need discipline. In hockey, Dan, if you don't skate back and help protect the goal, what happens?"

"You get a smack in the head," Martin says.

Before we part ways after class, I have a word with Dan Martin: "You got three or four right answers and then some nitwit starts making fun of you and you're playing dumb again. That nitwit won't be there to help when you're out looking for your first job, or trying to get into college." Martin studies the carpet, as I pat him on the shoulder. "Don't be afraid to be right, kid."

Walking into school the next day, I notice my former English teacher, Dan Herlihy, hair and beard gray now, striding out to the parking lot. During my senior year, Herlihy required our class to memorize the prologue from the *Canterbury Tales* and I refused, declaring that Middle English was dead. Now, as he passes me without a sign of recognition, I recall my advice to Dan Martin and how I never listened to anybody old enough to vote when I was Martin's age.

On that winter day twenty-five years ago, I shook my head "no" when asked if I was going to recite Chaucer, and then after class Mr. Herlihy overheard me declaiming the lines to a buddy in the hallway. I don't recall exactly what was said at that moment, but I remember thinking that I had outsmarted myself and gained an F in the process. It's a lesson I haven't forgotten.

The next day I spot my former teacher outside the cafeteria and hail him from a distance and go over. I say, "Sorry this assignment is a little late" and then recite:

Whan that Aprill with his shoures soote,
The droghte of March hath perced to the roote,

And bathed every veyne in swich licour
Of which vertu engendred is the flour

"Not bad," Herlihy says. "I'd give it a 'B.' " He shakes his head, smiling at me through his beard. "It's funny the things you remember."

A good friend of mine named Glenn Gallant was playing for St. Theresa's junior baseball league in 1968, when the kids took a field trip to the Museum of Science in Boston. Along the way, in Somerville or Malden someplace, they passed a variety store with the unusual name of Antronig-Parsha.

Glenn's coach said, "I bet no one remembers that name on the way home."

The young baseball stars visited the museum, ate lunch, and on the return trip to Methuen with no prompting from his coach, Glenn repeated the name of the variety store. No one else happened to remember it, but that's not the thrust of the story.

Decades after the trip, Glenn ran into his old baseball coach. He asked the fellow if he recalled going to the museum. Coach said yes. Then Glenn asked his mentor if he remembered Antronig-Parsha. Not only had the coach forgotten the name of the store, he didn't recall telling the kids to remember it. To an adult, it was a momentary thing. To Glenn Gallant—to a kid—a memory that will last a lifetime.

Before practice the next day, Albert Soucy, in skates and pads and a Holy Cross baseball hat, encounters sophomore James Girouard in the heated corridor adjacent to the rink. The slight, bespectacled Girouard is wearing his street clothes. "Hurry up," Soucy tells him. "Get dressed."

"I'm waiting to see the trainer," says Girouard.

“Whaddaya gonna say?” asks Soucy. “ ‘Oh, I got a big crack in my ass. Fix it.’ Go get dressed.”

Just then one of the girls from the basketball team passes by, spots the two hockey players, and bounces a ball to get their attention. She’s a head taller than Soucy. “Oh-oh,” she says. “It’s another ‘Al Soucy’ story.”

The little French Canadian practices his stickhandling with a crushed milk carton for a puck. “You wanna fight?” he asks the tall girl, smirking beneath the brim of his cap. “ ’Cause I’ll fight you right now.”

Robillard goes into the skate room and emerges with the box of practice jerseys. He lays them out in the corridor and the varsity players, in skates and pads, crowd around like kids at Christmas. Each “line,” or three-man squad of forwards, will wear a different color jersey. As captain, Chris Cagliuso selects the white jerseys for his line of Kevin McCarthy and Ryan Fontaine; Albert Soucy chooses the other Ranger color, dark blue; and Robillard assigns the black and the teal to the third and fourth lines, respectively. All the defensemen wear orange, and the two varsity goalies, Dan Bonfiglio and Dave Gray, also get Ranger blue.

Paul St. Louis, at 6' 2" and 258 pounds, fills the doorway when he comes in for his jersey. “Better sew two shirts together for Baby Huey,” says Coach Harb, a large fellow himself. St. Louis is a big kid, but a little slow-footed on the ice, and the coaches have been riding him.

Although Dan Martin’s brother Chris made the varsity as a freshman, Dan isn’t selected to receive a practice jersey. Assistant Coach Joe Harb, 29, a graduate of Tufts University and former college football player, is Dan Martin’s teacher for a course entitled “Science Topics.” While other teachers report that Dan is acting out in class, the freshman pays attention and works on his equations under the watchful eye of Mr. Harb.

"I have no problems with Danny at all," he says. But Harb has a fifty-inch chest, thighs like oak trees, and wears his black hair cropped close to his football player's brow.

Another teacher has accused Martin of throwing a five-pointed metal "karate star" in class. Luckily, no one was hurt. "A serious offense," Harb says. "I pulled him aside and he told me he didn't do it. See, Danny's problem is he never takes responsibility for anything he does. I told him, 'Don't pull that shit with me. I know your father.' "

Right before practice, Joe Robillard emerges from the skate room in his Methuen Hockey windbreaker and blue baseball cap with the embroidered white "M." He calls Dan Martin over and puts his arm around the kid's shoulder and walks off beneath the grandstand. Silhouetted in the beam of a klieg light mounted on the wall, they form the classic tableaux of coach and player: the taller figure hatted and bent to the young man's ear, the helmet nodding up and down, a slant of light showing beneath their skate blades.

When they're through, young Martin walks out and around the mass of bleachers, and Robillard clacks along the rubber mats in the peculiar gait of a man on stilts. I ask him what he has said to Dan Martin.

"That playing hockey is a privilege and from the things I'm hearing, he's in danger of losing that privilege," says Robillard. "I told him not to embarrass me or the program, and most of all, not to embarrass himself."

Coach Martin emerges from the jayvee locker room and whispers to me that he's just made some cuts: "Little Nicole the goalie was expecting it, but [a chubby 13-year-old defenseman] burst into tears. I took him out back and said, 'Keep skating and playing youth hockey. You're only a freshman. Try out again next year. Anything can happen.' But the tears were coming out, I'm patting him on the shoulder and I'm thinking 'Arrggh. Don't do this to me.' "

"How did Nicole take it?" I ask him, thinking of our extra practice sessions and the determined way that Nicole went about her work.

"Better than I did," says Martin. "I felt terrible about it. But she said her dad was a big track star in high school and she's gonna run track now, anyway." Always critical, Martin shows that he's impressed with the 100-pound field hockey goalie who dared to face the big boys. "She's a competitor. A tough little nut. It was her skating that held her back."

Since I'm a volunteer assistant without portfolio, I draw the most inglorious tasks: fetching the rink guy to clean the ice, opening and locking the skate room door, and keeping game statistics. This last one is the perfect job for me. Since the age of 11 I've been a meticulous recorder of athletic detail, storing my handwritten statistics in a blue plastic folder stamped with the logo of the Hanover Life Insurance Companies. All the way through high school, I'd spend hours in my room adding up numbers and arranging them in columns, clipping hockey photos from magazines, and doing push-ups and sit-ups. For instance, my records indicate that I played my first organized hockey game on April 18, 1970, at the Billerica Forum, splitting the game with another goalie, and allowing one goal in a 13-3 victory. Who else remembers that the first line center on the 1971 Methuen Junior High floor hockey champs was none other than my old pal Teddy Hajjar, and that Ted scored a team-leading six goals that year? Or that my goals against average for the 1971-72 Methuen Youth Hockey season was a stingy 1.90, and playing goal for the Methuen Flyers I shut out Lawrence 2-0 at the Frost Arena on January 30, 1972? No one but me.

Another thing I've noticed is that the players' gear is a lot lighter now: Kevlar and plastic and yards of black nylon, where once it was canvas, rolled woolen batting, and oiled calfskin. As a goalie, my weight would rise from 140 pounds before practice to 155 or so afterward, the heavy equipment soaked through with sweat and melted ice chips. For entertainment when we were teenagers, my friends Rick Angus and Dave Frasca and I would study the Ned Singer hockey catalog, filled with black-and-white photos of jerseys and helmets and goalie pads. If we'd saved money shoveling snow or delivering newspapers, once a year we'd order a pair of hockey socks or skate laces and then wait months for the mailman to deliver them.

Before they take the ice, Robillard draws his players around him and says, "The guy that busts his ass when no one is watching is the guy who's going to be a good hockey player. Remember that. I'm not all about winning and losing, I'm about giving 100 percent."

Albert Soucy maneuvers himself ahead of freshman Dan Martin in the line to go on the ice. "I can tell you what to do," he says. "I have juniority."

Nearby, senior defenseman Thom DeZenzo is standing with classmate Nick Maloney and jayvee goalie Becky Trudel waiting for the rink door to open. Grinning like a madman, DeZenzo nudges Maloney and asks the team's only female player, "Ever been to Joe Bertagna's goaltending camp?" Of course, this legend is emblazoned across Becky Trudel's practice jersey.

The blond-haired DeZenzo looks at Nick Maloney and they bump shoulders and laugh. This bit of humor from a guy who has his last name tattooed across his upper back in large Gothic letters.

I crook my finger and call Becky over. Methuen's jayvee goalie stands just five feet tall and wears her hair in a ponytail. A national champion at the all-girl level, she's Methuen's "second-best goalie," in Coach Martin's opinion.

"Next time Thom comes out with his shirt off, ask him if his name really is DeZenzo," I say to her. Trudel laughs.

While Robillard is off talking to the Zamboni driver, Dave Martin and I sit on the boards and he offers a "quick bio" of each varsity candidate as they skate past. "David George: tough as nails. Chris [Cagliuso] is Chris. He's good. That's Ryan Fontaine. We counted last year: he made three passes, all to himself." A dark-haired kid flies by, with compact strides. "Give us twenty Kevin McCarthys and we'll win the state championship every year: smart kid, works hard on every drill, and never says a word. James Girouard: great tryout player, hasn't shown it in games. Matt Zapanas: huge for a sophomore. Has what I call 'street hockey hands.' Good moves, but doesn't want to hit anyone. Chris [Martin]: talented player—not just because he's my kid, either. Last year I sat in the stands during tryouts and let Joe and Jon pick the team. Dan Bonfiglio: the goalie job is his to lose, but then he goes and dies last summer. Joe tell you? About his heart? Sometimes he's in his own little world. But that's a goalie for you." Martin smiles at me. "But you know all about that. Dave Gray: inconsistent goalie. Great one day, terrible the next. Becky Trudel: our most technically sound goalie. I like her chances."

"To make the team?" I ask.

"To start for the varsity."

A broad-shouldered kid with a familiar skating style lopes by the bench. "Who's that?" I ask Martin.

"Jarrod Trovato. He's a sophomore. His brother graduated last year."

Young Jarrod skates with a quick, powerful stride, just like his older brother, Jason. "His father the one that's sick?" I ask.

Martin nods. "Cancer."

Halfway through what amounts to a lackluster workout, Robillard whistles his squad to center ice. "Last year, there were games where we had no life at all," the coach says, noting how disappointed he was in their 6-12-2 record. "Heck, if you're going through the motions, I have to find a guy who's going to compete." He raises his whistle, adding, "I'm making some cuts today."

A few moments later, Dan Gradzewicz smacks one of the freshmen to the ice in front of Coach Morin, who jots down a note on his clipboard. Gradzewicz skates over to me. "How am I doing?" he asks.

"Knock a couple more guys down," I tell him.

It starts getting a little chippy. Sophomore Shane Wakeen slashes James Girouard across the midsection with his stick, and Girouard skates to the bench all doubled over. He lifts his jersey to reveal a six-inch welt that has already risen across his abdomen. "I'm dying right now," he says.

Senior Tim Parker, a lanky kid who's built like a pencil, laughs at Girouard. "Don't be a pussy."

In a three-on-two drill, Chris Cagliuso turns both defensemen completely around, slices toward the goalie at top speed, and fires the puck into the net, but loses an edge. He goes down in a heap and crashes into the boards, drawing the attention of all the coaches. The rink grows silent. Then Cagliuso staggers up; he's all right.

"That's the way to put it in, Chris," says Robillard, keeping an eye on his star forward. As Cagliuso goes this year—all 5' 9" and 160 pounds of him—so go the Rangers.

At the end of the workout, Robillard stands by the rink door with his clipboard and watches the kids file past into the locker room. Tapping his pencil on the metal clip, he studies his cut list until the rink grows silent. "I hate this part," he says, holding his stomach like he has indigestion.

I follow him into the locker room. The players are undressing, horsing around, but everything stops in an instant. In a soft voice, Robillard reads a list of players who are invited to practice tomorrow. "Anyone not on the list should report to the skate room, if you have any questions," he says.

When Robillard reads the brief list of seniors who have made the first cut, three-year player Nick Maloney doesn't hear his name and hangs his head and utters a quiet "shit." Immediately the other players shy away from Maloney's locker and avert their eyes. A year from now, he'll be in the Marine Corps. Robillard departs, and the only one talking is Chris Cagliuso, saying something about his new skates to Albert Soucy.

6

SANTA CLAUS IS COMING TO TOWN

METHUEN HIGH'S FIRST COMPETITION of the season is a round-robin scrimmage with Burlington and local rival Wilmington. Scrawled on the blackboard in the varsity locker room is the admonition: "100% of the shots you don't take, won't go in." Dressing in the corner is senior goalie Dan Bonfiglio, attaching his bulky leg pads with a series of interlocking straps. He's barechested and a raised red scar about two inches long appears on his upper chest, where the pacemaker was installed. Bonfiglio hasn't been his aggressive self in practice thus far, and Burlington, Methuen's first opponent this evening, will be a real test for him.

Dave Martin is in the locker room, keeping the guys loose with his friendly insults and masturbation jokes, and he stops at Bonfiglio's locker. In a loud voice, he proclaims that his starting goaltender must wear an extra chest pad or face the prospects of an early death. This seems crass, even for Martin. Bonfiglio replies that the pad is uncomfortable and he doesn't want to wear it.

But Coach Martin stoops over the goalie, avoiding the mass formed by his leg pads, and pats him gently on the shoulder. "I just don't think I could go through a season without seeing your smiling face," he says.

Outside the locker room Dan's father, Joseph Bonfiglio, is pacing the mats. A short, prematurely gray-haired man with a warm manner and ready smile, Bonfiglio speaks proudly of his two goaltending sons: Dan and Anthony, who played for Methuen and is now a sophomore at Boston University and participates in intramural hockey and rugby. Joseph Bonfiglio explains that Dan's pacemaker is a precaution, and that most people who wear one require assistance when their heartbeat becomes too rapid. His son's condition is rare. The device speeds up Dan's heart when his pulse drops to thirty, otherwise he'll pass out.

"Danny does not have a heart problem," says Mr. Bonfiglio. "Believe me, if there was any problem, we wouldn't be doing this."

Moments later, Robillard enters the locker room and tells the Rangers to play hard, work on the things he has emphasized in practice, and finish off their body checks. The team takes the ice in their motley practice jerseys; Burlington is in red. During the first shift, the Rangers are unable to clear the puck from their own zone and, within a couple of minutes, have given up three goals.

"Guys, it's a fast game," says Robillard to the players on the bench. "You're doing things in slow motion. Start moving your feet."

It's a long night for the Rangers. Although nobody is keeping score, they give up goals in bunches and both Dan Bonfiglio and Dave Gray look porous in the net. The only bright moment for Methuen comes when skinny sophomore Jeremy Abdo picks up a loose puck and slips through the defense with a nifty move and surprises Burlington's goalie. He makes the save but Abdo's linemate James Girouard skates in and shoots the rebound into the goal.

"Just like a street hockey player," says Martin, who's refereeing the scrimmage. He mimics Abdo's side-to-side moves, and laughs.

The Rangers play a little better against Wilmington but once again are outscored and outhustled. In the locker room afterward, they peel off their jerseys and throw them into a pile. "I'd have to say that sucked," says Albert Soucy, walking past in just his skates, socks, and hockey pants. "I have to get my thumb out of my ass."

Hovering around the skate room, the coaching staff is bewildered by Methuen's performance. "The worst opening scrimmage we've ever played," says Jon Morin. "Nowhere to go but up."

The only bright spot, according to Joe Robillard, is that his players won't be "going around thinking they're any good."

Sophomore Dan Gradzewicz comes in with his skates and leaves them on the shelf to be sharpened. He hasn't played very well, taking far too long to react to situations in his own end, according to Coach Morin. Gradzewicz is carrying a backpack and Dave Martin asks if it contains his homework. "I hope it's your history book," says Martin. "We must all learn from our mistakes."

Gradzewicz smiles. "I got an A in history."

"History of what? The Polish Revolution? Or History of Kielbasa?" asks Martin. He pretends to boot Gradzewicz in the ass. "Go home," he says.

After this moment of forced levity, the coaches are downcast. Robillard takes off his blue Rangers cap, scratches his head, and puts it back on. In his somber moments, which are few, he resembles the deadpan silent film star Buster Keaton. He says nothing for several moments.

"We've got a long, long way to go, Joe," says Morin. "Fundamental shit. Positioning. Basic things like that."

Robillard tries to find something positive to say about one of the freshmen brought up to skate with the varsity.

"He sucked," says Morin.

Robillard offers the name of a sophomore.

"Sucked."

Another sophomore.

"Sucked."

It's a cold, hard, impersonal but accurate evaluation. Robillard leans against the concrete wall, exhaling a slow breath. "Well," he says. "Back to work."

Liam and I arrive at Riverwalk Park in Methuen Square at quarter to six, just as carloads of children and their parents begin to show up for the Christmas tree lighting. We squeeze among the chubby Italian men in polyester pants and white bucks, their perfumed wives draped in gold necklaces; the teenagers strolling three or four abreast, the single mothers leading their broods of children, the hawkers, vendors, police officers, fire marshals, tattooed bikers clinging to their balloon-breasted molls; young girls with faces unlined and untroubled, like lilies, like dreams I used to have when I attended old brick schools and wore my hair long.

Next to the little white gazebo, which is decorated with evergreen boughs and contains a chair for Santa Claus, several volunteers hand out hot chocolate and tree-shaped cookies covered with red and green sprinkles. Liam is shivering with excitement when the mayor takes up the microphone and directs everyone's attention to the gates of the park. Three hundred children count down from ten to zero, and the mayor presses a button meant to illuminate the forty-foot evergreen.

Nothing happens. He tries again, but the tree remains dark.

Someone from the Department of Public Works rushes over and instructs the Mayor on the intricacies of the remote control. "I thought it was like a garage door opener," the mayor says. "Just push."

Suddenly the tree blinks on, festooned with red and green and blue lights. At the same time, a fire engine pulls up to the park entrance, its turret light throwing red swaths across the frozen lawn. Down leaps Santa Claus, waving and ho-ho-ho-ing and carrying a satchel.

"Wow. I didn't know Santa Claus had such a big mustache," says Liam.

While we're waiting beside the gazebo, the nosy young reporter from the *Eagle-Tribune* approaches and asks what's going on around town. "Santa is here," I tell him.

Our local paper is the *USA Yesterday* of tired wire stories, color photos, and high-tech graphics. Its strength lies in gossipy items about Methuen's and Lawrence's quarrelsome politicians, high school athletics, and the "Irish sports page"—the obituaries. You read the *Eagle-Tribune* in order to understand the world—if your world ends at the Haverhill-Methuen line.

The reporter glances over at Santa Claus. "He looks like a professional."

I point to the top of Liam's head and mouth the words, "Five years old."

At first the reporter doesn't get my point and goes on to make another hip, cynical remark about Santa Claus's plausibility. I make a cutting motion across my throat. The mayor saves the day by swooping down on the reporter, complaining that the *Eagle-Tribune* doesn't write enough "feel-good" stories about Methuen. He points to me. "If Jay wrote about this, you'd be able to visualize the scene," the mayor says.

"That's why Jay gets the big bucks," says the reporter.

Across the gazebo, Santa's beleaguered elf signals that the big man is ready for his next appointment. Liam rushes forward, and I tip my baseball cap to the mayor and the reporter. "Merry Christmas, gentlemen."

After visiting with Santa, Liam is ready to go home and we head out of the park, beneath the bare branches of the trees and through the iron arch. Liam gestures at the lights decorating the old-fashioned lampposts in the town square, and the wreaths suspended on loops of wire across Hampshire Street. "What is it, Dad?" he asks.

"We're celebrating the birth of Baby Jesus, who came to save us," I tell my son.

On the ride home, I can feel Liam's gaze on me from the backseat, where he's strapped into his safety seat. The house is dark and we go inside, turn on the Christmas tree, and Liam dresses himself in his pajamas. Then he climbs up next to me on the couch, and there are tears in his eyes. "I don't want you to get old," he says. "I don't want the angels to take you up to heaven."

"What makes you say that, Boo? I'm not going anywhere. I'm going to stay here and play hockey with you."

For a few moments, Liam is inconsolable. "I don't want Mom to get older either," he says, his arms flung around my neck. "I don't want to become a man."

7
OLD SCHOOL

EARLY IN DECEMBER, MY OLD Ranger teammates Ken Schelling and Curt Goulet and Gary Ruffen and I take the kids skating at the brand-new arena in Salem, New Hampshire. The "Icenter" features two beautiful rinks, a fitness club, and built-in hockey shop and café. "Where's the rusted chicken-wire fence and all the puddles?" asks Schelling, who was our team captain in 1975. "The urine-smelling locker rooms and surly attendants. I mean, what the hell kind of rink is this?"

At one point, the four of us are wheeling around the end boards and Gary Ruffen pretends to throw a hip check at Schelling. "Watch out for his prostate," I say.

"Don't laugh," Schelling says.

The next evening we rendezvous at Methuen High. Because it's warm and rainy outside, a layer of fog is wafting over the ice when I meet Ken Schelling in the rink lobby. A cheerful, dark-haired man who married his college sweetheart, Kathleen Duerr, and is father of three children—Keegan, Kelsey, and Kyler—my old teammate lives ninety miles away in western Massachusetts. Captain Ken is visiting Methuen for just one more night and I've arranged for him to skate with us; we spend fifteen minutes shooting the breeze about our kids, the varsity hockey team, and the old days. In the heated enclosure of the lobby, Ken asks how the players on this year's team are different from our era. Then Gary Ruffen enters the rink, he and Ken shake hands, and our conversation is suspended.

As we push through the heavy door to the locker room Ken starts shaking hands and ticking off the names of old friends and teammates, Gary Ruffen, Dennis Dube, Dave Martin, Mike Alianiello, and in the general uproar Dube calls out to me, "Jay. I got your title: 'Schelling's List.' "

Just before our game begins, I skate over to Ken Schelling and say, "The top players on Methuen's team are better skaters, better stickhandlers, better positionally, and much more technical than we were. But there's something missing, I don't know what you call it, a competitive fire or something. A kid gets cut, or sent down to the jayvees, and he shrugs it off and doesn't seem to care."

Ken's been coaching youth hockey players, including his own boys, for several years. "We wanted it more," he says. "Because we never had it before. They've had 'it' for years—all kinds of prime ice and traveling teams and tournaments. It's no big thing."

Schelling and I skate on the same line and work a couple of nice plays. Coming along the boards with the puck, he slides a nifty little pass behind the defense and I shift in alone on the goalie and slip a quick backhand under his pads. Ken skates up with a big smile on his face and we punch each other's gloves and Gary Ruffen, who's on the other team, glides by laughing at us and says, "The old magic."

Between shifts, Schelling apologizes for not playing in almost five years. But on the ice he's still slick and smooth and does intelligent things with the puck. Curling back along the boards under pressure, Schelling pulls up short and banks the puck to an onrushing teammate. It's a smart play, characteristic of our old captain. Ken Schelling is a clean, tough, precise, and durable hockey player.

When we were young, Ken's father built a makeshift rink in the backyard for Ken and his older brother Dennis and the other neighborhood kids to skate on. Mr. Schelling was a stickler for perfect ice and would spend countless hours preparing and grooming the surface. Early one morning, one of his neighbors called the police to report, "It's three A.M., it's five below zero, and the guy next door is watering his lawn."

For almost an hour after our game, Ruffen and Schelling and Alianiello and Dube and I hang around the locker room and recite our favorite *Three Stooges* routines and tell stories, like the time Mike Lebel pretended to flush himself down one of the industrial-sized toilets at the old high school. Finally the rink attendant comes around to lock up and outside beneath a canopy of stars the other guys drift off until it's just Ken Schelling and I chatting in the cold empty lot. We're each standing half in and half out of our cars, talking over my roof, and I say to Ken that if he were still living in Methuen I'd be pestering him to skate twice a week. But he shakes his head.

"You still have a passion for the game," Schelling says. "I love hockey, but I don't have to play anymore. I'm happy just to coach and pass on what I know to the kids."

During a brief practice before the scrimmage against Lynn English High School, Robillard bangs his stick on the ice and fumes at his team for being so casual an hour before their second real test. In my conversations with him, it's plain that Robillard is bothered by his players' lack of intensity more than anything else. Last year, when the Rangers lost games they should have won and the seniors on his team didn't seem to care, Robillard came very close to handing in his resignation midseason.

Dave Martin says that the "Old School" Robillard is growing sick of the typical Methuen player: pampered in youth hockey by indulgent coaches and parents, outfitted with a thousand dollars' worth of gear, and strong in the belief that a place on the varsity is a divine right for anyone who makes it to Bantam 'A.'

"These kids have no idea what it means to wear that 'Rangers' across your chest," says Martin, as we lean on the boards watching a drill. "With a few exceptions, they don't have enough heart."

His own coaches and several friends around the league convinced Robillard to stay with Methuen. But his temper flares when he notices a player coasting who ought to be sprinting, or catches someone laughing and fooling around when he's trying to instruct. Three players skate past, giggling like they're at a church picnic, and Robillard swivels his head around as they go by. "You want to fool around, get off the ice," he says. "Go run track or something. I don't want you."

In the locker room forty-five minutes before the scrimmage, the varsity are waxing and powdering their stick blades and arguing about who owes whom a roll of tape and who borrowed which CD. The close unventilated space reeks of moldy canvas and sweat, and the players joke that they have the smelliest training area of all the teams in Methuen.

Somebody's pager goes off and Dan Bonfiglio, half-dressed in his goalie equipment, clutches his chest near the pacemaker and feigns a heart attack. Then Dave Gray keels over beside him and pretty soon half the team is suffering from mild infarctions. It's their way of showing solidarity with their goalie and tri-captain. One of the freshmen turns off the pager and Gray and Bonfiglio laugh at him. Bonfiglio bends over to lace up his pads and tells Gray how he scared one of his teachers when he was wearing an electronic monitor to class and pulled the same prank.

"You should have seen her face," says Bonfiglio, as Gray straps on his own pads. Side by side on the bench, the two lanky, dark-haired goalies look like mirror images of each other. "I thought she was gonna have the Big One."

The seniors all join a discussion of team protocol and what the younger kids must do to stay in their good graces. The prime directive is that no freshman or sophomore can mock an upperclassman. "Anyone who disobeys that rule should have to have sex with our inflatable sheep," says Bonfiglio, assuming the role of clubhouse lawyer.

"Just for shits and giggles, what would possess anyone to purchase an inflatable sheep?" someone asks.

Bonfiglio nudges his fellow goaltender. "Gray bought it."

"Is he getting tired of his girlfriend?"

Busy fastening his toe strap, Dave Gray lifts his choirboy face and grins. Over the ensuing laughter, Bonfiglio says, "No. No. Anyone who gets it has to walk around with a sign that reads 'I like to have sex with . . . sheeps.' "

More laughter—this time at Bonfiglio's grammatical error. Blond-haired Thom DeZenzo points at me, sitting in the corner. "You gotta put the pause in," he says, appointing himself literary editor. "It's not as funny without the pause." I laugh along with the other guys but make a mental note: this is the first time any of the varsity players has acknowledged my presence, and my reason for being here.

Soon the room grows quiet and the players don their shoulder pads and practice jerseys, sitting on the bench with their caged helmets spread open on their knees. "Where's the all-star?" asks one of the sophomores, noticing for the first time that Chris Cagliuso is missing.

Someone replies that Cagliuso has another prep school interview and will be late. After starring in the prestigious "Hockey Night in Boston" summer showcase, the speedy Cagliuso is on the brink of a higher level when it comes to his game. Two or three years from now, when most of his teammates are playing in recreational leagues, or have enlisted in the Marine Corps and are retired from the sport, Cagliuso will probably appear on television playing for a major college.

"He's going all over the world—the all-star," someone says. But it's not sarcastic. The entire team respects Cagliuso's excellence and his commitment to the sport. He's their champion.

Outside the locker room, I ask Coach Morin if his defense is ready for tonight's contest. "No," he says, arms folded across his chest. "They're not ready to be ready, if that makes any sense."

While they wait for the Zamboni machine to resurface the ice, Dave Martin works at keeping the guys loose. He asks if any of the players clustered around knows what the "CH" in the Montreal Canadiens insignia stands for, and shakes his head at answers of "Canadian Hockey" and "Les Habitants."

"Notice that it's painted right in the middle of their rink?" he asks. "It stands for 'Center Hice.' So the dumb Frenchmen know where to drop the puck." As the Zamboni driver beeps his horn and rolls off, Martin lifts the heavy iron lever that holds the rink door closed, smiling at the news that Cagliuso is late. "Good. We'll see what we can do without him."

Compared with the abysmal effort of their first scrimmage, Methuen does quite a lot. In the first few minutes, freckle-faced Brian Mueskes, about 5 feet nothing and 120 pounds, flattens Lynn English's biggest player—directly in front of the Ranger bench. "Whoa," they all cry out, banging the heels of their sticks against the boards. "Oh no!"

Methuen scores four goals and gives up one, and after an hour, the teams break to clean the ice. Robillard collars Ryan Fontaine by the locker room door and compliments him for scoring a pretty goal. But before a smile can spread across the gritty winger's face, Robillard admonishes him for getting "too cute" with the puck in his own end—a mistake that led immediately to Lynn English's goal.

One of the few Rangers with a knack for putting the puck in the net, Fontaine has a reputation as a hothead on the ice and a wise guy in the classroom. After getting in a fight during the final game last season, this "loose cannon" received a misconduct penalty and was barred from the state tournament. Robillard says he'll have little tolerance for Fontaine's antics this year.

While killing a penalty in the last segment of the scrimmage, Fontaine hustles down the ice and ducks behind the Lynn English net just as one of their defensemen is coming out with the puck. Fontaine thrusts out his hip and catches his opponent across the thighs. The Lynn English player describes a 360 in the air and crashes to the ice with a thud. The Ranger bench hoots.

Fontaine is a solid, wide-necked kid, with thick shoulders and a definite mean streak. In the old days, the days of portable black-and-white televisions and circular UHF antennae, the Big Bad Bruins featured an undersized, pugnacious winger by the name of John McKenzie. Under normal circumstances, a lunch bucket player like "Pie" McKenzie would've been lost among a cast that included Bobby Orr, the horseracing goalie Gerry Cheevers, and several other characters. But Pie McKenzie, with his wicked grin and churning legs, was everywhere at once. He really stood out.

When Fontaine knocks the Lynn English kid on his ass and grins at the Methuen bench, I notice the resemblance. Dave Martin is refereeing the scrimmage and he skates over to me: "It's true what they say: 'Lynn, Lynn, the City of Sin, you never come out the way you went in.' "

We laugh, and I realize at that instant that I'm no neutral observer, or representative of the fourth estate. This year I want Methuen to win, and win big.

8
THE BLUE SANDS

On Saturday night I drive into Malden, Massachusetts, and take the Orange line trolley from Wellington station to Chinatown; I've been invited to a fancy Christmas party. After a ten-minute walk I arrive at the Tavern Club, a narrow brick building tucked into a lane across from Boston Common. The main room contains forty or fifty literary agents, lawyers, writers, producers, photographers, and wannabes clutching glasses of wine and gabbling in a huge, indecipherable mass. There's an open bar and a man in a tall white hat carving slices from a gigantic roast beef.

While securing a glass of beer from the red-jacketed bartender, I am accosted by a motormouthed stockbroker from Newton. Almost immediately he begins detailing the top ten moments of his life, including a backstage romp at the Phish concert the previous evening, and the swindle of box seats for a Red Sox/Yankees playoff game. The stockbroker says he's writing a marvelous screenplay about his adventures and when an agent wanders nearby, my new best friend halts his monologue and darts away.

Soon I join a little circle of various independent film producers and other gentry who are ticking off the names of the famous "intellectual property" attorneys they're associated with. Some wrinkly woman in a dress that looks like an inverted tulip asks what lawyer represents me and I say the public defender. The group dissolves like a smoke ring.

That's enough hobnobbing for one night. I leave the party early, heading for a ramshackle beer joint in East Methuen where I can "compose my notes." Three gents are clustered at the end of the bar, watching the Bruins game on television and fondling their drinks. The eldest of the three, stooped to the point where his chin nearly touches his glass, works his lips up and down and then erupts in several frightening coughs. Twice he announces to no one in particular that he has "missed something" by never having "had a dark woman or Asian girl."

"Too late now," says the guy in the middle. He's slick-haired and quiet, with deep pouches beneath his eyes. Mostly he just listens and nods to the slender, pop-eyed man to my immediate right, who talks nonstop. My neighbor at the taps is a positive-minded little barfly with gray hair and stunted fingers and a way of wrapping up everything he says with, "That's all right. What can you do? You can't do anything. So all right."

When I sit down, he's busy pontificating about a dive that he used to frequent called the Blue Sands. "It was filled with nice guys. You go in, drink whatever you want, vodka, rum, gin, beer, as much as you want, and nobody gives you a hard time, and it was all kinds: engineers, parking lot attendants, mailmen, lawyers, bus drivers, big guys, little guys, and everybody's talking, they laugh, they joke, no fights, no assholes. Good. So all right. And remember Jimmy? Loved rum and coke, Jimmy did. Young guy. What a character. He came in Christmas Eve one time and sang 'Con-nie Lingus. Con-nie Lingus' to the whole bar and they all laughed like hell. Blue Sands used to stay open till ten or eleven on Christmas Eve, past all the Chinese restaurants even, still open when you couldn't get a coffee at Dunkin' Donuts, and Jimmy went in there, went home, got up, went to his relatives' for Christmas and there's an argument, yelling, a fistfight, whatever. Next year, same thing, Blue Sands, home, his relatives', argue, fight, miserable. Three years of this, he says, 'Frig it.' He goes to Stop N' Shop, buys himself a nice turkey, half a gallon of coke, he has his ice cubes in the freezer, he gets up, it's Christmas morning, he turns on the television full blast, he cooks his turkey, he has four, five, six rum and cokes, he watches football, eats his turkey, good, fine, so all right. It's a nice Christmas."

"What's Jimmy doin' now?" asks the pouch-eyed man.

"Don't know. Got married probably. Moved to the South Shore, North Shore, uptown, downtown, three kids, who knows? Don't come in the Blue Sands no more, but that's all right. What can you do? You can't do anything. So all right."

Last period of the school day, I'm alone on the ice with its gleaming mother-of-pearl finish, half the rink lights turned out, an old Bob Dylan song playing over the PA. I make big looping figure eights, tracing my own skate trails, pieces of calligraphy etched onto the milky surface. Then the players start filing in, and I jump off and head for the locker room and a drink of water.

Some of the guys are lagging in their preparation, and tri-captain Thom DeZenzo glares at them. "Hey, St. Louis. Hurry up, get dressed," he says. "You have a lot of surface area to cover." The big defenseman looks puzzled and DeZenzo adds, "If you were in my calculus class you'd understand that."

While players buzz all around in the midst of various drills, Robillard works with the goalies at one end of the ice, Jon Morin underscores a point to the defensemen with vigorous arm movements, and Dave Martin whispers something off-color into Kevin McCarthy's cage, who rests his stick across his knees and laughs.

Everything is pointing toward the final preseason scrimmage with Triton, and Robillard sums it up by saying, "Dress rehearsal tomorrow. Look sharp."

As I enter Methuen High's rink the next day, I'm greeted at the ticket desk by ginger-haired Brian Mueskes, who's busy regaling teammates Dan Gradzewicz and Matt English about the time his older brother Brian shot him in the leg in their backyard. Apparently the two snipers were firing a pellet gun at an egg they had set out on a stone wall, and the lead pellet ricocheted up and was embedded in little Mueskes's calf.

"It's still in there," he says, pulling up his pant leg. "Sometimes I can feel it."

A pretty young brunette pays for her ticket and passes through the makeshift turnstile. "She's hot," Gradzewicz says. "She should get in free." The girl turns and smiles at him and the jut-jawed defenseman turns red. "Tell me she didn't hear that," he says.

Stepping over the velvet rope, I catch my foot and almost get knocked for a loop. "There's that old athleticism," says Jon Morin from across the lobby. I duck into the rink and witness a scary sight: Albert Soucy with a lit blowtorch, arguing about the best way to affix a stick blade with Chris Martin and Dave George, whose arm is in a sling. When I ask George if it's broken, the dark-haired winger says his elbow is so swollen the x-rays were inconclusive. The doctor applied a soft cast, and he has to have it examined again when the swelling goes down. George is a tough nut, and linemates James Girouard and Jeremy Abdo will miss him tonight—they need his grit.

Inside the varsity locker room, goalies Dan Bonfiglio and Dave Gray are getting dressed. They have dyed their hair a vibrant gold color, and passing through with an armload of game socks, Coach Martin takes one look at them and says, "Tweedle-dee and Tweedle-dumb."

Across the room Chris Cagliuso sits in his pants and pads, wearing a black Ozzy Osborne T-shirt with the sleeves cut off. Like many of the hockey players, he's lean from all that skating, his physique a weird mix of emaciation and muscularity. For sport, Cagliuso makes fun of the slim and bespectacled James Girouard, who's dressing nearby. "You and Parker are a couple of bobos," says the Rangers' star forward.

"What does that mean?" Girouard asks.

"Bobo. That's what you are."

Sitting around the locker room, fixing their equipment and bullshitting with each other, Bonfiglio and Gray and Cagliuso and Girouard believe that there'll be a million of these moments and they'll remember them forever. But this time in their lives will pass by so quickly, they'll forget most of it.

Tonight, in the showcase game of their annual jamboree, Methuen faces off against Triton Regional High School. At first Coach Robillard sticks with his bona fide varsity players and they acquit themselves well. Cagliuso and Fontaine combine for a scrappy goal, and a few minutes later Chris Martin rocks one of Triton's forwards and steals the loose puck.

"Nice job," says Coach Harb. "That's high steppin'."

In the second of two periods allotted in the jamboree format, Robillard experiments with a number of jayvee players and the results are disastrous. During one horrible sequence, Paul St. Louis gets turned by a speedy Triton forward who goes in alone and scores on the Ranger goal.

"St. Louis. Do you know what 'limitations' means?" asks Coach Martin when the huge defenseman returns to the bench with his head hanging. "Li-mi-ta-tions. Go home and look it up in the dictionary. Write the definition ten times."

Jon Morin hunches over St. Louis and instructs him to "stay in the middle. Use your size and strength, and make him beat you. If he goes around you into the corner, that's all right. He can't score from there."

Junior goalie Becky Trudel, who's been out with a pulled muscle in her thigh, gives up two weak goals and Ryan Fontaine smashes his stick against the glass when his shift ends. "What the fuck was that?" he asks. "Pathetic."

Cagliuso is frustrated. "She sucks."

Methuen loses 5-1. In the locker room, Robillard tells his team to forget about it. "Next week against Dracut, when it counts, I'm going with ten forwards, five defensemen, and a goalie, that's it. And I'm still looking," he says. "You gotta show me something in these final two practices."

Outside the skate room, Robillard and Harb and Morin discuss their options. As the season draws nearer, the coaches have one good line—Cagliuso's—one useful defenseman, Thom DeZenzo, and a lot of question marks.

"I'm going home to say my prayers," I tell Joe Harb, as we head out through the darkened rink.

9

THE SINS OF RYAN FONTAINE

TWO DAYS BEFORE THE RANGERS' first game, I'm buying gas down by the Loop when I run into Ryan Fontaine and a carload of his friends. It's lunchtime over at Methuen High, and that's where Fontaine should be. He tries to avoid my gaze but I call him over and with a sheepish look on his face, Fontaine advances as far as my rear bumper. When I ask the varsity winger what the hell he's doing, skipping school right before the Dracut game, he says that he doesn't like the cafeteria food and is out for lunch.

I've seen that same guilty smile on a bunch of hockey players, and I was one of them. Back when I was on the team, one of the other goalies, Mike Lebel, would take off his pads after practice and go through an ice dancing routine, pirouettes and spins and axels; he called it "performing an adagio." Coach Parker nicknamed him Dancing Bear, and he took his place alongside Nose and Blind Baby and Coma and Dust and Nigh and Gull and Heavy Lunch and Face and Truck and Skinner and Hibner and Stick on the rogue's gallery of the 1974–75 Ranger varsity.

Unlike most of us, Dancing Bear owned a car and one day at the height of our season he announced that the ice on Forest Lake was just like glass, and as soon as school started he was going to the nurse's office to say he was sick. Then he'd load up his Cutlass

Supreme with hockey sticks and beer, since today was probably the one and only day that the ice on the lake would be perfect.

Of course, we loved the idea. One by one, half the varsity trickled into the school nurse complaining of sore throats and diarrhea and a host of other maladies that were impossible to disprove. In between classes I learned that Rick Angus and John Sabbagh and Gary Ruffen and John Kiessling and Lebel were already out there, skating in the cold January sunshine and blasting the car radio.

Somewhere around ten o'clock I got up the nerve to sign myself out and walked home and started making phone calls. But everybody else had already taken off by then and I didn't have a ride, so I made myself a snack and lay down on the couch and watched *The Merv Griffin Show* on TV.

The next day Coach Parker called a team meeting. As we filed in, I saw that he had the previous day's "tardy, absent, and dismissed" roster in his hand and slunk to the back of the room. In fact, all the other varsity players were plastered against the rear wall, studying their fingernails. Parker went down the list of dismissals like a prosecuting attorney. Each of us was queried regarding our whereabouts between certain hours. With a cloudy conscience, I announced that I had suffered from gastric upset on the day in question and had gone home until it went away. My dear mother would attest to this fact, I said.

My best friend Rick Angus was the first to wilt under Mr. Parker's cross-examination. His testimony started off in promising fashion when the coach asked Rick why he wasn't home at nine-thirty when he'd called the Angus household. Our star defenseman reported that he'd taken a short walk for the "fresh air." Where did you go? he was asked.

"I walked down to the Square," Rick said. "I went to Merrill's Market."

Where were you at ten, when I called back? the coach wanted to know.

Rick began to squirm. "Walking around the Square," he said.

Everyone in the room was aware of the fact that Methuen Square is approximately fifty yards long and comprised of no more than two or three stores of even vague interest to a teenager. "Where were you at eleven?" asked the coach. "I called back at eleven."

Rick's face was like chalk. "Merrill's?"

Slowly Dancing Bear stood up and confessed, and we were all found guilty and sentenced to extra wind sprints. It was like a class action suit.

Standing on the concrete apron of the gas station, looking into the face of Joe Robillard's delinquent winger, I waver between the maverick attitude of an ex-player and my loyalty to the coaching staff. Ryan Fontaine looks terrified that I'm going to turn him in. But the kid has a certain rough-edged charm, and I like him.

"Get back to school," I say. "Don't piss off Mr. Robillard, and don't let the team down." Fontaine smiles at me, jumps back in his friend's car, and they zoom away.

Before practice that afternoon, I ask Chris Cagliuso to define a word that I hear a lot of the players using. "What the hell does 'bobo' mean? As in 'Tim Parker is bobo.' "

Cagliuso laughs as he tapes up his shin pads. Methuen's first line center is narrow and limber like a vaudevillian, with a pale handsome face, uncurved eyebrows, and a way of laughing in a single exclamation. "Goofy. Dorky," he says. "Parker and Girouard are definitely bobo."

Tim Parker comes into the locker room dressed all in white. "Going to your job at the mental hospital?" I ask.

"I live there," he says.

Cagliuso laughs again. "See?"

At the start of practice, Robillard tells his players to take a knee at center ice, so he can outline the team's goals for the new season. "Win more than we lose, and shoot for the state tournament in March," he says. Standing with his stick in one hand, Robillard gestures at the ceiling of the rink. "You have to come to play, every game. We can't afford—like last year—to take nights off. If you come to the rink with some heart, ready to go, we'll be fine."

Cagliuso's goals are loftier. He wants the Rangers to win the league outright and make it to the final rounds of the state tournament at the FleetCenter in Boston. On a personal level, he's shooting for fifty points and a spot on the all-conference team. He needs at least twenty-six points to break one hundred for his career and get listed on the trophy board in the rink, alongside his brother Brett, who finished high school with 104 points.

During the first drill, Cagliuso is motoring down the ice when he lands awkwardly and slides into the boards with a crash. "He hurt himself," says Robillard, gliding past with a whistle in his mouth. "That's all we need, right?"

But after flexing his left knee a few times and missing just one turn, Cagliuso joins back up with Fontaine and McCarthy for three-on-twos. During the water break, Tim Parker skates over and does his best Chris Cagliuso impression. Smiling over at James Girouard, the lanky winger throws his hands out, affects a facial tic, and says "Oh." Although Cagliuso is not amused, Girouard, another bobo, thinks it's hilarious. I recall that we used to mimic a quiet sophomore on our team named Dave April, who blinked his eyes frequently and had all the volatility of a mole, which was his nickname.

Cagliuso turns his back on his imitators. He and Ryan Fontaine stand to one side, leaning on their sticks. "They're crackpots," says Joe Harb. After a bad shift, Fontaine usually comes into the bench area and smashes his stick against the glass. Last year, Cagliuso "pulled a nutty" in the penalty box during the Methuen opener and was suspended for two games. Methuen lost them both.

The job of starting goalie appears wide open this year. The two seniors, best friends Dan Bonfiglio and Dave Gray, have been sharing time in the net, but junior Becky Trudel's return from a thigh injury clouds the picture. During practices, Bonfiglio and Gray warm up together and when there's any downtime, the two goalies stand helmet-to-helmet whispering and laughing, while Trudel waits silently off to one side. For obvious reasons, she has her own locker room and often seems distant from the rest of the players, who are all male.

Gray mentions that he and Dan Bonfiglio have been friends since youth hockey. When I ask him if it matters who becomes the number one goalie on the Ranger varsity, he says, "We don't care. I mean, we *care,* but it doesn't affect our friendship."

A little while later Gray is resting along the boards, watching his friend execute the "rapid fire" drill. While Coaches Robillard and Martin send a blizzard of rubber in Bonfiglio's direction, Gray says, "We try to beat each other out, but we don't get mad about it."

After picking up Liam, I drive along Howe Street to the home of senior defenseman Thom DeZenzo, whose family is hosting the annual preseason spaghetti dinner. Two illuminated reindeer stand in front of their home, set back from the road in a neighborhood filled with large colonials. All the players are arranged at three long tables in the DeZenzo living room, munching on Italian bread and watching a comedy on the large-screen television. They greet us as we come in, and Liam climbs on a chair beside good-hearted Jeremy Abdo and begins telling him about the "little-kid Rangers."

Also hosting the dinner are Horace Trovato and his wife, Joan.

We've never met, but I know a little bit about them. Last season, Liam and I were in the grandstand for Methuen's game versus Andover when Joan Trovato burst into the rink. Her face streaked with tears, Mrs. Trovato approached the stands and, with Methuen athletic director Brian Urquhart's assistance, removed her son Jason from the Ranger bench. Standing on the rubber mats in full uniform, Jason listened to his mother's report, hugged her, and then rushed into the locker room to change clothes. When Urquhart returned to the stands, he told us that Mr. Trovato had just undergone surgery for a brain tumor.

A year later, Horace Trovato is in remission. Although he wears a well-trimmed beard, his head remains bald and his eyes are deep in the hollows of his skull. Seated at the kitchen table among the coaches, Mr. Trovato breaks the half-cut slices from a stick of Italian bread and in a soft voice tells us how his temperature rose to 105 degrees while he was undergoing chemotherapy. He looks like a man who might die, an uncomfortably familiar sight to any man. Joe Harb and Joe Robillard and I stare at our plates and no one says a word.

Mr. Trovato still appears weak and his movements are slow and deliberate. When I look up, he's holding out the breadbasket with a sad smile on his face. It reminds me of my mother's emphysema, when she was drawing strength from the lake of life she'd created from old struggles, ancient happiness, and the flowering of her children and grandchildren. Sitting up with her, even that last, late November evening, the sky graying outside but enough light in the room to ingrain every object in deep detail, I asked her how much she had left. My mother knew exactly what I meant and replied, "A little," although she was weary, four weeks from the end, and starting to feel the great empty spaces looming beneath her.

Jarrod Trovato, a gangling defenseman who Coach Martin calls the "Ape Man," is seated across the room, clowning with his teammates. Like Chris Cagliuso and Dan Bonfiglio and Ryan Fontaine, he's another in the long line of younger brothers who wind up making the Ranger hockey team. (Jason Trovato graduated from Methuen High last spring and is enrolled at Worcester Polytechnical Institute.) The good-natured Jarrod is entering his first year of varsity hockey with his brother's skates to fill, and his father's illness hanging over his head. But he looks happy tonight.

After the huge meal of homemade ziti and meatballs, salad doused in Italian dressing, and chocolate cream pie, a group of seniors led by Thom DeZenzo and Dave Gray arrange a few chairs in the DeZenzo's dark and chilly backyard. Several players line up to have their hair dyed bright yellow, and the rest of the team and coaches stand on the deck above and gawk at the spectacle. Within minutes, Paul St. Louis, Dan Martin, Eric MacDonald, Jeremy Abdo, Matt Tetreau, Paul Sullivan, and Tim Parker ("Most definitely bobo," says Cagliuso) sit in the lawn chairs and come away with heads full of foam. In the dark, their hair glows like weather-resistant dandelions.

Standing next to me on the staircase, one of the freshmen says, "I'm sorry, but that's kinda gay." In the kitchen, Tim Parker admits that he is, finally and irrefutably, bobo. While Horace Trovato watches from the kitchen table, someone tells the slender, long-necked Parker that he looks like he has leukemia. The players laugh.

The next day, I spot Parker in the hallway of the North House and compliment him on his tint. The senior wing is a regular Ichabod, tall and skinny with a prominent Adam's apple and undershot jaw. "Everyone was doing it," he says.

"Dare to be different," I tell him.

Walking ahead to make his class, Parker turns and smiles at me. "You're only young once," he says.

10
DRIVING TO LOWELL

THE PHONE RINGS MIDMORNING in boys' phys ed. Joe Robillard swings around from his desk to pick up the receiver, and it's Dan Gradzewicz's father calling about the decision to move his son from defense to forward and demote him to the jayvees. Robillard tells Mr. Gradzewicz that nothing's definite at this point in the season, and that Danny's a big, rugged kid with a hard shot and may help the team at his new position. For a few moments, the coach listens to Mr. Gradzewicz and then thanks him for calling and gently returns the telephone to its cradle.

Robillard looks over at me. "Mr. Gradzewicz says that one of the coaches told Danny he was too stupid to play defense." Joe shakes his head. "I wouldn't take it very well if someone told my boy he couldn't play because he was too dumb. We can't have that."

Joe Robillard is a calm and contemplative man, and I have no doubt he will speak to each of the coaches privately, reminding them all of the job they signed on for. We're here to help kids, plain and simple.

In the skate room before practice, I ask Joe a trivia question: Who was the first goalie to represent Methuen in an interscholastic competition, what number did the goalie wear, and who was Methuen's opponent? Robillard shakes his head.

"It was me, I wore number 28, and we played against the Lawrence Voke on December 14, 1974."

Then it's Robillard's turn to surprise me. Fresh out of Boston University in the fall of 1974, he was hired as the head hockey coach at the Lawrence Voke and arranged a scrimmage against Methuen's brand-new varsity team. I was in goal for Methuen; Joe Robillard was on the bench for the Voke. While I mull that coincidence over, Joe retreats into the skate room and comes back with two gifts: a stiff blue baseball cap embroidered with "Methuen Hockey" in white letters, and an original varsity jersey from that first year, Ranger blue with gold and white piping and an "M" in script over the left breast. I haven't seen one of the old jerseys since I took mine off and when I thank Joe Robillard, the words catch in my throat.

On the ice before practice, Robillard tells me that he played goalie for the "Budmen" in 1974–75, a semiprofessional team in Concord, New Hampshire. The team was filled with colorful characters, including "Kangaroo" Hebert, a French Canadian who excited the fans before games by sprinting in from the blue line and leaping over the net, landing on his feet just in front of the boards. And Dick Kelly, who had perfected something he called the "kick shot." During warm-ups, Kelly would skate toward the net with the puck on the blade of his stick and the shaft of the stick slung in front of his right skate with that knee cocked. When he reached the top of the circle, he would snap his knee forward and kick his stick blade, propelling the puck "as hard as any slapshot," according to Robillard.

Hebert and Kelly picked up their esoteric skills simply by "rink ratting," says Robillard. "Those are things about the game of hockey that you never forget."

Today's practice is the last one before tomorrow's regular season opener versus Dracut. As we get underway, I spot Dan Gradzewicz in street clothes moping along behind the glass. I leave the ice and go over and pat him on the shoulder, telling him to skate hard in the jayvee workout. "Nobody wants you to succeed more than Coach Robillard does," I say. "Keep your chin up."

Dan Martin passes by in baggy shorts and a T-shirt soaked with sweat despite the chill of the rink. I ask him what's up and the freshman replies that he and some of the other jayvees have been "helmet boxing" in the locker room. "We put on our cages and gloves and whale the crap out of each other," Martin says. "It helps get the aggression out."

Joe Harb is standing nearby. "Crackpots," he says.

Even at 5' 8" and 155 pounds, Kevin McCarthy is a formidable presence on the ice. During a fierce one-on-one battle with Paul St. Louis, three times in quick succession Mac and Baby Huey charge at each other, ignoring the puck at their feet. St. Louis is six inches taller and more than a hundred pounds heavier, but the soft-spoken McCarthy stays on his feet, his shoulder pads hunched up and helmet askew.

A few moments later during a top-speed drill, St. Louis loses his footing and crashes into the boards. I call Jon Morin over. "Mr. Parker used to say, 'If you don't—' "

Morin finishes the quotation for me. "—fall down once in a while, you're not skating hard enough, and he was right."

Just then, Shane Wakeen rides James Girouard into the boards, their feet get tangled, and somehow the tip of Girouard's skate flies up and catches Wakeen beneath the chin. Instantly there's blood on the ice and the injured player gets up clutching his neck. Girouard is in a heap, the wind knocked out of him. He has asthma and stumbles to the bench for his inhaler. Coach Martin whisks Shane Wakeen from the ice and leads him into the locker room, then runs off to fetch the medical kit.

Wakeen is hunched over the bench, trying to unlace his skates with one hand. He's a smooth-faced kid with short brown hair and gobs of blood are seeping between his fingers. I tell him to sit up straight, tilt his head back and put pressure on the wound, and then I drag another bench over and begin stripping off the laces of his skates.

Martin runs in, flips open the kit. No rubber gloves. He instructs the 16-year-old player to move his hand away. "You ain't HIV positive, are you Wakeen?" he asks.

The cut is a little more than an inch long and an eighth of an inch wide, located just beneath the left side of Wakeen's jaw. By luck, no major arteries have been nicked but there's a substantial amount of blood on Wakeen's hand and on the floor. Martin swabs the wound with gauze and flourishes a bottle of disinfectant. "It's gonna hurt like a bitch," he says.

Martin sprays on the orange liquid. "Oh, *shit,*" Wakeen says.

"Told ya," says the coach. Then he applies a pressure dressing and fastens it with strips of adhesive tape. "I'm gonna take you to the hospital," Martin says. "You need a stitch."

While Wakeen puts on his sneakers, Coach Morin bangs through the door of the locker room. He takes a quick look at Wakeen, leans on his stick, and says, "You're all right. That's nothing." Morin nods at me. "What was it Mr. Parker used to say? You're not a real hockey player until you get a hundred stitches in your head."

On February 10, 1975, I was at varsity hockey practice when my neighbor and teammate Dave Frasca skated toward me with the puck during a two-on-one drill. I remember gliding out toward the play, dropping into a crouch, and setting up for the shot. His legs whirling, Frasca cut from left to right through the circles and unleashed a drive that rose at a steep angle. It was like a blurry piece of unreality coming straight for my head and I hunched up, figuring the mask would protect my face. Then I went away somewhere, into the darkness. Later, who knows when, I was on my back looking up at the rink lights and trying to recall what day it was. I could feel something running down my forehead, stinging my eyes. It tasted salty.

Mr. Parker and Coach Cullen got me up and called my dad and he drove to the rink and took me to the hospital dressed in my goalie gear. An emergency room doctor shaved a patch of hair and sewed up the gash.

By midmorning I was back at school and went looking for Mr. Parker. Like most of the guys on the team in '75, I had long hair and had combed it over to hide the stitches. Coach Parker brushed my hair back and examined the cut and nodded with approval. It was a badge of honor, he said, and I should be proud of it.

After Elmwood Cemetery, Chuck Trudel wheels the bus past the Methuen Rod and Gun Club and the Dracut Legion Post and several miles of darkened farmland. For the next three and a half months, we'll log plenty of miles over two-lane blacktop, Routes 110 and 113 and 97, alongside Little League fields and country stores and olive-drab World War II ordnance, the half-tracks and tanks and artillery pieces that dot the various squares and greens spread throughout the valley. In this part of the country, the family Bibles have dust on them; the towns all have a history.

As we pull up to the rink, Tim Parker and Paul St. Louis and I sing along with "Proud Mary" over the bus radio. Obviously we are a team to be feared, and passersby give us a wide berth when we climb off the bus.

The Janas arena in Lowell is a cookie-cutter state facility: rubber-matted lobby with wooden benches that are bolted to the floor, pro shop and concession stand to the right, four tiny concrete locker rooms to the left. Hockey tape and hot chocolate are sold from the vending machines, and the rink smells like frosted mold and cleaning fluid.

The Ranger locker room is so crowded two players have to dress in the lobby, just a few feet away from Dracut's starting goalie, who's in the same predicament. The opposing players do not speak or even look at each other. But the coaches shake hands and chat amiably, renewing acquaintances from old campaigns and other chilly rinks.

Youth hockey teams occupy the other two locker rooms and Joe Harb nudges me as a little six-year-old waddles past in his gear, followed by a middle-aged woman wearing a purple running suit. "The time commitment and cost commitment (for hockey) far exceeds that of any other sport," says the crew-cutted Harb, who also coaches football at Methuen High. "It's to the credit of the parents."

Five hundred kids between the ages of 4 and 18 spread over six divisions are currently enrolled in Methuen Youth Hockey, which was established in 1972. (I played for MYH during the first three years of its existence, on the same team with Dave Martin.) Although the Learn to Skate participants in Methuen, including my 5-year-old, are only charged $125 for a weekly hour of ice time from September to April, players in the other age divisions are charged $625 to compete in one league and $900 for two. Despite the fact that hand-me-downs are common and several area hockey shops sell used equipment, the cost of outfitting a player is quite high. When a top-of-the-line pair of skates costs over $400, parents are hard-pressed to equip a child at almost any level for less than $1000.

As a favor, my old friend Jim MacDonald has calculated how much money he's spent on hockey for his two sons, varsity player Eric and 12-year-old James, over the past ten years. For league tuition, head-to-toe outfitting, skate sharpening, sticks, tape, home hockey nets, equipment bags, and league jackets, MacDonald figures that he's shelled out $18,500. "And the equipment was discounted fifty percent by a buddy of mine," he told me, delivering a spreadsheet that breaks down the expenditures by category. "Look at it this way, you can always take out a second mortgage so Liam can play."

Even this year, Liam's first in organized hockey, I've spent about $500 for tuition and gear, including a pair of adjustable in-line skates for dry land practice. Hockey school this coming summer, if he decides he really wants to attend, will run another $300. But it's a small price to pay for the friendships Liam will develop through the sport.

Joe Robillard beckons all his players into the locker room and squeezes the door shut. As the kids sit bareheaded, hunched over their sticks, Robillard says, "Play hard—the way the game is supposed to be played. And stay out of the penalty box."

Robillard signals to Coach Martin to open the door. "We'll find out what kind of team we are tonight," he says.

Methuen plays in the hybrid Merrimack Valley Conference/Dual County League, competing against some of the best and some of the middling hockey talent in the region. Situated in the middle of the three-tiered MVC/DCL, the Rangers play two games apiece versus the teams on their level and one game against the old MVC teams above and below. This configuration limits many of the mismatches that were plaguing each league, while maintaining traditional rivalries like Methuen-Dracut.

The grandstand inside the Janas rink is filled with Dracut fans to one side and a gallery of familiar faces to the other: Donita and Ray DeZenzo; the white-haired Gerard Soucy, Albert's father; Jim MacDonald and his dad, Frank; and a host of other parents and grandparents and friends. Especially at the high school level, hockey players, coaches, and their fans are a collection of diehards and fanatics. Accustomed to paying exorbitant fees for equipment and ice time, playing and attending practices and games at all hours of the night, and often returning home bruised, bloody, and exhausted, hockey teams and those who follow them are a tightly knit bunch.

As the teams warm up at either end, skating in circles until their jerseys blend together like an amusement park ride, I lean over to Joe Robillard and ask him if he has butterflies. He nods, handing me the statistics sheet. "When I'm not nervous anymore, it'll be time to get out," he says.

Although Dracut peppers starting goalie Dave Gray with shots in the opening moments, the yellow-haired senior plays his angles well and makes the season's first brilliant play. The Dracut center drifts into the slot and receives a quick pass, chooses the low corner of the net and fires the puck. Gray flops out his right pad, stops the shot, and covers it with his huge webbed mitt as the snow flies and Thom DeZenzo knocks the Dracut player on his backside.

"That's it, Dave," says Robillard. A moment later, after Methuen wins the face-off but one of the defensemen makes an errant pass, Robillard sounds like an owl with the hiccups. "To who? To who?"

Ryan Fontaine muscles his way to the front of Dracut's net and golfs in the rebound of a Chris Cagliuso shot for the Rangers' first goal of the year. He comes back to the bench with joy painted on his face and several teammates reach over the boards and punch him in celebration. From the very start, it's clear that Methuen has team speed. Cagliuso and Fontaine and Soucy and McCarthy and DeZenzo take turns buzzing up ice and by the end of the second period, Methuen is ahead 5-3.

In the locker room, the Rangers are excited but conscious of last year's third period collapse against Dracut, when they surrendered a two-goal lead and lost Cagliuso for two games after a tantrum in the penalty box. Robillard, a former goalie and defensive-minded by nature, reminds his team that they can win without scoring again. All they have to do is backcheck.

Over in the corner Ryan Fontaine stands up, buckling his chin-strap. "Just to be on the safe side, guys, let's score a couple more goals," he says.

I whisper to Dave Martin: "Ryan, the Zen master."

Martin presses his hands together and bows in Fontaine's direction. "Ooommm," he says.

The third period passes quickly, each shift like the blink of an eye. Late in the game, Dave George, a tough little player, stakes out a patch of ice in front of Dracut's net. Two Dracut players collide nearby and the puck bounces to George who shoots it underneath the flabbergasted goalie. With less than three minutes to play, the Rangers have built up a 6-3 lead.

After the cheers subside, a voice floats out from the grandstand: "Don't get cocky, Methuen."

But the coaches won't allow that to happen this year. When Dave George returns to the bench after his goal, Robillard congratulates the hard-nosed winger for scoring and then faults him for poor coverage in the defensive zone. "You can't let that guy stand there," the coach says. "Get on him and stay on him."

George bites on his yellow rubber mouthpiece and nods his head up and down. His face is smooth and boyish inside the cage, and there's a glint of determination in his eyes. Dave George's two goals—and two each by Cagliuso and Fontaine—carry Methuen to its first victory of the season.

11

SOMETHING HITS THE FAN

BEFORE METHUEN'S HOME OPENER AGAINST Bishop Fenwick, I pass through the Ranger locker room. Dan Bonfiglio occupies his usual seat and is sitting in T-shirt and boxer shorts, taping his stick. Joe Robillard has just told the laconic senior goalie that he'll get the start tonight.

"Nervous?" I ask him.

Bonfiglio shakes his head. "A little anxious."

"That's good," I say, and leave him with his cronies.

Just as the players have a whole culture that lies beneath the coaches' radar, the adults who run things must keep their peeves and peccadilloes under wraps, as much as possible. When those two worlds collide, however, there can be some awkward—and funny—moments. In the corridor outside the skate room, Dave Martin is relating an argument he had with one of his jayvee players, and later, the player's father. For the first time in his lengthy coaching career, Martin has been accused of playing favorites when it comes to apportioning ice time.

"It was like they stuck a friggin' knife in me," Martin says. His eyes are bulging, and he gestures with his hands. "I might tell you something you don't wanna hear, but one thing I ain't is political. Man, I was so upset, I went around the locker room pointing at each player and asking, 'Do I know your father? Do I even know you? I don't know you. Who's your father? Who's your uncle?' I pointed to my own kid and said, 'I don't know you. I don't know your father. You're not playing tonight.' I tell you, Joe, I was having a friggin'—"

At that moment Paul St. Louis comes looking to have his skates sharpened and Martin stops in midsentence. His face and scalp turn crimson, and he snaps off his last word and tries to gather it back in. As Joe Robillard shepherds St. Louis along the corridor, Jon Morin and I loll against the cinder block wall, wagging our fingers at Martin.

A few minutes later, Methuen takes the ice with Ozzy Osborne's "Crazy Train" blasting over the PA. In their white home jerseys, the Rangers wheel around the rink, alternately stretching and sprinting. Bishop Fenwick comes out of the locker room in their ugly brown and gold uniforms, and the coaches from both teams waddle to the bench, holding the dasher. Methuen trainer Kevin MacLennan loses his balance and falls hard on the ice, legs splayed.

I'm going off the rails on a crazy train

Jon Morin and Dave Martin laugh at their trainer. "The ice is extra slippery tonight," says MacLennan.

Recruited to operate the game clock, Horace Trovato smiles wanly and totters down from the grandstand. He looks ill but he's manned the timekeeper's bench at every Ranger home game for the past five years, since his older boy Jason was in ninth grade. The players clap their sticks against the boards as he goes past, and at center ice the referee holds up the puck like a jewel.

Fueled once again by Cagliuso's line, Methuen takes a quick lead and by the end of the first period is ahead 4-1. Field hockey goalie and late cut from the Ranger varsity Nicole Pienta has been assigned the task of recording shots on goal. As the players file into the locker room, she hands me the shot sheet, an 8½" by 11" facsimile of a rink. Little X's dot the ice, each one representing a shot on net from a particular location. Four of the X's are circled in Bishop Fenwick's end, signifying Methuen's four goals. Nicole has also drawn a stick figure that represents the opposing goalie.

The figure is lying prone on the ice, with a balloon rising from its head like in a comic strip: "I suck." Wearing an oversized varsity jersey over her sweater and jeans, Nicole Pienta laughs when I spot her embellishment. Dave Martin comes out and shoos her away from the locker room door.

"There's half-naked boys in there," he says.

"What's wrong with that?" Pienta asks. "After all, I am part of this team."

"Get going," says Martin. He turns to me. "She wouldn't get in any trouble, but we'd be screwed."

In the second period Methuen is victimized by what appears to be a terrible call by the referees. Skating from right to left in front of Methuen's goal, a Bishop Fenwick player blasts a shot that flies over Bonfiglio's shoulder and clangs against the metal crossbar of the net. Immediately the puck bounces out toward the middle of the ice; the Bishop Fenwick players raise their arms in celebration. But is it a goal?

The two officials stare at each other for a moment, while players fight for the loose puck in front of the net. Suddenly one of the referees blows his whistle and points to center ice, signaling that a goal has been scored.

Robillard erupts on the bench. "That wasn't a goal," he shouts.

But it stands and Bishop Fenwick has new life. Soon they score again, and when James Girouard's line returns to the Ranger bench, their heads hanging, Thom DeZenzo turns from watching the game and says, "Abdo, you're not Gretzky. Dump it in and chase like everybody else."

Jeremy Abdo, who has sticks for legs and an awkward skating

style but a slick pair of hands, doesn't respond. DeZenzo is one of the captains and Abdo's a lowly underclassman. He knows better.

Ryan Fontaine, however, doesn't always know how or when to keep his mouth shut. The fiery winger gets in a shoving match on the ice and gets sent to the penalty box. A moment later, Chris Cagliuso, who's already being targeted as a player to hinder and hack at, retaliates when he's elbowed in the throat, and then swears at the referee for penalizing him. He receives a penalty for hooking and another for unsportsmanlike conduct. Then Ranger defenseman Chris Martin is whistled off for holding and Methuen's penalty box looks like a barrel of monkeys: three irate Rangers contained in a tiny space, waving their fists and shouting. Dave Martin looks over at me and rolls his eyes.

During a stretch of furious action, Thom DeZenzo breaks his stick, tosses it over the glass, and borrows another from the bench. When he comes off the ice, he fires the stick into the corner and gropes through the pile for a new one. "That stick blows," he says.

Dave George is leaning up beside him. "Where's your other one?"

"Busted."

"Your *other* other one."

"Don't have one. I'm poor."

"Me, too."

Last season Methuen succumbed to the pressure in a very similar situation and got off to a horrible start with two losses in a row. But led by Thom DeZenzo's steady quarterbacking on defense and penalty-killing specialist Albert Soucy, Methuen escapes a whopping six minutes of shorthanded play and makes it to the end of the period.

Robillard enters a subdued locker room. He stares right at Cagliuso and says, "Anyone gets a misconduct, sits out the next game."

"Is that a league rule, Coach?" asks one of the players.

"That's *my* rule. Play the game the way it's meant to be played." Robillard raises his voice for the first time since tryouts. "Let's finish them off. You're all business out there now."

Late in the third period, with Methuen leading 4-3, hardworking winger Kevin McCarthy knocks a loose puck into the open corner of Bishop Fenwick's net and Methuen has their second win in two games. The players from both teams line up at center ice to shake hands and Dave Martin slips and slides across the ice, joking with the referee about Bishop Fenwick's phantom goal. Together they shuffle over and study the net where it occurred. Martin returns to the bench with a sheepish look on his face.

"Sure as shit, that was a goal," he says. "The ref showed me the mark on the padding where it hit." Martin shrugs. "We win. What the hell."

A half hour after the game, the locker room contains only Cagliuso, sitting exhausted on the bench in his hockey pants and socks, and Ryan Fontaine, who's busy having a cut on his chin attended to by the trainer.

"Have you ever started a season two-and-oh since you've been here?" I ask Cagliuso.

"We've never been one-and-oh. We've lost the opener every year."

Cagliuso heads into the shower as Fontaine comes out. "How's the cut?" asks Cagliuso.

"Pain doesn't bother me at all," says Fontaine.

The two players, who skate on the same line and have known each other for eleven years, couldn't be more dissimilar. Cagliuso looks at ease in a suitcoat and tie and is headed for prep school. Fontaine is barely surviving high school and has the reputation of being a troublemaker. The plug-headed winger looks over his shoulder as Cagliuso goes into the shower. He grins and says, "I pissed in there. Sorry. I couldn't wait."

Cagliuso dances over the tiles. "Which one? Which one?" And Fontaine just laughs.

Right before the game against Boston Latin, I discover that I've bet the wrong end of the player/coach wager. Ryan Fontaine has been suspended for truancy, after being pulled over at lunchtime by Methuen police in a car filled with wise guys. One by one, the Ranger coaching staff learn of Fontaine's transgression while I lean against the doorway of the skate room feeling pretty stupid. When I caught Ryan cutting class the previous week, I counseled him to be a good boy and go back to school. Fontaine gave me a choirboy look and nodded his bullet head up and down. I never mentioned the incident to Joe Robillard or any of the other coaches.

Fontaine didn't need a handshake deal for a second chance—he needed a little discipline and I understand now that I wasn't the person to deal it out. The man in charge is Coach Robillard, and like the star of an old black-and-white television show, he truly knows best. In fact, when I look at men like Joe Robillard and his colleague Fran Molesso and longtime Ranger football coach Larry Klimas, I see that their ideals are rooted in the culture of the 1950s, i.e., home and family and faith and school and team. Corny as it may sound, adhering to these notions is what distinguishes the hockey players from the general population of Methuen High.

Ryan Fontaine comes into the skate room with a penitent look on his face and apologizes to Robillard. Busy fixing a pair of skates, Robillard tells his hard-charging winger that he's benched indefinitely and that further disciplinary action will be determined after consultation with the team captains and Fontaine's teammates. The coach turns around and makes brief eye contact with his player and then resumes working on the skate.

For a moment Fontaine stares at the back of Robillard's head and then departs without another word. Immediately Chris Cagliuso and Thom DeZenzo, two of the tri-captains, march into the skate room. "I've known Ryan since we were 7 years old," Cagliuso says. "He's a good kid, coach. He just makes bad decisions sometimes."

"What bothers me is that Ryan chose to be with those cronies of his instead of thinking about the team," says Robillard, turning to face his players in the cramped space. "Like I said, I'm not going to make my decision now, because you're not going to like it. And neither is Ryan."

DeZenzo and Cagliuso eye each other, and then withdraw. Coach Morin enters the skate room, keying his voice to the timbre of an adolescent. " 'Oh coach, it wasn't me. It was the other guys,' " he says, mimicking the repentant athlete.

Robillard is disgusted. "He was supposed to be in my class that period. It would be bad enough to skip class or miss a practice or two, but on the day of a big game?" He makes the sound of a buzzer. "Forget it."

A short while later, Morin and I are inside the varsity locker room when Fontaine bursts in. "Sorry, guys. I fucked up," he says.

While Fontaine gathers his gear, Cagliuso asks Coach Morin, "Why does he have to sit out tonight? He didn't really do anything to hurt the team."

Morin crosses his arms over his chest. "Yes he did. Because he represents the team. No individual is greater than the collective unit."

Fontaine picks his way over the various pieces of equipment and Cagliuso grabs him by the arm. "You better apologize to Mr. Robillard again, because he's really pissed off. And you better be sincere. None of this 'I fucked up' stuff."

Fontaine stares at the floor. "I fucked up. I did."

Joe Robillard enters the room as Fontaine is leaving, and coach and player avert their eyes and pass each other without speaking.

Robillard calls his team into the center of the room. "We haven't seen a team like this yet. Here's where we find out who has big balls," he says. "These Boston kids get a little cute with the stick. Let the referee call that. Don't retaliate." The players lean in, forming a tight mass. "Get your hands in here. Give it everything you got tonight, boys. Ready: one, two, three . . ."

"Rangers!"

During the national anthem, from my position atop the bench I look down the gauntlet of Methuen players lined up along the blue line. Gazing at their faces—some hopeful, some hardened, all full of youth and promise and many topped with bright yellow hair—I realize this is a twice-in-a-lifetime opportunity for me. Jon Morin paces back and forth on the bench and then glances over with a smile on his face. "Here we go," he says.

The game is scoreless after one period. I look down at my statistics sheet and count the tiny X's that represent shots on goal. The Rangers have mustered only two. At the other end of the rink, Dave Gray has made twenty-five saves, some of them miraculous. Heading into the locker room, Dave Martin imitates the goalie's puck-stopping gyrations. "He's like one of those ducks in a shooting gallery at Salisbury Beach," says Martin. "Bing-bing-bing."

Robillard allows his team five minutes alone in the locker room, where they loosen their skates, shed their jerseys, and remove their shoulder and elbow pads. In profane language, the players describe the dirty tricks used by certain Boston Latin players and their plans to get even. Then Robillard comes in and the room falls silent. Coach Martin ducks his head in and says that the Zamboni machine is making its final pass around the rink: two minutes.

The players tighten their laces and don their pads and jerseys. They mill about in the doorway, waiting for the signal to go out, hardly making a sound. "Let's get fired up. It's like a morgue in here," Robillard says. Then the former Boston University standout brings the whole experience to a point of summary: "Shit, I wish I was playing."

Although Chris Cagliuso scores two goals, Methuen loses the game 5-2. Boston Latin was the best team in the league last year, and defeating the Wolfpack is high on Methuen's wish list this season. They'll meet again in February.

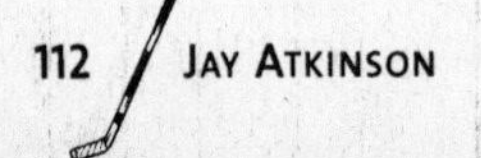

12

THAT'S MR. BOBO TO YOU

CHRIS CAGLIUSO AND TIM PARKER have invited me to address Mrs. Borucki's accounting class, but since I'm ignorant of even the most basic accounting principles, I give a long-winded speech about following your dreams, etc. Somehow I get sidetracked into a discussion of role models for youth and mention that in junior high school I had a poster of Boston Bruins' goalie Gerry Cheevers on my wall. In retrospect, a better choice from that era would have been my seventh-grade math teacher, Mario Pagnoni. Now in his thirtieth year of teaching and currently stationed at the high school, the wisecracking Pagnoni was a rookie in 1969–70, teaching mathematics and coaching flag football, basketball, and floor hockey after school. I saw more of Mr. Pag that year than my own father, who was busy working.

After my speech, Cagliuso and I proceed to Pagnoni's new course entitled "Internet Management" where he rates his students on test grades and "EPA"—Effort, Participation, and Attitude. "Everyone should have a picture of Mr. Pagnoni on their wall," I say aloud to the class. "He's a dedicated public servant."

"Mr. Pag, I have a picture of you," says Cagliuso.

Hopping from computer to computer, Pagnoni rubs his stomach and asks, "What, have you got a wide angle lens on that sucker?"

Cagliuso mentions that Albert Soucy is his best friend on the hockey team, but mostly he hangs out with his buddies from football. Two of them are in Mr. Pag's class, and the threesome retreats into the corner to work on a group assignment. Someone like Tim Parker, who's also a senior and has played hockey with Cagliuso for years, he sees only at the rink.

"Parker is bobo, pure and simple," Cagliuso says. "Everybody has gone to high school with someone like Tim Parker."

Parker is an ungainly kid with large blue eyes set far apart and a pointy chin. When he sees me in the corridors of the high school, he addresses me as "Bobo" until I correct him: "That's Mr. Bobo, to you." In class, Parker calls his good-natured accounting instructor by her last name and when she catches him at it, his wide-eyed look is so guileless the teacher refers to him as Parker and they both start laughing.

Down in boys' phys ed, Joe Robillard is discussing the Ryan Fontaine incident with his colleague Fran Molesso. "This hurts me, right here," says Robillard, pointing to his heart. "I was so upset last night, thinking about it, that I ran a red light on the way home. Practically got myself killed. I'll probably let him come back. But if he makes one more little mistake, he'll have to transfer to Acton-Boxborough or something. Because he'll never play hockey for me again."

Leaning back in his swivel chair, Molesso winks at me and says, "It's good to see you're doing the right thing, Joe. At least this year."

"Whoa," says Robillard, leaping up. The two gym teachers begin wrestling, Molesso still in the chair and Robillard on his feet. "That was a cheap shot."

When the buzzer signals the end of the class period, Molesso goes out to monitor the hallway and Robillard sits down again. "People say about Ryan, 'Oh, it must be a hard decision for you.'

But it's not," says the hockey coach. "If I'm going to be consistent with the rules, it's not a tough one. Not at all."

When I run into Dan Bonfiglio, who along with Chris Cagliuso is a consistent Honor Roll student and member of the National Honor Society, he expresses his dissatisfaction with Ryan Fontaine. "He can't be too interested in hockey when he goes and does something like that," says Bonfiglio, the most reticent of Methuen's polite young captains. He slides his gaze up and down the corridor and lowers his voice. "He kinda fucked us over."

The senior goalie adds that he and fellow tri-captains Chris Cagliuso and Thom DeZenzo plan to meet with Mr. Robillard about Fontaine, but "if Coach has made up his mind, there's no use trying to convince him otherwise."

At practice I catch up with Thom DeZenzo on the ice and he says, "The fact that [Fontaine] would do something like that before a big game really bothers me, 'cause he's a big part of our team." The defenseman snaps his chinstrap into place and hefts his stick. Before he pivots and skates away, DeZenzo says, "Everybody does stupid things, but you gotta be smart during the season."

Robillard blows his whistle and instructs his players to take a knee at center ice. Although it's time to move on and prepare for Westford Academy, he wants to say a few words about the Boston Latin game first. Robillard sensed between the second and third periods that his team wasn't going to win even though the score was only 2-1. "But I also could tell afterwards that you weren't happy with your performance either, and that's a good thing," he says.

Joe Robillard is not given to speech making. He's a simple, straightforward guy, and he expects his team to play a straightforward, aggressive style of hockey. But while nineteen kids stare at him through the bars of their cages, Robillard summarizes the situation as eloquently as a poet. "A high school season, a high school career, comes down to one game, one moment. Seize that moment.

Because it will come and it will pass away quick. So thank God you've got another game to play, which happens to be tomorrow night."

After practice Coach Martin is in the locker room, talking about Ryan Fontaine. "He shouldn't have been doin' what he was doin' and was stupid enough to get caught, to boot. That's my two cents," he says, turning on his heel. "I'm gonna leave now, and let you mull amongst yourselves."

In the skate room, Joe Robillard explains his position to the three captains. "I'm an educator first. And I care about people," he says. "I'll let Ryan come back. But if he screws up once more, he's gone."

The oldest player on the team at nineteen, Thom DeZenzo glances at Cagliuso and Bonfiglio and adopts the role of spokesman. "We like Ryan as a player and a friend—he brings a lot to our team—but we're behind you a hundred percent, coach," he says. "If you say he goes, we're with you on that."

That night, Dave Martin dusts off his old equipment and skates with our group at nine o'clock. Early in the game, he and I are jousting in front of the net. As I slide back and forth, trying to establish position, Martin pitchforks me between the legs, holds my stick, and shoves me in the back of the head. I pretend that I'm Dave George and fight back. A 42-year-old man emulating a 16-year-old boy and it feels completely natural.

It's almost midnight when I come out of the locker room with my equipment bag. Suddenly there's a loud click and the overhead lights go out; off in another part of the rink a door closes with a metallic boom, and I'm alone in the darkened lobby. Outside the moon is big and full and the stars are like little jagged fires in the sky. In Methuen, you don't have to pay two hundred dollars an hour to see a therapist. You tell your problems to your accountant, your dentist, and the girl who cuts your hair. Or you play a game of hockey and get smacked around a bit, throw a couple of wild elbows, and sweat until the water pools inside your skates. Then you sleep.

Joe Robillard and I are in the skate room filling our pockets with the hard candy he keeps in a margarine container when two figure skaters pass by in the corridor. "*Phew.* Mr. Robillard. You guys smell," one of them says.

"Thanks a lot," the coach says. "I bet your locker room smells, too."

"Not like that."

The girls are right. Perhaps they have a rancid sneaker or two in there, but nothing that compares to the hockey team in olfactory insult. Picture an unventilated cinder block room, approximately 30' by 15', lined with perforated metal lockers. Into those lockers every day go nineteen sets of sweaty hockey equipment and a like number of wet towels. This routine continues for months. The result is a vast penetrating smell that mingles damp canvas and mold with refrigerated perspiration, Zamboni backwash, and industrial toilet cleaner. The white wax pucks in the urinal add to the bouquet, as well as the occasional whiffs of cologne or hair gel. It is a stench familiar to hockey players everywhere, and we surely do love it.

Right before the road game versus Westford Academy, the players are milling around the entrance to the rink, dressed in their blue game jerseys and neckties. Dave Martin hollers from the doorway that it's time to leave, and the players hoist their equipment bags and head for the bus. An inverted Tim Parker walks along the rubber mats on his hands.

"Hey, we're in the circus," says jayvee call-up Matt English.

Skate 3 in Tyngsboro is a labyrinth of cinder block corridors painted red and white, with three ice surfaces going around the clock. It's a hockey world unto itself, filled with players of every age and description and the shrill tweet of whistles and muffled shouts and buzzers. Wandering through the corridors I come upon Methuen winger Kevin McCarthy carrying a droopy slice of pizza on a paper plate. It's twenty minutes before game time.

"Kevin. That'll make you sick." I take an energy bar from my coat pocket and hand it to him. "Here. Eat this instead. And drink some water with it."

The shy junior mumbles his thanks and stares at the foil-wrapped bar in his hand like he's never seen one before.

Outside the locker room, Joe Robillard and Dave Martin renew acquaintances with the opposing coaches. Skate 3 is next door to a nightclub that features adult entertainment, and Westford's head coach tells a story about walking into the rink manager's office to find two exotic dancers in skimpy dress. "Evenin', ladies," he said. "Here for a skate?"

The coaches shake hands again and retreat to the dressing rooms. The Rangers are solemn, almost to the point of distraction. No one says a word. This is a game they must win, against an opponent that has not performed well in the Merrimack Valley conference. Yet they look like a bunch of guys waiting in a doctor's office, no emotion, and no chatter. Nothing.

Every rink has it stories. As the grinding noise of the Zamboni echoes throughout the complex, Joe Robillard tells me about the 1994 Christmas Tournament that was held here. Methuen was in the championship game opposite heavily favored Acton-Boxborough, leading by a goal with less than two minutes to play. Suddenly an extra puck that had somehow been lodged inside the ceiling fell to the ice behind Methuen's net. The Ranger defense, confused for a moment, stopped playing and Acton-Boxborough scored to tie the game.

Robillard was certain that the referees would nullify the goal. But they ruled that the second puck had not interfered with the play. Shocked and dispirited, Methuen lost in overtime.

In the first period of tonight's game against the Westford Academy Grey Ghosts, the referee slams the puck down for a face-off and it breaks into two pieces. Ranger Dave George skates off with one fragment while two players battle for the other. "It's been a while since I've seen that happen," says Robillard, standing on the bench.

Years ago, pucks were made from two halves cemented together. But the modern puck is one solid piece of rubber. "This must be the rink of the jinxed puck," says Dave Martin.

The Rangers certainly appear to be afflicted by sprites and fairies as they skate all over the Grey Ghosts but find themselves losing 2-1, deep into the second period. The opposing goalie is a smallish kid with a big mouth, taunting Methuen's forwards when they miss the net, and Dave Martin is incensed. In the locker room after the second period, the battered old defender stomps his feet against the rubber matting and waves his arms.

"Whiz it by his ear a few times. Hit him in the face. Shut him up," says Martin. "Score a goal, for crissakes. PLAY SOME HOCKEY."

Martin bangs through the door into the corridor outside. His hands are shaking. "Jesus Christ," he says. "Kids these days."

Robillard tinkers with his lines in the third period, searching for the right goal-scoring chemistry. Using these new combinations, Methuen overwhelms the Grey Ghosts, tossing in four goals over an eight-minute span. In one sequence, defenseman Chris Martin knocks two Westford Academy players to the ice and clears the puck out of his zone. One foot up on the boards, Dave Martin is riveted on his son as he skates past the bench. "Attaboy, Chris," he says.

The bus is rocking after the game, the players scarfing down French fries and pizza from the concession stand and bombing each other with wads of friction tape. They have reason to celebrate: this is the Rangers' best start in over a decade.

13
FLEETING MEMORIES

I REMEMBER THE NIGHT IN 1969 when my father escorted me to a Red Sox game at Fenway Park for the first time. We hurried through the turnstiles and beneath the understructure of the stadium, past the ushers and policemen and up the narrow concrete runway, clutching our ticket stubs. As we emerged onto the grandstand, a great rush of sound enveloped us: thousands of excited fans chattering at once, punctuated by the cry of vendors and the dramatic thrum of John Kiley's organ. Light streamed from the giant poles surrounding the park, and the grass was a deep luminous shade of green.

I glanced around at the tiered seats, back to the diamond, and then up at my father's gently smiling face. I didn't know what to say, or how to express the thrill I felt.

"Dad, can I have a hot dog?" I asked, inhaling their smoky scent. "And later, can we get a pennant?"

My father swept his hand across Fenway's glowing vista and replied that I could have anything I wanted. "This is your night," he said.

I've waited thirty years to express that sentiment to my own son.

Liam and I enter Boston's North Station and are heading upstairs to the FleetCenter for the Bruins game. Nearby, a small boy takes a foam rubber bear's head from his pocket and slips it on.

"Wow," says Liam. "Can I have one of those?"

"You can have whatever you want, Boo. It's your night."

The gates open, and we go up. For the first half hour, Liam holds tightly to my hand, speechless at what Bruins owner Jeremy Jacobs has wrought. No matter where we turn, someone is trying to sell us something. With all the credit card pitches, merchandise kiosks, and "signage," it's like being trapped inside a surreal television commercial. But we eventually find our seats behind the Bruins' net, shed our coats, and head back to the promenade for snacks and souvenirs.

They're not reasonably priced. A soda is $3.50 and M&Ms are $2. (It cost $17 to park, and our tickets are worth $150—compliments of a rugby friend, Randy Reis.) We find a walk-in shop and purchase one of the flimsy bear heads for $10. In his size-too-small Bruins jersey and new *chapeau,* Liam thrusts out his chest proudly, smiling at the passersby who laugh and point at him.

"They like me!" he says. "They like my bear's head. Do you like it, Daddy?"

"Of course I do." Even in the guise of a bruin, my son resembles nothing so much as a baby bird.

We return to our seats to watch the Bruins warm up. Now don't get me wrong, I enjoy loud music. I grew up on it. But the tendency in postmodern arenas and stadiums is to blast high-decibel rock music, simulated crowd noise (what on earth for?), and nattering advertisements every second that the game is not actually being played. There's no room for quiet father-son conversation, no chatting with your neighbors, no time to think.

The most obnoxious gimmick appears on the Jumbotron, exhorting fans to "Make Noise!" while the mercury rises to various heights reflecting the crowd's effort. It's ironic that the highest possible attainment is "Boston Garden" level—the amount of noise made in the old barn by fans who didn't need to be prompted when

Bobby Orr or Bill Russell or Larry Bird created their moments of magic.

Today, major league sports franchises are nothing more than marketable products, and the FleetCenter is their container, full of sound and fury, signifying nothing. The frenetic gyrations of one popular vendor underscore that fact. Amid a chorus of jeers, the vendor dances madly while autographing overpriced boxes of Crunch n' Munch. He's a young fellow, and I don't begrudge him a living. But there's a clear message in this "entertainment": *we will do anything to separate our customers from their money.*

The game is terrible, and during the third period a bunch of drunks in the section above us start a fistfight and then an all-out melee. Brown-shirted security personnel arrive when the punches are flying on all sides, and it takes a few minutes to separate the idiots and throw them out. As the pugilists are being led down the steep stairs of the balcony, a young man rises from his seat and bellows at the security guards.

"You're Jeremy Jacobs' stooges," he says, invoking the Bruins' cheapskate owner. "Arrest the real perpetrators."

Thankfully, Liam is oblivious to all this. Late in the game, with the score tied, an opposing player takes a slap shot that streaks through the air like a dotted line. Gliding out of his crease, Bruins goalie Byron Dafoe does a complete split and snags the puck in his catching glove. With no prompting from the Jumbotron, the crowd begins cheering and Liam hollers along with them. The magic, if only for a moment, is back.

"By-ron *Da-foe,*" Liam says. "By-ron Da-foe for Christmas."

14

MERRY CHRISTMAS, MR. PAGNONI

DAN BONFIGLIO IS A LADIES' MAN. Strolling the corridors of Methuen High like a latter-day Valentino, understated and suave, the yellow-haired goalie exchanges brief greetings with his pals.

"Keep it real, Dan," says a kid in a striped shirt, leaning against the wall.

Bonfiglio nods, clasping his friend's hand for a moment. "Keepin' it real," he says.

In Mr. Fuller's environmental science class, the senior goalie makes up a quiz while the rest of the class listens to Christmas carols. Next to Bonfiglio is a fresh-faced Amerasian girl named Emily who plays on the field hockey team, and the two teenagers chat throughout the hour. Emily was Joe Robillard's choice for homecoming queen, and I can see why. Just before the bell, the young beauty hands Bonfiglio a small package of cookies she has baked for him and the goalie blushes. At this moment, he's more adolescent than matinee idol, and then the buzzer sounds, ending the class.

"What are you waiting for?" I ask Bonfiglio, as we pass through the crowded main hallway. "Ask her out. You've obviously built up some points there."

Bonfiglio shuffles along with his hands in his pockets, dressed in skateboarding sneakers and stovepipe dungarees, his hair a vibrant yellow and a string of wooden beads around his neck. "She has a boyfriend," he says, glancing at me.

"Every nice-looking girl has a boyfriend," I say. "Don't let that stop you."

It strikes me that girls from Methuen, at least from certain neighborhoods, are caught between their femininity and their surroundings; tough chicks in leather jackets and push-up bras, with fobs on their key chains big enough to put out an eye, and narrow rooms filled with teddy bears and rosary beads and jewelry that looks like pieces of armor. But Bonfiglio's crush has a face like an orchid, delicate and soft, with a gentle personality and tender way of speaking.

On the way to a holiday band concert, pretty young Emily gives me one of the cookies she made. It's crumbly and sweet, dusted with red and green sprinkles. On the downward-sloping concourse, other students pass between Emily and us and I shake my head at Bonfiglio. "She bakes you cookies and everything," I say. "She's too good to be true."

"Isn't she?"

"Man, you better play your cards right with this one. Feel free to come to me for advice anytime. I'm very experienced in these matters."

Against the blue curtained backdrop of the stage, Methuen's acclaimed concert band plays "Angels We Have Heard on High." When the number is finished, Frank Savory, the tuxedoed band director, thanks the audience while a hulking, goateed trumpet player standing behind him picks his nose. It's just the right mixture of elegance and comedy to remind me I'm back in high school.

Thinking about my own days at Methuen High, and their contrast to middle age, I can't help but wonder how fortunate I am and, also, why I've been so lucky. I've known this town and this school all my life, and examining them so closely has brought a lot of feelings and memories rushing back—about youth and desire and how being with a beautiful girl affects you when you're young. Watching Dan and Emily sitting together at the band concert makes me feel like a kid again, reprising some moment that I'd lost.

Down in the computer room, my old mentor Mario Pagnoni is serving chocolate Santas and regaling his class with stories of the good old days. He delivers a piece of candy to me and says, "My name is Mario, and I'll be your waiter this evening."

In the late 1960s, Pag was coaching basketball in a rough section of Springfield, Massachusetts. "One day kids came to practice wearing Bob Lanier's sneakers and Oscar Robertson's game jersey," he says. "They broke into the Hall of Fame and stole them." During another game versus a team from the suburbs, an opposing player ran by Pagnoni's bench and shouted "Guinea, guinea, guinea," at his collection of Italian hoopsters. A brawl ensued.

"My kids smashed open a glass case and beat them with their own trophies," says Pagnoni, with a chuckle.

Suddenly music is heard in the corridor. Half the concert band is assembled there, dressed in tuxedo shirts and blue silk cummerbunds, serenading the classrooms with "Deck the Halls." As the last strains are heard, an earnest young clarinetist says, "Merry Christmas, Mr. Pagnoni."

My old goaltending rival and eventual all-around buddy Mike Lebel, the Dancing Bear, died on December 23, 1996, from injuries suffered in a plane crash. Lebel, always a daredevil in cars and on the ice, had taken up flying and acquired a pilot's license and a four-seater Piper Cherokee. He was practicing his "touch and goes" at the Beverly airport and encountered some engine trouble, crashing in an attempt to land on the taxiway. Mike was an intelligent and capable flyer, and later I heard he had saved lives by forcing his plane down in the airport while avoiding the suburban neighborhoods that surround it. But Mike Lebel always was a technically sound, confident son of a gun.

Growing up, my best friend was stocky, blond-haired Rick Angus, an all-around athlete and one hell of a hockey player. Besides Rick and me, one of the great hockey friendships of the 1970s was between Gary Ruffen and Mike Lebel. The hub of both friendships was the defenseman-goalie relationship, the intuitive on-ice bond between the keeper of the cage and his extra set of eyes, his guardian. Gary and Mike attended the Orr/Walton Sports Camp in Orillia, Ontario, and they lived in the same neighborhood and played street hockey for hours on end, just as Rick and I did across town. Mike was an aggressive goalie who had the big time written all over him, but he didn't go to college and never really caught on with a marquee team after high school, despite flirtations with junior and semipro hockey.

Since only one goalie usually plays in each game, the fact that I was on teams with Mike Lebel meant I was often in his shadow. His father Ray was head coach of the Methuen Flyers and one time when Mike was injured I played back-to-back games, winning 5-4 and 2-0. I remember because I still have the pucks, with the scores printed on the side in whitewash. There was talk of a rotation after that, but soon Mike returned to the cage and I was back on the bench. It was relief to move on to youth hockey and a new team and to play every week.

As I got older and established myself, I began to appreciate Mike's practical jokes and love of life. Once after a high school practice, Lebel ran into the shower wearing nothing but a pair of knee-high rubber boots—after Mr. Parker told us to wear shower thongs to prevent infection. Lebel stomped around in the puddles on the shower room floor and rubbed himself with soap-on-a-rope, drawing gales of laughter from the other hockey players and Coach Parker from his office. Even the old stone face himself couldn't help cracking a smile.

Mike Lebel was an exceptional skater and rink general, who looked older than he was and routinely played and fought with grown men. He had a sly sense of humor and a commanding verbosity and was a natural comic. At the first alumni game in 1979, all the ex-Rangers were introduced at center ice and Mike came wobbling out from the bench like he'd forgotten how to skate. Then he decided to play forward instead of goalie, no shin pads, no nothing, and he was "out there making moves for no reason," said Gary Ruffen. "He was always mimicking guys he'd seen in the NHL, except he'd exaggerate—their facial expressions and everything."

Every night I say a Hail Mary for my old teammates Bill Tinney, Jim Concannon, and Mike Lebel. They're all dead now: Billy from the aneurysm, Conk from a heart attack at age 40, and Mike in the plane crash. It was almost thirty years ago that we played together, on the old rinks and swamps of the valley, but I haven't forgotten them and I never will.

15

THE TOWN AND THE CITY

SURROUNDED BY THE WARM SCENT of turkey, cloves, and evergreen, I stretch a little in the kitchen, chatting with Liam. Then I zip up my windbreaker and go outside, down the snow-dusted walk. With a gingerbread man in his fist, Liam watches for a moment through the curtains, shaking his head.

Running has always connected me to the landscape and made it mine, no matter where I've been. But some territory has to be claimed again and again, trod constantly to keep it close and familiar. Home ground is like that. The landscape presents a new face every time out, and each successive run has its own personality, each day its particular color. Only one place at one time of the year has stayed the same through my years of running. It has a perennial character, a flavor all its own. Christmas Eve in Methuen.

I run with the north wind at my chest, blowing straight through me. The final shifting rays of the sun gild the pavement as I turn onto Baremeadow Street, a vestige of rural Methuen in the heart of town. Dropping from the glacial escarpment into a deep valley, Baremeadow is a scarred old Indian trail that runs across a half mile of bottomland, the remains of Nimmo farm. With a broad plain on either side, the lane is bordered by cat-o'-nine-tails, tall drooping sunflowers that look like rusted showerheads, and the frozen silver ribbon of a brook.

Across the stippled fields are majestic new homes described in strings of light and the elongated H's of horse fence, silhouetted in the dusk. I climb from the bowl at the far end, traverse Milk Street, and weave my way along a stretch of Prospect Street before descending a long S curve toward Searles Pond and the forest that rings the high school. The landscape is empty at this hour, not even a car passing for minutes at a time, and I trot across Jackson Street and enter the woods.

Searles Pond is skimmed over with ice, and the empty gray stalks of the trees cover the hillside like bristles on a brush. Finding a trail in the dimness, I traipse over the backside of the high school grounds, climbing all the while toward the huge illuminated cross atop Holy Family Hospital. I was born there, although that event is a little dim. And when I was a kid, we used to play army in the surrounding woods, shooting at German soldiers who were disguised as squirrels. These days, I run early-morning laps around the hilly parcourse that's dedicated to my father and two other deceased Rotarians. My dad died in the Cardiac Care Unit at Holy Family, pretty much a botched case. And my mother's bumbling, incompetent doctor worked out of there, and that's where the ambulance took her the last time, a preliminary stop on the way to Massachusetts Respiratory Hospital and her lonesome death on Christmas Eve 1990.

Holy Family used to be named Bon Secours, from which it took the nickname "Bon Voyage," and oddly enough it's been the scene of Methuen's bloodiest violence in recent times: a man went crazy there and stabbed somebody in the chapel. Several years ago on Christmas morning, a Methuen policeman was shot with his own gun in an adjoining neighborhood, and just last year a plastic surgeon confronted his ex-wife's lover in her sickroom and shot the man to death as nurses watched in horror. Physician: heal thyself.

So when I emerge from the darkening woods and run through the Holy Family parking lot, my head is crowded with thoughts of the day Liam was born and crazy doctors shooting at people and my younger brother Jamie's life-threatening abdominal surgery back in 1985. At the bottom of the driveway, there's a plaque commemorating the old Meeting House of 1727. As a boy, I always called this steep band of pavement Daddy Frye's Hill and never knew why until I read Ernie Mack's wonderful little book, *Bridges from the Past: An Introductory Sketch to the History of Methuen.* The hill was popularly named for Jeremiah Frye, who for many years operated a tavern at the intersection of East and Brook Streets.

The trees inside Ye Old Burying Ground are black against the sky, their branches like capillaries. Here are the thin granite headstones of the town fathers, weathered with age, the families who lived and loved among these streets and then traveled to their rest. According to froggy-voiced local historian Ernie Mack, the gravestones face westward so those interred will meet the dawn on Resurrection Day.

HERE REST THE REMAINS OF

JOHN DAVIS
Born March 30, 1732
Died Nov. 17, 1815

JOHN FRYE
Born January 2, 1798
Died
July 10, 1878

I lope over the empty squares of the sidewalk. At the corner of Sunset Avenue is Mrs. Maloof's house, the place my mother sent us when we were kids to smooth the rough edges of the neighborhood.

Mrs. Maloof ran a sort of finishing school for local toughs; in her basement was a bare room with a linoleum floor and a wooden stage at one end. On Saturday mornings I would join a small class of wise guys who were expected to memorize speeches by Abraham Lincoln and walk around with books on their heads to improve posture. At Mrs. Maloof's insistence, "cahh" became "car" and "dahkness" was transformed into "darkness." On those rare occasions that I attend a cocktail party, my ability to walk upright and pronounce words like *arthritis* has proven more valuable than my college degrees, thanks to Mrs. Maloof.

The first single-family home my parents ever owned is at the corner of Sunset and Mayflower. Although the place is covered in vinyl siding now, it's the same shade of yellow it was when they purchased it in 1962. My sister Jill was born the next year and while my mother was recuperating in the hospital, my dad attempted to paint the house before she returned. Falling a little short, he brushed "Welcome Home Mama & Baby" on the side of the house in gigantic red letters.

Growing up in the Depression, and then again in the early days of their marriage, my parents could stand in one spot and survey all the rooms of the family residence. Here on Sunset Avenue was a house with two full stories, six rooms in all, and a basement and bulkhead and cobwebbed attic. There was a gravel driveway leading to a garage that resembled a little cottage, and a sticky pine tree and old car tires my father had split open and painted white, turning them into flower planters. During football season, we would arrange the tires in double rows and run through them like we were in training camp. Usually, I'd forget to put them back and catch hell for it.

Tonight there are decorations on the house, plastic candy canes and wreaths in the windows, but it looks deserted. For a long time now, whenever I find myself in parts of town that I haunted as a child, I get the strange feeling that the place isn't real anymore—

that I'm visiting a full-scale replica or museum exhibit. Like if I glanced behind the house on Sunset Avenue I'd find a façade propped up with two-by-fours, and a monument commemorating the place that once stood here. The moments that occurred in those rooms are gone forever, taking the rooms that I once knew along with them.

Four miles into my run, I stop and drink from my water bottle so I can take a close look at the house. Places and objects always seem to shrink over time, as the side yard hardly looks big enough to contain the football games we used to play there. The window of my old room is around back, on the second floor. From that perch very early on the morning of December 25, 1964, I spotted a sleigh and eight flying quadrupeds in the narrow slice of sky between the Russos' and the Suslovics'. By the following year, my schoolmates had convinced me that I had been mistaken. So I had my last glimpse of innocence from that very window and haven't been the same since.

Time to get moving; it's growing dark and the temperature is sinking. I raise my water bottle and toast the old house, old times: my mother young again and beautiful, my father clean-shaven, wearing fedoras and narrow ties, the evergreens that filled our living room to the ceiling and acres of brightly wrapped packages. Our laughter echoed throughout those rooms, and the scent of turkey and tree filled the space. It was the house of my early Christmases.

Down the hill I go, toward the Lawrence border and the granite wall that surrounds Howard Park. As a youth I was small and skinny and there was a nasty kid who lived in the three-decker across from the park. He was about fifteen pounds heavier than I, a year or two older, with black hair and a fierce-looking eyebrow that ran straight across his forehead. Every summer when I tried to go swimming in the shallow concrete fountain, this particular kid would terrorize me. His favorite trick was to sneak up and hold my head under water until I thought I was going to die right there, in the warm dirty water of the fountain. I wonder if my tormentor still lives in the old family house. When I was out to dinner a few years ago, I saw him sitting alone at the bar, slumped over his paunch, a sad, rumpled man with a cigarette smoldering before him and a glass of hard liquor. I hadn't seen him in more than thirty years but it was the same guy, all right. You never forget a bully.

I gazed at him across the restaurant. For a minute or two, I considered introducing myself and then throwing a punch. But I kept going, out and around the bar and back to my table. The guy looked like he'd taken quite a few punches already, and mine wouldn't have made much difference.

I run beneath the iron arch of Howard Park and skirt the edge of the baseball field. Five Latino boys dressed in hooded sweatshirts are coming toward me, descending in age from 13 or so, the last kid holding a football.

"Merry Christmas, boys," I say to them as they pass, and they return the greeting.

There isn't another soul in sight, and the playing fields are shrouded in darkness. One by one the boys climb the granite wall and drop out of sight, and as I move away from them, the last little boy waves his football overhead and calls out, "Happy New Year, too."

The turnaround point for my annual run is the Arlington district, the poorest neighborhood in town. Located on Broadway is a dilapidated liquor store that once contained Atkinson's Bakery, the family business where my grandfather began working in 1932. His signature item was the pork pie, and I remember visiting him as a child, a short, pudgy man with white hair, and the weight of the pie in my hand. We were taught to eat them cold, with ketchup, and although a meal of salted pork and larded crust is something I usually avoid, one pie a year on Christmas Eve is a reminder that my family worked hard to move up the hill.

On Railroad Street, I pass the shaded glass front of Thwaite's Market. In business for seventy-seven years, Thwaite's would be known as a "pork store" in England. It's the last local bakery that continues to use old English recipes to turn out its products, and all the cooking is still done by hand. The market, operated by Ken Greenwood, is an example of old-fashioned perseverance, a place where teamwork, customer loyalty, and family tradition are upheld.

"I like what I'm doing, I just wish I didn't have to do so much of it," Ken Greenwood had said, when I visited his bustling shop this morning. He employs twelve workers, nine of whom are relatives. "Family are the only ones you can count on."

At one time pork pies were common in Methuen. My paternal grandfather Wray Atkinson and his brother Harvey began making them in the twenties. Working out of a cellar, they baked at night and then drove around in a panel truck delivering the pies. Wray carried a huge ring of keys and would let himself into the speakeasies around the Merrimack Valley, where pork pies would be sold two for a quarter with the bathtub gin. As I climb Oakland Avenue, an hour into my run, the pain collects in my lungs and legs and I reckon my grandfather's short hard life, dead at age 54.

I run down Osgood Street and make a left turn through Methuen Square. All the shops are closed, Emblem & Badge, Rostron's Liquors—even Kam Sing, the Chinese restaurant. At the crest of Hampshire Street is the 1859 House, a neat, brown-shingled building with a gabled roof. It's rumored that my neighbor Peter Miville is selling the town's best eatery after twenty-five years in the business. Miville is a tall, barrel-chested man with a pencil mustache and deep rumbling voice. A good friend of my dad's, the 60-year-old restaurateur has given me plenty of useful advice over the years, seated in his office above the kitchen, surrounded by vintage model trains.

Just the other day, I stopped into Sheehan's gas station on

Lawrence Street and said to Bob Sheehan Sr., "The 1859 won't be the same without Peter."

Mr. Sheehan shook his head. "I'm sure the new owner didn't go to the same charm school," he said.

"That would be the School of Hard Knocks. It closed up a while ago."

"About forty years ago," said the white-haired Mr. Sheehan.

Each house is draped with glittering strings of light, and a decorated fir tree shines from every picture window. It starts to snow, as I zoom past the Anguses and the Frascas and the Comtoises, my childhood friends. All have moved away, married, their parents live alone now. The terrain is familiar, but still somehow distant, dreamlike in the falling snow. I can describe every room in those houses, though I haven't set foot in them for years.

Almost home, and I feel a great expectancy spilling onto the streets, a vibration generated by a thousand neighborhood children concentrating on their individual wishes. But a collective wish arises from all—comfort for the old and infirm, understanding among races, peace for the tortured corners of our world and hope for the nations in the coming year.

A message that began with the birth of a child two thousand years ago has echoed like footfalls throughout the centuries. God bless us and keep us. Merry Christmas, one and all.

16

TWO GOOD SONS

BEFORE THE NORTH ANDOVER GAME, I visit with Dan Bonfiglio in front of his locker. "How's Emily doing?" I ask.

The goalie says that he spotted her at the mall with her boyfriend, a former wrestling team captain who graduated from Methuen High last year. Bonfiglio has a lovesick expression and I tell him to keep working on little Emily. He sees her every day at school and the boyfriend doesn't. "When the cat's away, the mice will play," I tell him.

"You bet."

Ryan Fontaine has returned from his suspension. In the locker room he's sitting in his customary seat between Chris Martin and Thom DeZenzo. He hails me with his eyes and I go over and ask him how he's doing. "Jesus Christ. I made a mistake," Fontaine says. "What can I say?"

"That you're a stupid ass?" asks DeZenzo, sitting beside him. He looks over at me and shakes his head.

Waiting for the hubbub to rise around us, I pitch my voice beneath it so only Fontaine can hear me. "In another week, it'll be a new year and a new start," I tell him. "Make something of it."

His eyes unblinking, Fontaine sits on the bench in his pants, socks, and skates. "You're not gonna write about my suspension are you?" he asks.

"Of course I am. The question is, what's going to happen now? Will you make a comeback and be one of the heroes of the story? Or will you crash and burn?"

The stakes of his predicament seem to dawn on the hard-nosed winger for the first time, and he sits there dumbfounded while DeZenzo snickers beside him.

"You'll be seeing a lot of me," I tell Fontaine. "Happy New Year."

Kevin McCarthy is eating a jelly doughnut at the other end of the room and I hand him an energy bar on my way out. "Get rid of that thing," I say. "Hockey players don't eat junk like that."

The Rangers burst onto the ice led by their two goalies, who look like space-age beekeepers in their helmets and extra padding. Before the game, Robillard agonized over his choice of goaltender: Dan Bonfiglio, or stick with last year's backup, Dave Gray. "No question," said Jon Morin, shaking his head. "It's gotta be Dave. Dan's off his angles, he's sitting way back in the net. He just doesn't have it right now."

"He's struggling, huh?" Robillard asked.

"Struggling? Joe, he's terrible."

As we take our places behind the bench, the Rangers and their opponents warm up to the thumping beat of Static-X blaring over the PA. "This sounds like Satan's music," says Robillard, covering his ears. "No more of this crap."

Morin laughs when I ask if Mr. Parker ever played music before their games. "No way," he says.

"If anything, it would've been Chopin or Mozart," I say. "Something to stimulate the mind, quicken your response time."

Robillard calls his team to the bench. At center ice, the referee holds the puck in his hand and blows his whistle. "Work hard.

Shoot the puck and get in there and pick up the rebounds," Robillard says.

In an odd reversal from the previous season, when Methuen started sophomore Becky Trudel in the net against North Andover and was blown out 7-2, the Scarlet Knights have a young woman in goal and find themselves being peppered by the Ranger forwards. Methuen leads the game 4-0 after two periods.

Chris Cagliuso sits at his locker drenched in sweat. "This is the last level you're going to see a girl goalie. Time to put a bunch of pucks in the net," I tell him.

"Easier said than done," says Cagliuso, swigging from a plastic bottle of water.

The boys line up at the door, ready to go back out there, and mild-mannered Eric MacDonald takes some ribbing about a nasty cross-check that left him lying on the ice. "He's a tough kid," says Kevin McCarthy, apparently coming to his teammate's defense. "He's a golfer."

Bonfiglio is downcast, about not playing again and perhaps about his fortunes with Emily. "Come on, good son," says Joe Harb, whacking him on the cage. Harb turns to me. "Bonfiglio. That's 'good son' in Italian."

Early in the third period, hustling winger Dave George finds a loose puck near North Andover's net and flings it over the sprawling goalie for his fifth goal in five games. "Who was that?" I ask, as Rangers cheer all around me.

"Dave George again," says Harb. "He's got the knack."

Everything is not rosy for Ryan Fontaine. Even though he collects two assists, the feisty winger is unhappy about being relegated to the third line and comes back to the bench angry after a bad shift. He smashes his stick against the glass. "I fucking hate this," he says.

"Don't play then," Robillard shoots back. "Sit for a while."

Dave Martin is everywhere, jumping over the glass to repair his son Chris's broken skate, joking with several of the guys on the bench as well as principal Ellen Parker, who's standing nearby with Brian Urquhart, the athletic director. Martin even calls over one of the referees during a lull and chats with him. "I can brownnose the refs better than anyone," he tells me, when the zebra skates away.

Soon after, Methuen scores their seventh and final goal during a controversial pileup in front of North Andover's net. "Hey, ref," someone shouts from the stands. "Next time use your good eye." Martin turns around to me and laughs.

Several of the Rangers have career nights, including Kevin McCarthy. Skating from end to end like a man possessed, Mac bangs in two goals and sets up another. While killing a penalty to Chris Martin, McCarthy takes the puck the entire sheet of ice and misses tucking it beneath the goalie by half an inch. Robillard hollers from the bench, asking his stalwart winger if he's tired and wants to come out. Albert Soucy is standing nearby, ready to leap the boards and replace McCarthy.

Bent over his stick, McCarthy shakes his head. "No, coach," he says.

"How'd you like to have twenty of him?" Dave Martin asks. "Geez . . ."

Coach Robillard sends Dan Bonfiglio into the game for the final eight minutes. North Andover musters only a handful of shots and none go in the net. Still, Bonfiglio is upset over the mop-up duty and when the Rangers return to the locker room after the game, the senior goalie fires his gloves against the wall and quickly strips off his equipment.

Dave Gray is also somber, and Al Soucy saunters past in just his skates and oversized hockey pants, grabbing a can of soda from the case Robillard provides after home games. "Cheer up, ladies," Soucy says to the glum netminders. "We won."

"I took it as an insult," says Bonfiglio, sitting in goalie's corner. "Why not let Dave finish up?"

I look Dan in the eye. "Believe me, it's better to play a little than not at all."

Kirk Walsh, one of last year's captains, is home again from Brewster Academy and visits his pals in the locker room. After shaking my hand, the rugged blond defenseman notes how the team lockers form two distinct Ranger neighborhoods. "From McCarthy and Mueskes on down: Girouard, English, Trovato, Zapanas. They're the rich dicks. Now up in that corner. Fontaine, DeZenzo, Martin, Parker. They're just like me. Abdo. Cagliuso. All like me. The goalies are the goalies. They're different."

Coach Martin walks by and Walsh attempts to trip him with the stick he is fooling with. Whirling on his former charge, Martin presses a booted foot against Walsh's groin. "You're gonna push one time too much, Walshie," says the coach, in the midst of general laughter. "And then you're gonna lose that left nut."

In the locker room before practice, one of the players nudges the guy next to him. "My sister wants you bad," he says.

"Tough luck for her. She's ugly as hell."

The other guys start laughing and the chivalrous brother shoves his teammate over the bench and laughs, too. "If she's so ugly, how come you never stop talking about her?"

The players dress and tramp onto the ice. It's school vacation and there's liberation in the air; during the three-on-three "Northeastern drill," where players on both squads can shoot and score on either goalie within a confined area, the boys get rambunctious and start playing the body. Guys are sprawling all over the ice and the goalies are scrambling. It's near the end of the century now, and Joe Robillard looks on with approval.

The hour ends, and Robillard calls the squad together by clapping his stick on the ice. "I don't expect it to be rah-rah in here all the time, but it was good to hear some noise the last ten-fifteen minutes," he says. "Maybe as you get older, you develop more passion for the game and you guys just aren't there yet. I don't know. But it seems you're too grumpy sometimes."

The veteran coach surveys his team for a moment, a reflective look on his face. Then he taps his stick on the ice a few times and the echo travels across the empty grandstand. "Take those shirts home and wash them," says Robillard, wrinkling his nose. "The stench."

Dan Bonfiglio drops by the skate room in T-shirt and boxer shorts, looking to stow his pads.

"I take it you were pissed off when I put you in the other night," says Robillard, as Jon Morin and I look on.

The inscrutable goaltender hangs his dyed blond head. "Yeah. I was."

"That's good. A goalie needs a little fire. If you want that starting job back, I need you to work for it."

Bonfiglio nods, turns around to go. "I'm on your side, kid," says Robillard. "Remember that."

When Bonfiglio departs, Morin leans against the cinder block wall of the corridor and stares after him. "We're gonna need him, Joe," says Morin. "If Graysie gets hurt or something . . ."

"We need two good goalies this year," says Robillard, nodding.

17

TIME AND TIME AGAIN

HALF AN HOUR BEFORE THE annual Methuen High Alumni hockey game, there are only seven players in the dressing room. Most years, the December classic attracts more than forty ex-Rangers and Joe Robillard arranges for two separate games: odd years versus even years prior to 1990 and post-1990. It was my job to call the details into the *Eagle-Tribune* this year, but the item that ran was microscopic and included the wrong date.

Jon Morin and Dave Martin think this is hilarious and while we put on our gear they pester me to reveal my "connections" at the newspaper. "What's your profession again?" asks Martin, bending close with his hand to his ear. "Writer. Author. Journalist. Ha! Bullshit."

Martin charges out through the door half-dressed. Across the room, old rugby friend Jeff Barraclough, who graduated in 1986 and was coached by Martin in youth hockey and high school, shakes his head at these antics. "He's like a cartoon character," he says.

Gary Ruffen is the only other guy who shows up from the 1974–75 team. We dress side by side, talking in shorthand, having a few laughs about the old days. Now there are fifteen guys in the room, including Jason Daigle, a 20-year-old goalie whose father, Bob, was on our team. After Ruffen and I don the white alumni jerseys and skate through our warm-up, we spot Bob Daigle sitting in the stands and go over and bang our sticks against the glass, telling old man Daigle to suit up and get out here. Shaking his head, Daigle laughs and waves us away.

In front of the net, Jason Daigle, fresh from junior hockey in Canada and now playing for Wentworth Institute, warms up like a gymnast. He executes a full split in either direction, and then leaps to his feet with a single powerful movement.

"How come your dad's not out here?" Ruffen asks him.

"He's too old," Jason says, grinning through his mask.

Ruffen and I glide away. "He's younger than we are," I say to my old buddy.

The sporting life at age 42 comes with far greater mental, emotional, physical, and financial struggle than it did just a few years ago. These days I have all the classic impositions of budding career, continuing money woes, a young child who needs and deserves my attention, and a body that's still supple but constantly on the verge of major breakdowns: ankles, knees, neck, hamstrings, and just about everything else. But once the game begins, particularly if I take a hit early and the adrenaline makes me fearless, I can still play like a kid.

We line up at center ice for the opening face-off. I'm playing right wing. There's a 24-year-old kid at center and our left wing is 20—a star forward at Plymouth State College in New Hampshire. Martin and Morin are the defense pairing for the blue team. The two of them stare at me like they're driving steamrollers and I'm a squirrel.

Suddenly it occurs to me that, twenty-five years removed from the Ranger varsity, I can't skate, I can't carry the puck, and positionally I'm a mess. The first few minutes of the game are a buzzing, blooming confusion, much faster than the competition on Monday nights and more frenzied than the pickup games we play in Joe Robillard's gym class. But with so many good skaters on the ice—mostly on our team—space opens up and my own game moves to a higher level. Racing down the wing, I can hear the wild breathing inside my helmet and feel my heart thumping against my clavicle.

In hockey, the area surrounding you is exaggeratedly clear, devoid of sound and slow moving like syrup. Outside that circle everything is blurred, whipping past at incredible speeds. The game moves at the quickness of thought, the puck shifted from player to player, suddenly appearing on the blade of your stick. Decisions are made in an instant—skate with it, pass it, snap off a wrist shot—and mistakes bring that blurry onrushing violence right to you. Four minutes into the alumni game our best player, the college star, flies the length of the ice and shoots at the sprawling goalie and the rebound comes straight to me in the slot. In one motion I bury it into the back of the net.

"Oh, Jesus," says Dave Martin, who has just been burnt on defense. "That's gonna be in the book. Chapter Twenty: 'I scored the first goal in the alumni game.' "

"That's Chapter One," I tell him, skating away.

As it turns out, I score the first two goals of the game within a couple of minutes. For all my weaknesses as a hockey player—which are various and glaring—I have decent vision, quick hands, and I can pass the puck. When I was a teenager, I used to play floor hockey for hours in the confines of our basement, with my 6-year-old brother Jamie as goalie and 3-year-old Patrick on defense. Now I'm pretty accurate from fifteen feet out.

Although I have two embarrassing pratfalls, am knocked on my ass several times by Jon Morin, and am wheezing like an asthmatic, I can't stop grinning after the second goal. Both shots are one-timers right along the ice, sneaking just inside the post to the goalie's right. As a former goalie myself, I always look for that little patch of space in the lower left-hand corner as I approach the net. Even the best goalies have an Achilles heel, and it's usually a quick shot just beyond the heel of the broad, unwieldy stick they all use.

Most of my time, in one way or another, belongs to someone else: paying my bills, waiting in line at the supermarket and doctor's office, bulling through traffic. But for a few thrilling moments after each of those goals, all the time in the world belongs to me, an expanse that reaches out to the future and back to every other moment when I felt the same way. From my sweaty gray hair to the tips of my scrunched-up toes, I'm alive. That's the reason I've introduced Liam to sports, and why I started taking him to the rink when he was only 4 months old. I'd choose these goal-scoring moments over any other, and for my child to experience them is more precious to me than money, or real estate, or power of position. What could I pass on to Liam that's more valuable than joy?

On the ice everyone is equal and when Kirk Walsh swings a pass to me, he just says "Atkinson." Later he and I are jousting with the opposing forwards and when we clear the puck out of the zone, Walshie says, "Nice job, coach." That makes me feel good, because around here "coach" is a title of respect.

We win 10-3. In the locker room, Dan Bonfiglio's older brother Tony, also a goalie, is dripping with sweat. "I'm too old for this," Tony says, removing his helmet.

Nearby is Gary Ruffen, hunched over the bench. He asks Bonfiglio how old he is, and the kid throws out a number. "Jay: he's 19," Ruffen says to me. "Double that and we've still got four years on him."

A few years ago we organized a special alumni game for our twentieth reunion and then had a party at the 1859 House in Methuen Square. Heavy, vaporous light mingled with the smell of roasting meats inside the tavern, blurring the figures ranged along the bar and in front of the fireplace. As I moved through the crowd, receiving the various insults and pats on the back, I was looking for one guy in particular, a teammate I hadn't seen in twenty-five years. Then I heard his voice, booming over the din. He was telling a waitress that the service was too slow.

A gifted athlete and an opinionated and controversial fellow, John Sabbagh has always been a beloved friend and someone I'd genuinely missed over the years. Right after I graduated from Methuen High, I learned that Sabbagh had stopped playing sports and then he just seemed to disappear. When he got married a few years later, none of his old teammates was invited to the wedding. Hearing his voice from the bar, I was struck by a realization: I had not seen John Sabbagh since he was 16 years old.

He was about thirty pounds over his playing weight, in a cream-colored shirt with fish printed on it and a clipped black mustache that made him look like a Mexican bandit. But it was the same old Sabbagh, all right, charismatic and profane, with a keen eye for summing up a situation. He sat with me and Gary Ruffen, in a loud voice questioning the identity of some of the other former Rangers at the party. "Who's that? Where did he play? Just trying out for the team doesn't count," said Sabbagh.

As usual, John talked of his carnal desires, of body parts, and of his flippant attitude toward the conservative and sanctimonious, refusing to give an inch to his many critics. "Let's have a sex reunion and all swap," he said. "One of the coaches grabbed my testicles and that's not right in an organized program. Look at that guy over there. I'd rather be me dead than him alive."

After dinner, Sabbagh and Ruffen and I made plans to meet across town at the Fireside Pub for more drinks. To my surprise, Sabbagh showed up and we drank beers and told stories until midnight. At one point, Sabbagh said, "I miss you guys. You guys were the top, the best." He gestured at the clatter and ruckus of the bar. "This is great. But it's great because we didn't do it every night for twenty years."

Then John Sabbagh shook my hand and sauntered out of the bar. That was five years ago, and I haven't seen him since.

At closing time Gary Ruffen drove me home, past the granite walls around the old Tenney High, Nicholson Stadium, and the playing fields beyond. Gary confessed that he'd nearly skipped the party because he hadn't seen John for so long and had felt slighted when Sabbagh stopped calling all his old friends.

"We owned the town in those days," I said, musing as it rolled by the windows of Gary's car. "And we were always trying to cram everything in and slow things down. But it only speeded things up. Even back then, we could see it was coming to an end."

The night of the alumni game I enjoy five or six hours of itchy, endorphin-laced sleep, and then I'm back at the rink with my skates and gear. It's New Year's Eve morning and keeping with tradition, Coach Robillard transforms the final practice of the year into the Rangers' annual ball hockey tournament played on ice. I've been invited to participate, and I come limping into the dressing room with a foggy head and sore right hip.

Two nets are facing each other at either end of the rink, and the varsity is divided into five squads of four skaters each. The teams will play a series of ten-minute games in round-robin format, similar to the "shinny" played in Methuen High gym classes but much faster and more skillfully.

Although my legs are dead after last night, I plan to continue my goal-scoring ways. But Robillard is short a goalie and putting on my skates in the locker room, I survey the other three volunteers—Ryan Fontaine and the two "bobos," Tim Parker and James Girouard—and begin to consider playing goal. Other than a little street hockey here and there, I haven't put on a set of goalie equipment in twenty-two years. But Dave Gray is offering his gear and it looks about my size . . . what the hell. I raise my hand.

"I'll do it, coach."

The locker room erupts in catcalls and warnings. "Mr. Bobo, you must be nuts," says Tim Parker, half-dressed in goalie equipment himself.

The street hockey balls are so light, there's very little chance of injury from being struck by one, especially in full gear. But the odds of pulling a muscle, wrenching my back, and/or humiliating myself are about three to one, I figure. Judging by the smirks I'm getting from around the locker room, I've entered into a fool's wager.

Dave Gray sits beside me and helps with the bulky leg pads. He's owned them for years and has a few tips on managing the worn leather straps that hold the pads in place. As I kneel on the matted floor of the locker room and buckle up first the right pad and then the left, a weird sense of déjà vu settles over me. I'm popping a light sweat and my heart rate is up a bit. Do I still have any game?

Soon I'm suited up from head to foot, including Gray's distinct black helmet and mask. Out by the rink door, several players are milling about, hardly glancing my way because most of them don't know who it is. I'm Dave Gray's 42-year-old doppelgänger, and only when Albert Soucy gets real close does he start up with laughter. "Oh, it's you, Mr. Atkinson," he says, and laughs. "*Good luck.* I thought it was Dave."

There on the rubber apron is where the resemblance ends. At the far end of the building the Zamboni machine finishes its circuit and eases from the ice into its stall. Emerging from the rink office, Joe Robillard stalks over to me on his skate blades and offers some advice. "Play the angles, and just let the ball hit you," he says. "I remember about three years ago I played in goal and hurt my back pretty good. Tried to make a quick reaction to a shot and *whammo.* I mean sharp, shooting pain."

This isn't very encouraging. I take the ice and wheel around the rink, more or less anonymously. I was always a pretty good skating goalie and adjust to the girth of the pads right away. But my old buddy and youth hockey adversary Jim MacDonald, there to watch his son Eric play, is standing beyond the end boards and recognizes me. He makes a theatrical gesture with his hands, like he's calling for divine intervention in my plight, and then laughs soundlessly behind the glass. For Jimmy MacDonald, the entertainment factor of the ball hockey tournament has just risen considerably.

The first game begins. Lucky for me, Jon Morin's team is defending the goal I reside in, and with his keen sense of anticipation I don't face many back-to-back rushes or flurries. After a couple of decent saves I begin envisioning my comeback as a goaltender. There are vague hints of the trouble to come, but intoxicated by my athletic success over the past eighteen hours, I pay little heed to the signs. The first clue that there's an ordeal ahead is the multiplying effect that gravity begins to have on my reflexes. Although the goalie equipment is comfortable when I'm just standing around, and much lighter than when I played, after I sprawl on the ice half a dozen times and jump back up, it feels like I'm wearing chain mail long johns and a suit of armor. This stuff gets heavy real fast, and glancing up at the scoreboard clock, I see the first game isn't even half over.

My other problem is seeing the pale yellow ball as it whirs through the air. Although I have 20/20 vision, the street hockey ball is difficult to pick up against the milky backdrop of the ice. And although it's much lighter and less threatening than a real puck, these kids can zing it around like a laser beam. Sharpshooter Chris Cagliuso scores two goals in under a minute, but Morin's bunch hangs on to win 5-2. So far I'm undefeated.

The second game is the most dangerous because I make an impossible save with the blocker pad on my right arm and begin to acquire an inflated sense of what I can do. In this sort of hockey, there's no defense to speak of, just four guys whaling away in the offensive zone and hoping their goalie comes up big when two or three opposing players steal the ball and go racing the other way. Even though I'm stumbling around back there, I manage to fling myself in front of unguarded portions of the net and the ball springs off my skate or arm or chest and bounces the other way. We win again.

Between games, I take off the mask and gloves and leave the ice for a drink of water. Mostly I'm stalling for time; I'm lightheaded and my legs are numb. Moving along the rubber mats behind the grandstand, I weave back and forth like a sailor too long at sea, my left shoulder bouncing off the cinder block wall.

Jim MacDonald pokes his head around the grandstand while I slurp from the bubbler. "Making a comeback?" he asks.

"Discovering my limitations."

MacDonald laughs at me. "Is it bringing back any bad memories?"

Instantly I flash on pucks streaming over my shoulder, between my legs, along the ice, and up high in the corners; a hailstorm of vulcanized rubber, nearly all of it eluding my desperate gymnastics. I reply to Jimmy Mac with a familiar barnyard epithet and he laughs again and disappears.

In the third game, Jon Morin is leading the other team and my secret horror manifests itself. My lungs feel like they're an inch deep and my peripheral vision is so bad, it's like playing goal in a subway tunnel, only a tiny point of light out ahead and even that's rocketing toward me. Within about twenty seconds, Morin deposits one shot over my left shoulder and another one through my legs.

"Whee-ee," he says, skating around the net. "Five hole."

We lose big, and at the end of the game I'm lying exhausted in the crease and Joe Robillard skates over. "Enjoying it?" he asks.

"Yeah. Love it."

"Great. One more to go." Robillard pivots and skates away, trailing his stick like a little kid. "Big, big game coming up," he says.

I feel like I'm going to pass out. My head throbs and a hint of nausea curdles my stomach. All around me, 15- and 16-year-olds are shooting pucks off the boards, etching the ice with their skate blades, and gabbling like pigeons. The only encouraging sight is Ryan Fontaine, local tough guy, who's minding the net opposite. For several minutes after the third game, he remains prone on the ice. Finally he rises to his knees, struggles upward, and skates to the bench on shaky legs. Dave Gray is leaning against the boards, talking and laughing with Dan Bonfiglio.

"You goalies are stupid," says Fontaine. But he's not angry or abusive. He's enlightened.

The last ten minutes of the morning commence with a buzzer resounding throughout the rink. I make a nifty skate save, just as quickly give up a bad goal, and stand in front of the net exhausted. I glance up at the clock: seventeen seconds have elapsed. As Methuen High football coach Larry Klimas is fond of saying, O Mother of Good Counsel!

Buoying our little squad for the final game is Joe Robillard, whose tactical sense, enduring athleticism, and sheer love of playing dominates a wide strip of the ice in front of my net. Robillard knocks the ball away on defense, makes slick little passes, and scores goals, while maintaining a steady commentary on the game. As we've all done as children, he executes every move like he's being watched over by a play-by-play man who never tires or goes away.

When Robillard steals the ball from Dave George just as he's about to shoot, the coach yells, "What a play by Mario Lemieux," and the kids all laugh. A few moments later, I wave at the ball and it goes in. "Atkinson beaten from center ice," says Robillard.

Then I suffer the goaltender's most dreaded indignity—I allow another goal on the very next shot. "Sieve, sieve, sieve," Robillard says, chuckling at me.

Beyond the glass, Jimmy MacDonald throws his hands in the air. It's his imitation of a particular 15-year-old goalie, circa 1972, when young Jimmy Mac scored a goal just seven seconds into a youth hockey game. It was the shock of the season, and as soon as the puck blew past me, I started screaming and swearing at my defense. Now, lying on the ice, I'm too tired to flip Jimmy the bird.

There's under three minutes to play and the score is 2-2. The ball is rolling around the end boards and one of their players carves it away and flicks a shot on goal. The ball hits me—I don't know where—and for a maddening instant, I can't find it. Then someone darts in and taps at my feet and the ball is behind me, rolling in the net. One arm flung over the crossbar, I dangle to the ice like a shattered marionette. I can't breathe. I can't see. Death is approaching, as Joe Robillard picks the ball out of the twine with his stick blade and they all go flying the other way.

Within seconds, not near enough time to catch my breath, the opposition has returned and is cycling back and forth in front of my net. One moment I am covering the right post, my head curled around to the right, trying to stay fixed on the pale yellow shadow of the ball. Suddenly it goes zipping across to my left, toward the open half of the goal. Somehow I throw myself down and slide hard, flinging my left leg and left arm in the air. Pain shoots through my left shoulder like a bolt of electricity and the ball, fired at the goal in the blink of an eye, tips off my extended skate blade and goes wide.

"GREAT SAVE, ATKINSON," says Coach Robillard, who scrambles after the loose ball.

Seconds later, we score again, and the final game ends in a tie. The kids leave the ice, piling into the locker room amid holiday chatter and the banging of their sticks. I make my way to the first row of the grandstand and collapse there. Stripping off the mask and gloves, I feel the sweat running down my back. It pools against my tailbone and instantly turns cold. In the distance, the Zamboni grinds over the ice and I lean back on the lower benches, waiting for my energy to return.

In years gone by, I would play entire hockey games with real pucks flying at me and then shower and go home like nothing extraordinary had occurred. I'd practice at 5 A.M., play games on consecutive nights, and fill the hours in between with floor hockey tournaments in my cellar. Certain things I can still do and I'm proud of those things, which means I've maintained my love of sport and haven't given in to middle-age complacency. But running and cycling and lifting weights won't turn the clock back to 1975. It will, however, allow me the opportunity to suffer the way I have this morning. And that deepens my appreciation for the current Ranger varsity and the talent they have, as well as the game I used to play in the musty rinks of long ago.

By the time I head into the locker room, most of the kids are gone. Piece by piece I stack Dave Gray's gear in his locker and then sit on the bench in my long johns. Always polite, Albert Soucy tips his baseball cap on the way out. "Happy New Year, Mr. Atkinson," he says. "Nice game today."

"You too, Albert. And many more of them."

In a few minutes I'm alone on the scarred old bench, too tired to get dressed. Joe Robillard makes a pass through the room, picking up spiky balls of tape and splinters of wood. He smiles at me, doesn't say anything, and goes out. From my appearance and body language, Joe probably figures I'm having deep thoughts and want to be left alone. But my mind is pretty much blank. Here at the end of the century, I'm just a heart beating. I'm a guy sitting on a bench, happy to be alive.

From the rink I drive straight home and sleep for several hours. When I wake up, it's four o'clock on New Year's Eve and already growing dark. I have a stiff neck and rise slowly into a sitting position. This is the season for taking stock and within a minute or two, after a jangly circuit around the living room, I catalog my latest ailments. My right hip feels bound by last night's contusion and hinders my gait. Both sides of my groin—muscles a goalie uses to push back and forth across the crease—have tightened up like piano wires. Running over my left shoulder to where it attaches beneath the scapula, a narrow band of muscle has sprung loose and refuses to act in concert with the rest of the group.

Despite these irritations and the throb of a significant headache, I'm feeling pretty good at the close of the year: there's nothing new to enshrine in my personal museum of debilitating injuries. Certainly there's no concussion like in 1975, when I was knocked out by that Dave Frasca slap shot. No stretched knee ligaments of '77, dislocated shoulder of '78, perforated rib cartilage of '81, or chest hematoma of '82. No torn tendons in my right ankle like '84, left ankle '85, torn upper rib cartilage of '89, compressed cervical disk '91, torn right hamstring of '93, broken right cheekbone and fractured eye socket of '96, torn cartilage and surgical repair of right knee in '97, several deadened teeth and hundreds of bruises and contusions and stitches, all of these maladies the result of an unrestrained passion for hockey, rugby, soccer, and wrestling.

My passions have left their mark on me. Look straight on and you'll see that my right shoulder, separated during a wrestling practice in college, drops about three inches lower than my left. On those rare occasions when I visit my tailor, the white-haired

Lebanese gentleman always insists on padding that side of my sports jackets. Invariably I refuse, keeping in mind Bruce Parker's dictum about exhibiting your war injuries.

Torn up by twenty-two years of rugby and thirty-one playing hockey, sometimes my ankles lock up, transforming my smooth athlete's gait into a painful shamble. I can't turn my head very far in either direction because of frayed and flattened cervical disks, and when I'm tired, shooting stars appear in the periphery of my right eye and it refuses to track properly. The whole mess on that side of my face was caused by a running blindside punch in a rugby game, and I remember when the swelling improved and I went in for oral surgery. The dentist was amazed at the number of root canals I had already received, a sum that was pretty high for my age, 38 at the time. He asked if I recalled taking any sharp blows to the head. I started laughing so hard, the little air suction hose got stuck on the underside of my tongue and nearly strangled me.

All this, and my addiction to heavy exercise and competition continues unabated. It's what I know.

18

ANGRY JOE

In Ryan Fontaine's art class, I discover that the hockey team's bad boy is a paragon of self-discipline and etiquette compared with some of his peers. Six large wooden tables dominate the room, scattered with bits of construction paper, glue pots, papier-mâché residue, and tubes of scented wax. A large kiln stands to one side and a series of wire cages for drying out greenware. While sitting at a table, I'm joined by a short, chunky kid named Joe who refuses to participate in the class activity—designing a clay valentine—and curses in the teacher's face. Joe is a small, round ball of rage and even though I fancy myself invisible, the kid draws me into his private circle of hell by grabbing one of my notebooks.

"That's not yours, buddy," I tell him. "Put it back."

Angry Joe pauses for a moment, giving me the eyeball. "I don't give a shit whose it is."

I stare him down and Joe pitches the notebook back on my pile of stuff. Again the teacher comes over to prompt the kid and he rebuffs her with an expletive. I'm in shock. But the teacher is hailed from across the room and departs without another word. Over in his group, Ryan Fontaine works on his clay turtle and flirts with the pretty girls. A halo appears in the air above his head.

Angry Joe is a refugee from the Behavioral Resource Room, an unfathomable kid who despises everything he looks upon. After class, Ryan Fontaine says that even he's had problems with Joe. "He said my girlfriend had a nice ass. I told him he was lucky he was too small to hit."

Later the art instructor stops to discuss Joe's behavior. Apparently he's one of eight special education kids in the ceramics class. "If I had just those eight, I could manage," the teacher says. "But with all the rest of the kids . . ."

"What kind of home life does Joe have?" I ask.

"There's definitely something going on in that household," she says. "Something bad."

In Ellen Parker's office, I outline for the second-year principal some of the things I've noticed as I visit certain classrooms and follow hockey players around. In a few departments, there's major audiovisual abuse going on, as instructors show movies instead of teaching, raising the noise level in the adjacent class spaces by making the other instructors lecture over the roar of the soundtrack. Also, the classes are poorly supervised in many cases; too many kids making thirty-minute trips to the bathroom or just drifting through the space between dividers and clogging up the hallways. And there's a distinct cadre of "students" who are disrupting classes and contributing nothing to the academic climate of Methuen High.

I throw a name out and Parker looks the kid up on her computer. His grades for the first two quarters are four F's and two D's. He is an 18-year-old freshman/sophomore. Ironically, he's passing history, where I've observed him on three occasions and where he's in constant conflict with the teacher.

All of my comments reinforce Parker's own thoughts about the school's weaknesses. She believes it all comes back to the teachers, and the quality of instruction they provide. "We need more teachers who can motivate and engage kids from the first moment of class to the last," Parker says. "Too many times, our worst teachers are assigned the lowest classes and the worst kids. The chairpersons think the smartest kids are the hardest to teach. It's the opposite."

I tell her how much fun I'm having as I float through the rink, the field house, and the classrooms, eyes and ears open. "Enjoy high school," Parker says. "Not many people get a second chance."

Before hockey practice, I relate my experience in Ryan Fontaine's class to Joe Robillard and Joe Harb in the skate room and they run through Methuen High's roster of topnotch idiots—the worst kids they've had in recent years. Usually a Puritan in speech, Robillard cannot resist telling me about one hyperactive kid who popped off at his Spanish teacher in the cafeteria. The woman tried to admonish her charge *en español* and the punk was having none of it.

"Fuck you, nacho lady," he said.

As a classroom teacher and two-sport coach, Joe Harb sees a wide range of personalities in the course of a school year. "Ryan Fontaine is an 'in trouble' good kid, but [Angry Joe] is an 'in trouble' sneaky kid," he says.

"Give me the kid I can see coming from the front over the kid coming from the back," I say. "Angry Joe is the devil in baggy pants."

Harb adds that hockey player Dan Martin has been a handful lately. That morning, Harb was conducting a discussion on the ramifications of mandatory academic testing. While the other students weighed in with various opinions, Martin kept bopping the kid in front of him on the head. Finally Harb approached, looming over the slightly built freshman. "What are you doing, Martin?" he asked. "Don't be a dink."

The players begin coming into the skate room so we shift topics of conversation. Dan Bonfiglio appears with his skates in hand, which haven't been sharpened in two years. Chris Cagliuso, who puts a new edge on his blades every few days, is surprised at this.

"How else will a goalie slide back and forth?" asks Bonfiglio. "It doesn't take a physicist to figure that out."

Cagliuso shrugs. "I'm gonna be a business major," he says.

Just as the players take the ice, I notice that Dave Gray is missing. "You wrecked his equipment," says Robillard.

After my heavy and awkward use of his gear during the ball hockey tournament, Gray's appearance at practice has been delayed by a broken toestrap and missing buckle on his leg pad, and a stripped screw on his mask. Twenty minutes into the workout, Gray shows up and I wave him over.

"Sorry, Dave. I was so tired afterward I didn't even notice."

Gray chucks me on the shoulder with his glove. "Don't worry about it," he says.

A couple of minutes later, I figure it out. "Hey, Graysie. Next time you want to miss half a practice, why don't you let me borrow your equipment?" He and Bonfiglio grin at me through their masks.

During the practice session the coaches watch Albert Soucy fly up and down the ice, scratching their heads over the winger's scoring slump. "One assist all year," Robillard says. "That's it."

Soucy is a charming, talkative fellow, and during the water break he tells a story that illustrates his love of hockey. After night games when he can't get to sleep, Albert digs an old stick out of his bedroom closet and sneaks down the back stairs. Across the street from his parents' house is the Mount Carmel churchyard. During storms, the municipal plows leave giant mounds of snow that melt on sunny afternoons and then refreeze overnight, forming strips of ice about twenty feet long and five feet wide. Scurrying across Lowell Street, Soucy hops the wrought iron fence in the moonlight and dumps a bucket of pucks on the glossy blue apron of ice. Listening to music on his headset, he'll fire pucks into the snow mounds until he grows tired and can sleep.

"I like that," says Robillard. "It's Old School."

When practice resumes, smooth-skating Matt Mueskes, little Brian's older brother, doesn't hustle one bit while Kevin McCarthy charges up and down like it's the state championship. McCarthy wears his dark hair bootcamp-style, ears protruding, and is the sort of kid who would run through a wall if you pointed at it. What players like McCarthy already know and ones like Matt Mueskes will eventually find out was revealed to me a long time ago, before they were born: time inevitably passes, and if you work *through* the time, you'll get results.

During one of the drills, Mueskes skates until he reaches Joe Harb and then glides when he's behind the coach's back. It reminds me of '75 and how one time in the locker room I told Rick Angus that the way to survive all the conditioning was to go at three-quarter speed and make it to the end of practice. Rick paused in tightening his skates and looked over at me. He was the chipped-tooth hero of our neighborhood, star of every sport in season, and my best friend growing up. "Go all out, until you can't go anymore," he said. Rick Angus's theory was to give one hundred percent all the time, and your tolerance for the pain would increase. And he was right.

Jon Morin arrives late for practice and notices that one of his defensemen is missing. "Where's Chris Martin?" he asks.

Robillard tells his assistant that "just like last spring" Martin doesn't want to go to school anymore. Tri-captain Thom DeZenzo, Martin's partner on defense, is out with the flu and has been dispatched to talk with Chris.

Morin takes this all in, chewing his gum. He nods to me and skates away to start a new drill. The other Martin, freshman Dan, is also struggling. He's been ruled ineligible for today's jayvee game versus Acton-Boxborough because of an in-school suspension.

"Any other good news?" asks Dave Martin.

Dressed in his lineman's overalls and nursing a giant cup of coffee, Martin is stricken with the flu and looks haggard and weary. His Christmas holiday has provided new strain, as he's buried a favorite aunt and spent half the week away from his kids because of the divorce. Dave Martin's first reaction is to jump all over his two oldest kids and he goes tearing through the rink looking for them.

I catch up near the jayvee locker room. "Easy, Dave," I say to my old friend. "Don't pop a gasket."

Nearby, Cagliuso asks Robillard about Chris Martin. "You guys have to talk to Chris," the coach says. "I tried, but he thought I was going to yell at him. And his mum was crying. I felt bad."

Cagliuso says that Martin has insomnia. He frets aloud over the state of the Ranger defense minus the stewardship of DeZenzo, and without Martin's grit. "This is the best we've been as a 'team' since I've been here," he says.

Athletic trainer Kevin MacLennan appears at the rink door. "Who's the victim tomorrow, Coach?" he asks.

Joe Robillard shakes his head. "The Lincoln-Sudbury . . . what's their nickname?"

"Rich Folk?" asks MacLennan.

19

HANGERS, HACKERS, AND DANGLERS

I'M A RINK RAT AND ALWAYS HAVE BEEN. Even now, I'll go to the rink for public skating, then home for lunch and out to find a pond hockey game in the afternoon. That's where the best ice time and purest hockey is played—on the ponds. Here at the apex of winter, there's usually a small season where the natural ice is thick and solid and the weather is just right for hockey. That's when I drive around with my gear in the car, ready to play.

At seven o'clock on a weekday morning, I cruise past Hillsie's pond behind Mann Orchards and spot ice that has been covered with a thin layer of water and then refrozen. While motorists on their way to work gawk at me, I change into my windsuit and grab my skates and stick from the trunk and get out there for a workout. By visiting one of the local farmer's ponds, I'm following a long-established precedent of Methuen leisure. On January 16, 1878, 18-year-old orchard keeper Charles W. Mann wrote in his diary, "Went down to Deacon's Pond skating with John Crosby. The hog was brought home. It weighed 222 lbs. A cold windy day. Ther. stood at 13."

I can feel the edges of my skates chattering over the little bumps and imperfections in the ice. All that water underneath provides extra buoyancy, allowing me quicker cuts and faster turns than a man-made surface. In just five minutes, the tips of my ears are burning in the cold, my face grown stiff as leather. This is open ice skating: an acre of glass, marked here and there by the cross-hatchings from yesterday's hockey game. Looking down the broad sheet of ice, they're like hieroglyphics, messages that can't be read so much as felt as I skate over them.

At the end of a long sprint, I make a jump stop—throwing up shards of ice like a thousand tiny white sparks. Then I reverse direction. Skating backwards is all in the hips, not the legs; a quick glance over my shoulder for the bumps, a long double S curve left along the surface in front of me. The scratch of my blades on the ice is deep and loud, echoing in the still morning air.

True pond hockey enthusiasts always work on their moves in secret. In my neighborhood, we called it dangling: holding on to the puck much longer than you would in a real game. Alone on the ice at Hillsie's, I practice this art. The basketball equivalent would be a lot of dribbling, never giving up the ball except for a hot dog shot or a fancy behind-the-back pass. In pond hockey, the dangle of choice consists of letting the puck drift close to your opponent, and then when he lunges for it, you "pull the string." Drawing the puck away, you slip it through the defender's skates and pick it up on the other side. That's a behind-the-back dribble and slam dunk all in one.

A few days after my solo skate at Hillsie's, I'm in western Massachusetts visiting friends and decide to go look for some ice. Outside a convenience store in Ludlow, I ask a video-stunned teenager where I can find a game of pond hockey. The kid shakes his head, jerking his thumb toward the arcade behind him. "They don't have that game in here," he says.

Although the origins of hockey are unclear, historians suppose that it evolved from Northern European stick and ball games dating back to medieval times. In fact, the word *hockey* is derived from the French *hoquet,* or "shepherd's crook." Forms of "hurley," "bandy," and "shinny-on-ice" were played in Canada and the northeastern

United States during the 1800s, with some of the participants on foot and others on skates. In 1862 an indoor skating facility called the Victoria Rink opened in Montreal and a local man named J. G. A. Creighton encoded a set of rules for ice hockey. Teams at the Victoria Rink played the first game before spectators on March 3, 1875.

I stop at no fewer than nine ponds in Ludlow, Wilbraham, West Springfield, Enfield, Springfield, and Longmeadow before Officer Parsons of the Longmeadow Police Department directs me to Heritage Park in East Longmeadow, a quaint little recreation area that only the day before had been "teeming with kids," according to the barrel-chested policeman.

But with six inches of new snow covering everything, Heritage Park is deserted. I haul a shovel out of the trunk and start clearing the ice, like spreading crumbs in the backyard to attract birds. The sun is brilliant overhead, in a ceramic blue sky. On shore, the picnic tables are frosted like two-layer wedding cakes. A man in a station wagon filled with kids pulls up and watches me heaving snow for a few minutes, then drives off again. A while later, the station wagon returns and four new shovelers pile out with skates and sticks slung over their shoulders. Pond hockey has a definite protocol: if you don't shovel, you can't play.

The cleared space on the ice grows larger. Another car arrives containing two mothers and four more kids who clamber down the embankment and join in. The only equivalent to this sort of effort was when barn raisings and quilting bees brought out the whole community to help. Children soon dot the ice, in their colorful snowsuits and ski masks like innocent little bank robbers. An instructional clinic develops, with 3-year-old Connor from Springfield enjoying his first whirl with a hockey stick in his hands while his older siblings and neighbors battle for the Heritage Park Cup.

The kids have no memory of pain as they trip over bumps and land hard on the ice. A smile through the face mask and they're up again, chasing the puck. I take a hard spill going backward that jars my vision and throws a wicked jolt up my funnybone. (I'm not on my skates again as quickly as the kids are.) When we're through, the other players have their mothers handy to take their skates off and fortify them with hot chocolate.

The next day, my search for a more competitive game leads me to Baboosic Lake in Amherst, New Hampshire. My rugby pal Dave Rolla and his wife Kristynn spend most of their free time grooming the ice in front of their house. This is a professional pond hockey outfit: a rink-sized space and a snowblower to clear it with. Each week, the local volunteer fire department resurfaces the ice by pumping a new layer of water over last week's ruts and divots.

By one o'clock, a dozen cars are parked in front of Dave and Kristynn's place and the hockey players are suiting up. Standard equipment is skates, stick, gloves, and elbow pads. Too much equipment and a player is identified as a potential "hacker"—someone who can't skate very well and uses his or her stick to slow down the opposition. In the hearth on shore, a fire is lit and someone has their trunk open with the stereo blasting Pearl Jam and Tom Waits and the Smashing Pumpkins. Against the backdrop of pine trees and buttoned-up summer cottages, the snow-covered lake extends for a mile or two in the distance, crossed by roaring snowmobiles and the occasional Nordic skier.

Teams are chosen by throwing sticks down on the ice and then separating them, one to each side. At Dave and Kristynn's rink, the goals are made of two-by-fours and plastic mesh. They're a regulation six feet wide but only a foot high (instead of four feet), and they look like weird lobster traps or equipment for the Lilliputian hockey league. Slap shots and lifting the puck off the ice are not permitted, but the goalies wear street hockey pads just in case.

Pond hockey is different from rink hockey in several ways. Of course, body checking is outlawed—until someone gets whacked in the ankle and tempers run high. There are no shift changes, no referees, and no offside rules except when someone spends too much time in front of the other team's net and is labeled a "hanger." Hangers are dealt with at some point—and I've got the welts to prove it.

We end up with teams of seven players, including three women who play every week and are good skaters. On the ice are a collection of former high school and college athletes, some experienced hockey players and a few hackers. Amazingly, the stick selection method has resulted in a pretty even matchup.

In the brisk, rarefied air, the game goes back and forth, punctuated by some good passing and nifty maneuvers along with a few spills on the chippy ice. Our team falls behind 3-0 in a game to 15, but we rally back and score three quick ones and then go ahead 5-3. The puck comes to me and I deke the goaltender, and then slip the puck behind him. I wheel around and my wingman Kevin Moore skates past and slaps my gloved hand. We're not kidding out here.

The score is 10-10, and we take a short break and change ends. Long blue shadows stretch across the lake as the sun goes down, and the smell of wood smoke drifts over the ice. The makeshift rink is even equipped with klieg lights, and someone goes over and cranks up the generator. Now some of the laughter and joking goes away, and in the corner elbows fly, the no-checking rule is suspended, and players end up face first in the snow. Suddenly, there's no room out here for the casual hacker.

We're ahead 14-12. With the puck coming to me on the right wing, I chip it along through the rough ice and see Duke Cronin streaking toward the goal. He and I've been playing rugby together for fifteen years and I anticipate where he's going and make a blind pass behind my back. Duke shoots the puck at the goalie and it breaks ever so slowly behind him and trickles into the net. A big cheer comes from our team, and everybody skates off for one of the bottles of Winter Ale stuck in the snow and what Jason Massa calls "gourmet fire food"—steak and chicken and a smoky cabbage stew that looks like Russian gulag cuisine but tastes delicious.

A dozen hockey players cluster around the fire on bales of hay as the first stars appear over Baboosic Lake. The players and their dogs, Alaskan malamutes, Siberian huskies, and a Newfoundland-Labrador mix, linger by the blaze into the middle of the evening. There won't be too much more pond hockey this year, and we want to make it last.

20

THE MAN FROM LINCOLN-SUDBURY

As I enter the locker room before the Lincoln-Sudbury game, Dave Gray says, "I got a story for you. One of my old girlfriends called me last night and asked me if I went out with [new girlfriend] the other day. I said yeah. She started screaming and swearing and said the only reason why I was so popular was because she went out with me."

Nearby, Dan Bonfiglio is pulling on the blue turtleneck he always wears beneath his game jersey. "File that under the heading 'Psycho Girlfriend,' " he says.

Methuen is sluggish as the game begins and Lincoln-Sudbury scores the first goal and then hangs onto the lead until the waning moments of the first period. Because he's been absent from school for the previous two days, Chris Martin is dressed but remains on the bench for several shifts. During a break while an injured player is helped off the ice, Dave Martin sidles over to Jon Morin and motions toward his son. Chris is staring at the gritty rubber mats beneath his feet.

"How long is he gonna sit?" asks Dave Martin.

With one foot up on the boards, scrutinizing who he has on the ice, Morin shrugs. He doesn't say a word or turn to look at his colleague. As much as we need young Martin's tenacious defense,

Morin wants to send a message: self-discipline and dedication to the team come first. Realizing this, Chris Martin's father retreats.

At the end of the period, down 1-0, the Rangers bump into the locker room and are barely seated when Chris Cagliuso lights into them. "That's the worst team defense I've seen in four years here," says the senior tri-captain. "Time and space, guys. Take away their time, take away their space."

"You know how they scored?" asks Thom DeZenzo, from his spot in the corner. "We tossed the puck out through the middle. We've been playing hockey all our lives. You don't throw it up the middle. Ever. Bang it off the glass. We do it enough in practice."

Methuen scores in the first few seconds of the middle period and powered by Cagliuso's line, surges to a 4-1 lead. After a questionable call by the referee, Lincoln-Sudbury's coach mouths the word *asshole* and gets tossed from the game. Teenagers in the stands begin hooting and hollering. They swear at the referee and throw popcorn boxes and a baseball cap onto the ice. The referee asks Methuen athletic director Brian Urquhart, who's the ranking official on site, to remove the offending fans from the rink.

Urquhart dispatches two of the punks, and I'm standing near the rink door when he returns. At the same time, a large, bulky man in his mid fifties lurches down from the grandstand and follows Urquhart along the runner. Right when Urquhart stops, the man barges ahead and shoves him to one side. It isn't a hard shot, but still premeditated.

Brian Urquhart is surprised. The jug-eared former wrestler glances at me and swings around to look at the pushy man, waiting for an apology. None is forthcoming.

As the man walks away, heading for the Lincoln-Sudbury bench, Urquhart goes after him. Standing only as high as the man's shoulder, Urquhart clears his throat and says, "Excuse me, but something odd just happened. Did you push me?"

"I said 'Sorry,' " the man replies.

"Well, I didn't hear you," says Urquhart. He's calm and patient, so far. "I'm the Methuen athletic director and I think we need to talk about this. Let's go out to the lobby."

The man has a large nose and beefy, sulking face. "Leave me alone," he says. "I'm watching a hockey game."

The third period begins, and I'm back on the bench. From the corner of my eye, I notice Urquhart striding toward the bleachers with a hardened look in his eyes. The Lincoln-Sudbury man is about five rows up. Urquhart speaks to him again, shakes his head at what he hears, and goes to the rink office to call the police.

Dave Martin is also watching. "You know what it is? Rich people," he says. "They think they don't have to be polite."

Two Methuen police officers show up, wearing their dark blue commando sweaters and sidearms. They beckon to the man but he refuses to come down from the bleachers. "I'm watching a hockey game," he says.

"Come down here or I'm going to arrest you," says the larger of the two cops.

Reluctantly the Lincoln-Sudbury man climbs down from the bleachers and leads a small contingent toward the lobby. Walking a few strides ahead of the police officers, he turns to Brian Urquhart and says, "You're a fucking asshole."

Later, Urquhart will say, "My balls were swollen"—he holds his hands apart—"this big." It takes all his composure and maturity to restrain himself from making a comment, or throwing the guy to the floor with a double-leg takedown. It turns out that the Lincoln-Sudbury man is the goalie's father and has been muttering throughout the game how the lousy officiating is victimizing his son's team.

Long after Methuen has eked out a 4-3 victory, the rink is dark and I'm standing with Joe Robillard in the illuminated corridor outside the skate room. "If it was just these kids on a pond somewhere, they'd scrap with each other and then they'd all go home friends," I say. "When the adults get involved, it gets screwed up."

Robillard notes that during the game, Thom DeZenzo lost control of his stick and bashed Lincoln-Sudbury's star player across his cage. After the kid appealed to the referee and was told it was an accident, DeZenzo skated over and whomped him on the ass with his glove and it was over and forgotten.

Loopy with the flu, I've been off the ice for a few days and have to watch Liam's Saturday morning practice from the bleachers. My sense of physical detachment and the distortion of the glass that encircles the rink enhance the dreamy quality of the experience. I see Liam in a series of snapshots, little cameos that feature his tiny shape independently of the other children on the ice. He's small, even for 5 years old, with his slender legs clad in gray sweatpants and bound with strips of athletic tape, the dark blue jersey hanging to his knees, and the helmet like a bubble on his head.

Right after Liam's practice the varsity will embark on a trip to Haverhill, and Jeremy Abdo enters the rink dressed in shirt and tie and wearing his blue game jersey over them. Abdo is a quiet, polite kid, the puck wizard of Methuen's third line, and he nods as he walks along behind the glass. The sophomore wing asks if my son is on the ice and sits beside me, watching Liam skate. He's a good kid, this Abdo.

While four instructors try to corral two dozen toddlers, Liam drifts in and out of the session, stopping when the whistle says go, skating clockwise when told to make circles in the other direction, and performing several impromptu swan dives on the ice. But I can tell that he's acquiring control of all four edges, growing more comfortable on his skates, and if Liam seems to resist all attempts to focus his efforts, he's learning to change directions on a whim and go wherever his heart takes him. There'll be plenty of time to skate his lane as he grows older.

When Liam's indifference to the coach's whistle grows absurd, he just leaves the ice, five minutes early. Walking to where Jeremy Abdo and I are sitting, he plops down on the bench and watches his teammates finish their workout.

"All done, Boo?" I ask.

Liam stares at the ice through his cage. "Yeah. All done today."

"You remember Jeremy, don't you? From the big-boy Rangers. You sat next to him at the spaghetti dinner."

Liam raises his glove. "Hi."

Jeremy says hi back, grinning at us. He's as shy in my presence as Liam is in his. When I prompt him, Jeremy opens his jacket and shows Liam the varsity jersey he's wearing. It's nearly identical to my son's: dark blue with the white silhouette of a skating Ranger in a coonskin cap.

"That's cool," says Liam.

I pull him into my lap and together we contemplate Jeremy Abdo's tall slim figure. "Keep skating, Boo, and someday you'll get one of those. Right, Jeremy?"

Abdo nods his head, smiling broadly. He's proud to wear Ranger blue.

On the bus ride to Haverhill, Joe Robillard uses a little chalkboard to show Dave Martin and me something called the "inverted triangle plus two." It's an aggressive forecheck, designed to create havoc in the other team's end.

"Haverhill thinks they know what we're going to do," Robillard says. "But they won't be expecting this."

For just a few thousand dollars beyond his teacher's salary, Robillard stays inside the frigid confines of the Methuen High rink

until 6 P.M. every weeknight, coaching two practices. League games are played on Wednesday and Saturday nights, sometimes including long bus trips and late-night telephone calls to the newspapers to secure press coverage for the sport. On his off nights, Robillard attends interconference games among the Rangers' key opponents, scouting their tendencies. He knows Haverhill has been watching Methuen's games, in preparation for today.

Martin wants to know if they'll employ the same daring forecheck next week against Billerica, long among the wood of the Massachusetts first division. Robillard flips the diagram over and illustrates "triangle plus two," a much more conservative tactic used to clog the center of the ice against good skating teams. Now that Methuen is 5-1, the better teams are gunning for them.

"Keep 'em guessing," says Robillard.

Haverhill is overwhelmed by Methuen's team speed and surrenders a goal to Ryan Fontaine just nineteen seconds into the game. Although a traditional rival of Methuen's in every sport, the "Hillies" are struggling on the ice this year. Still, they're a competitive, chippy bunch, and both of their wins have been engineered via last-period comebacks.

On his first shift, Albert Soucy buzzes past our bench and dumps the puck into Haverhill's end. A second later, Soucy's opposite number steps up, shoves Albert's head into the stanchion where the glass ends, and completes the dirty maneuver by giving our kid a "face wash" with the palm of his glove. Robillard whistles between his teeth and Soucy's line comes off.

"I'll get that bastard," says Soucy, his head hanging between his shoulders as he gulps air.

"You know him?" I ask.

"Yeah. He's just pissed 'cause I tuned him up in Midgets last year."

Methuen leads the game 5-1 in the third period. Ryan Fontaine, who's been reinstated on the first line with Chris Cagliuso and Kevin McCarthy, has three goals. The Rangers' second line, made up of Albert Soucy and Tim "Bobo" Parker, centered by Eric MacDonald, is being shut out, but it's not for lack of trying. During one shift, MacDonald rings a shot off the goalpost, and Soucy whistles one over the crossbar that bangs off the glass. When the trio comes off, Soucy is so agitated that his father, Gerard, leans over the Ranger bench in concern.

"I can't buy a goal," says Albert Soucy.

Tim Parker is beside him. "Mr. Soucy, will you please give Albert some money so he can buy a goal?"

"That's pretty funny, Bobo," I say, nudging Parker with my foot. But he's not through.

"And I'll take a couple of bucks, too," Parker says to the white-haired Mr. Soucy. "I'd like to buy me one of them-there goals myself."

Not known as a physical player, the tall, pencil-thin winger is banging bodies today. Swinging around the Haverhill net, Parker throws his shoulder into a chunky Haverhill defenseman and knocks the kid on his rear end. A few seconds later, Parker comes off the ice to attaboys and applause from his teammates and the coaches—a rare occurrence.

On the bus ride to Haverhill, while other kids listened to head-banging music on their CD players, Tim Parker was caught singing along to a sappy romantic ballad playing on the radio. When he takes a seat on the bench, I rap on his helmet and ask what's gotten into him today.

"It's that easy-listening music," says the pop-eyed Bobo. "It makes me crazy."

Methuen wins 7-1, and Ryan Fontaine comes away with six points: three goals and three assists. All told, his line accounts for fifteen of the nineteen points that Methuen players are credited with during the game. Coming out of their own end, Fontaine, Cagliuso, and McCarthy are like a jailbreak: more speed and sheer talent than most local teams can handle.

In the locker room Fontaine is soaring on adrenaline, his mouth going like a machine gun. "It's gre-a-aat to beat such a bunch of pussies," he says.

Chris Cagliuso is sitting across the room from Fontaine. Cagliuso's gray T-shirt is drenched in sweat, and the two-week-old charley horse on his left hip is mottled brown and purple. I pick my way over the discarded equipment and nudge Cagliuso's shoulder. "Look at Ryan," I say, and Cags glances over at his linemate, who's in the midst of a profane rant. "Somebody's got to make sure that he's a good boy tonight."

"I'm not his mother," says Cagliuso, shoveling his elbow pads and helmet into a large canvas bag. I hover there for another moment and Cagliuso looks up at me, studying my expression. Then he swivels his gaze over at Fontaine again. "You're right, Mr. Atkinson," he says. "I'll say something to him."

Out in the hallway, I'm leaning against the cinder blocks with Joe Harb when Fontaine passes by with his gear. "Be smart tonight," I tell him. "Take it easy."

"Why is everybody telling me to take it easy?" asks the pugnacious junior, throwing his arms out. "Am I an idiot or something?"

"It's only because we care about you, Ryan, and want you to have a safe night."

Fontaine's reply is an expletive and he passes around the corner with his bag. Harb arches an eyebrow and pushes off, heading for the team bus. I stay there in the dank hallway, wondering and worrying about Ryan Fontaine's plans for the evening. All because I remember myself on Saturday nights, when beer was two bucks a six-pack and I thought I would live forever.

21
EDUCATIONAL TV

IT'S 11 A.M. AND I'M ENTERING Methuen High when I spot Ryan Fontaine emerging from a car in the parking lot. He's carrying a bag of fast food. "What?" asks Fontaine. "I had to get my lunch. I can't eat that food in there."

This is the very thing that Joe Robillard has warned Fontaine about. In his meeting with the captains after Ryan's suspension, the coach said he wouldn't stand for any more nonsense from the troubled winger. I shake my head and keep on walking, even though Fontaine is still saying something to me. Probably something about it not being his fault. I hear that a lot.

Inside the school, I go looking for phys ed instructor Fran Molesso. He's sitting in the office and I crook my finger, asking him into the hallway. He's been a teacher for twenty-five years and knows Joe Robillard as well as anyone. Because of my cloudy role here, I need Molesso's advice on Fontaine.

Molesso thinks I should go straight to Joe and tell him what I saw. "It's not about winning," he says. "Ryan's behavior tells me that he doesn't give a shit about the team. Hey, better to know he's gonna wash out now than right before the state tournament. Give Joe the chance to try somebody else."

Robillard's at his desk. He's dressed in green nylon windpants and a Big Dog T-shirt, and he smiles when I approach. But Robillard's smile drops away when he sees the expression on my face. "What is it?" he asks.

I tell Robillard the story and he lets out a long, slow breath. "It's frustrating," he says, rubbing his scalp. "The kids have a real good thing going here, and Ryan doesn't care."

At practice, Robillard catches up with Fontaine during the warm-up laps and skates beside him. The coach speaks for about twenty seconds, Fontaine glides along with his head down, and then Robillard disengages from him and comes over to the boards. When I ask him about it, he says, "I told him that if he ever gets caught off school grounds, he won't skate for me the rest of the year. And not to bother coming out when he's a senior."

In the field house the next day, Thom DeZenzo is stretching out before gym class and I put on my sneakers and join him. Today's activity is indoor soccer and Joe Robillard invites me to come out and get a game. I sit down next to DeZenzo, who was all-conference in soccer, and ask if he's heard about Fontaine's latest screwup.

DeZenzo's close-cropped hair is dyed almost white and his eyes are like two blue marbles. Squatting on his haunches, he says, "Kids go out to lunch all the time. I do it. But I told Ryan not to fuck us over again. We put our necks on the line for him."

DeZenzo is also concerned about Chris Martin, who stays up half the night with what the doctors call a sleep phase delay/circadian rhythm disruption and is in jeopardy for excessive tardiness. For the past week, DeZenzo has arrived at Martin's house before 7:30 A.M., roused his defense partner from bed, and driven him to school. "It's not just for hockey," DeZenzo says. "I've known him most of my life, and I don't want to see him get in trouble."

If high school in general is a long-running program with a host of characters both major and minor, points of high and low comedy, and constant dramatic tension, then the members of Methuen's varsity hockey program are responsible for some entertaining moments. On this particular day, several players have spent the afternoon spreading a rumor that Albert Soucy will be hosting a spaghetti dinner at his home tonight. Although he has no such plans, Soucy goes along with the fun, telling the gullible underclassmen to "bring their own booze" because his parents don't care.

Nothing entices a hockey player more than home-cooked pasta and some of the boys are calling for Soucy's head when they learn it's a ruse. "We should buy five pounds of spaghetti and bring it over to his house and say 'Cook it up, bitch,' " says one of the juniors.

As practice begins, Ryan Fontaine slams a wrist shot into the bench area and knocks over the milk carton that contains the extra pucks—something he's been trying to do all season. I shoot a look at him and he raises his arms in celebration and smiles at me through his cage. Fontaine is a beaut, all right.

Between halves of the practice, Bonfiglio and Gray flank me on the bench in the locker room. "How does it feel to sit in 'Goalie's corner'?" Bonfiglio asks.

"Privileged," I say. "But even though it occurred before you were born, I feel as though I've earned it."

Gray has a bum shoulder and he goes into detail about his inflamed bursar sac and weakened trapezius and deltoid muscles. "It feels like something's burning in there," he says.

"It could be worse," says Bonfiglio, hunched over his giant leg pads. "You could have a pacemaker."

Hockey is a rough and sometimes bloody sport, and since all of Methuen's coaches have played hockey for a long time they understand the violent heart of the game and so share an understanding with their charges that wouldn't normally exist across such a gulf of years. Inside the locker room, on team buses, and on the bench, there's a familiarity and profane equality that would shock even the parents of these children in its intimacy. What happens in this world, for the most part, remains here. But some moments are too good not to share.

Before the annual junior varsity game with Central Catholic, there's a sense of urgency crackling across Methuen's rink. Inside the Ranger locker room, Dave Martin is about to deliver his annual lecture about the importance of beating Central. Dressed in blue power company overalls trimmed with reflective silver tape, Martin kicks aside some loose gloves and sticks, taking his place in the center of the room. For the young freshmen who make up most of the jayvees, what's about to transpire is a mystery although they have heard various rumors concerning Martin's oratory. Crowded against the outer walls of the tiny cinder block room are Coach Morin, the trainer Kevin MacLennan, and eight members of the varsity, who've heard Martin's speech several times over.

"Shit, I should charge admission," Martin says, grinning. He scratches his balding pate and raises his voice into a formal register. "Today, gentlemen"—he spots goaltender Becky Trudel, standing in the doorway in her gear—"and lady, we face Central Catholic, another team that I despise immensely. And on this occasion, since this is a school and we are all concerned here with your education, I will deliver a talk on 'The Mating Habits of the Sperm Whale.' "

Giggles erupt around the room, and beside me, Jon Morin stifles a laugh and raises his eyebrows.

"Gentlemen, please," continues Martin, raising and lowering his hands. "This is a true story. It has to be. I saw it on public television." More laughter. "Did you know, gentlemen, that it takes two males to impregnate the female sperm whale? That's two on one. And that's what we like in hockey. We like to have two of our players—with the puck—against one of theirs. Now, in her state of excitement, the female sperm whale turns on her back. Because she could drown this way, the second male, poor bastard—let's call him Gradzewicz—swims beneath her and holds her up for his buddy."

The players roar and blond-haired Dan Gradzewicz turns crimson and accepts a vigorous pounding on his shoulder pads from the guys on either side. Martin raises his voice over the din. "And here comes his buddy, the other whale, Shane Wakeen, with a shaft"—Martin makes a huge circle with his hands—"three feet in circumference and eighteen feet long. And that's us. That's Methuen. Because we're gonna two-on-one 'em, we're gonna beat the living shit out of 'em, and boys and girls, we're gonna win!"

Martin hops up on the bench. "Let's go, Methuen. Let's beat Central."

The players leap to their feet and pile out of the room. Pressed against the wall beside me, Jon Morin's face is only a few inches away. "Fifteen years, and I never get tired of hearing it," he says.

As a prelude to the varsity game with Central Catholic next month, the Ranger jayvees prevail, 2-1.

22

INDIAN FIGHTERS

BILLERICA INDIANS. Just the name of the town and the team conjures up a hard-skating swarm of green jerseys, the premier high school hockey team in a prime hockey region. When I played for Methuen, Coach Parker had a standing offer: any Ranger team that beat the Indians would be treated to expensive dinners at the Hilltop Steak House in Saugus. We never got to eat there. In fact, according to Joe Robillard, Methuen varsity teams have only defeated Billerica three times in more than forty games over twenty-five seasons. But the Rangers have traditionally played well against Billerica—the Merrimack Valley farm team for Division I colleges and the National Hockey League. All the kids get excited when Billerica comes to town.

Half an hour before the game, Methuen's locker room is an odd mixture of tension and comic banality. While Tim Parker and James Girouard and some of the other underclassmen in the bobo section snap each other with towels and goof around, starting goalie Dave Gray has a heavy look on his face, stretching and limbering up. "Hey, assholes, get your heads into the game," says Gray.

"If we don't come out scoring goals, Billerica's gonna kick our ass," says Bonfiglio, dressing alongside Gray. The bobos clam up and begin putting on their equipment. Then Bonfiglio turns to Gray with a piece of friction tape stuck on his upper lip like a mustache.

"Quit screwing around," says Gray. "This is serious. What if I get hurt and you have to go in?"

Bonfiglio stands up, crosses to the trash can and throws the tape away. "I'll be ready," he says. "Last year they were talking like they were gonna kill me." Bonfiglio pantomimes a skate save, a glove save. "But I shut 'em right down."

"We lost four to two," says Gray.

"Whatever."

Dave Martin charges in to tell a story about the bizarre sexual experiences of an old man in a nursing home. Some tight laughter ensues, and then Joe Robillard enters. Outside the close warm stench of the locker room, the Zamboni machine can be heard grinding around the arena. "They got some young kids who can fly but don't think for a second that you can't beat them," says Robillard. "You just gotta skate—all night."

In their white home jerseys, the players crowd the doorway, waiting for the Zamboni to finish so they can take the ice. Their faces are red, they whoop and curse, and squeeze their sticks tightly. "This is our fucking game," says Tim Parker, as the pep band crashes away in the grandstand and the buzzer sounds for the warm-up period.

Jon Morin is exhorting his defense to clear the puck away from Methuen's goal. "Nothing fancy," he says. "Skate hard, and fire it off the boards."

The players go out and we follow them to the bench and jump up to survey the ice. Billerica's team is big and fast and execute their warm-ups with professional crispness. The grandstand is more crowded than for any game this year, and there's electricity when the starting lineups are introduced. Singing from the timekeeper's bench, orchid-faced Emily, Dan Bonfiglio's crush, renders the national anthem in her lovely soprano and the players all clap their sticks on the ice.

Cagliuso's line skates the opening face-off straight into Billerica's end and takes the first two shots on goal. Along the bench Methuen's players are up and yelling, the veins popping in their necks, stick blades pounding on the boards. They know that for the first time since the seniors were freshmen, they can compete with the best teams in the valley. In goal, Dave Gray is like the elastic man, throwing up arms and legs, blocking, deflecting, and catching a slew of blurry pucks from the Indian attack. The period ends 0-0 and the boys rush into the locker room.

"Now we know we can play with 'em," says Cagliuso. "Let's go out and beat 'em."

Beside him, Kevin McCarthy sits with his game jersey off, hands knotted in front of his face, looking like a young combat soldier between firefights. Although McCarthy is one of Methuen's best players, he's only 16 years old and quiet by nature. Listening to Cagliuso exhort the team, he drops his hands and speaks aloud for the first time all year.

"Remember the state tournament," McCarthy says, and around the room heads start nodding.

Last year, the Rangers qualified for the Division II state tournament on the last day of the season and drew the Beverly Panthers as their first-round opponent. I attended the game, sitting in the stands at the Chelmsford Forum with Liam and my old teammate Gary Ruffen. Suffering from the jitters, Methuen fell behind early, rallied to go ahead in the third period, and then gave up the tying and losing goals in the last three minutes of the game. It was a heartbreaking example of being almost, but not quite good enough to win.

In the grandstand afterward, Gary Ruffen and I were reminiscing and he said, "If there's one thing I wish I could do, it's go back and sit in the stands and watch us play."

Robillard enters the locker room in his blue Ranger jacket and holds his arm out and points around the room. "There's nobody on our schedule we can't beat, so long as we come to play," the coach says.

"Every loose puck should be ours," says Coach Morin, leaning against the wall.

The Zamboni is beeping in the distance and then the buzzer sounds, calling the teams out. "The pressure is all on them," says Ryan Fontaine.

Deep into the second period and the game is still scoreless. For such a fine skating club, Billerica clutches and grabs and hooks the Methuen forwards away from the puck. McCarthy and Fontaine and Cagliuso jump back over the boards after a shift complaining what pussies they're up against. When Dave George gets tackled in front of the Methuen bench—a gross case of interference—Dave Martin is apoplectic. He leaps onto the dasher, screaming at the dour-faced referee to wake up and call something.

Martin turns to me, his face red and steaming. "Goddamn it, get me a razor and a helmet," he says, indicating his furry brush of a mustache. "I'm gonna shave and go out there and play."

Finally one of the Billerica players is whistled off for interfering with Thom DeZenzo and Methuen has the man advantage for ninety seconds. As soon as the Indian penalty begins, DeZenzo wins the puck at the Billerica blue line, slides it through the middle, and Eric MacDonald snaps a wrister into the open half of the net. Methuen leads 1-0.

Our bench erupts. Robillard has his hands thrust out, calming everyone. "We need another one," he says.

With just six seconds remaining in the period, fleet-footed Albert

Soucy finishes his check at the red line, corrals the loose puck, and races in alone on Billerica's goalie. Even with Soucy's speed, one of the Indians' defensemen is nipping at his heels, trying to drive him away from the slot. Along the bench we all crane our necks, leaning that way, shouting for another goal. With his legs pumping, little Albert fires the puck up high, over the goalie's shoulder, aiming for the top corner.

The shot misses. The period ends. We all crowd into the locker room. Limping on his bad leg, Cagliuso comes in last, using the butt of his stick like a cane. He takes his usual seat in the middle of the room and surveys the reddened faces around him. "Play this last fifteen minutes like it's the last time you'll ever play," says the centerman. "This is our last chance to beat 'almighty Billerica.' "

"Yeah. Come on you guys. We can beat these guys," says Bonfiglio, standing up from the bench. No one responds, and the soft-spoken goalie, an all-star last year and currently reduced to Dave Gray's backup, sits down again. "How come nobody ever takes what I say seriously?" he asks me.

"It was inspiring, Dan," I tell him.

A big topic of conversation is how dirty Billerica is playing. "They're provoking you, so you'll retaliate and they can go on the power play," says Dave Martin. "Don't fucking do it."

But these kids are too young to know what I learned the hard way: throwing a punch doesn't mean you're tough. It's taking one.

"Take a slash in the throat if you have to," says DeZenzo.

Ryan Fontaine laughs. "I don't think I'm gonna go that far," he says. "But let's go out and skate our balls off."

Impressed by the atmosphere, the coaches glance at each other and withdraw. Cagliuso stands in the middle of the room, motions for everyone to put their hands in, and is buried inside a circle of helmets. "This is the biggest period of the season," says Cagliuso.

The players grind their faces together, and Cagliuso barks out the cadence: "Rangers!"

On the way to the bench I notice Horace Trovato being led out of the rink by his wife, Joan. He is wrapped up in a scarf and overcoat, his face pale against the dark-colored fabric, and there's a hush as he passes by. Over the last five years Mr. Trovato has attended each and every varsity hockey game, and there must be something wrong if he's leaving early.

Just thirty-nine seconds into the third period Billerica scores a goal to tie the game up. This energizes their bench and they come at Dave Gray in waves, piling up the shots on goal. One puck zings past his ear and seems destined for the upper half of the net. Suddenly Gray's arm comes flying out and he batters the puck away with the web of his catching glove.

"That's it, Dave," cries Robillard, the old goalie.

Soon after, Methuen is awarded another power play and Cagliuso finds a loose puck down low in the Billerica zone. Canting his body to one side and leaning hard on his inside edges, Cagliuso sidesteps one defender and fends off another with his arm and shoulder. Slipping the puck through his opponent's skates, Cagliuso rides the man away from the net and Eric MacDonald darts over and swats the puck into the Billerica goal. With less than seven minutes to play, Methuen leads 2-1.

The Rangers on the bench are boiling with excitement and the high school kids lining the upper grandstand are screaming and waving. I can't hear what he's saying in the din, but Billerica's coach is shouting and gesturing at his players. For the next few minutes, the Rangers hold off a number of desperate charges into their end. At times, Methuen's attempts to clear the puck seem impeded by extra gravity while Billerica players flash back and forth like they're weightless. But our kids plug away, and time ticks off the clock.

Billerica's captain is a rangy, hard-skating kid with a slick pair of hands. He also has a nasty side, and the provocative nature of a bully. All night, Chris Martin has battled with this kid, watching for the high elbow, the butt end, all the dirty tricks. Now, with three minutes remaining, the Billerica star escapes a tangle near center ice and bears down on Martin with the puck.

It all goes wrong in a single, horrible moment. The Billerica kid sweeps over the blue line, cutting right to left, and pivoting with him, Martin catches a rut in the ice and falls down. There's no other player between the Billerica captain and the Methuen net, except for goalie Dave Gray.

The kid wheels toward him. On the bench, we all watch in silence, suspended over the dasher, mouths agape. One piece of razzle-dazzle stickhandling, a quick, last-second swerve, and Billerica's captain buries the puck inside the net.

Beside me, Dave Martin swings a fist at the empty air and lets out an agonized snarl. His head hanging, Chris Martin picks himself up and trudges toward the bench. The teams gather at center ice for the ensuing face-off and Jon Morin gestures Chris away. "Stay out there," he says. "Get it back."

But the feeling of doom that seems to trail Methuen into big games hovers over the team tonight. Billerica is a perennial Division I champ, and they sense their opportunity. Twenty-three seconds later, they score again on a freak deflection and the game ends that way. Billerica 3, Methuen 2.

"We can play with anybody," says Robillard to a somber locker room. "Get those heads up."

An emotionally and physically drained Chris Cagliuso sits in his soaked boxer shorts, unraveling the wrap on his left thigh. "Everyone in this room should be proud to be a Methuen Ranger," he says in a hoarse voice. "Everyone here should be proud to put on this fucking jersey."

A short while later, I encounter Kevin McCarthy in the long corridor leading down to the field house, against the glass case where they keep all the Hall of Fame plaques. He's wearing a black Red Sox cap, bright yellow parka, and breakaway nylon pants and he greets me with his typical shy politeness. When I ask him about the game, McCarthy says, "Too many guys are happy just because we played well. I'm mad. We should've beat them."

On my way home, I'm thinking about McCarthy and how much he wants to win, and about Cagliuso's remark. A skater's moon has risen, silvering the evergreens and oaks and throwing their ragged shadows across Ranger Road. I turn the corner onto Pleasant Street and the moon reappears above the bulwark of Nicholson Stadium, huge and bright like a coin. There's a mountain of desiccated Christmas trees in the stadium parking lot, threaded with strands of tinsel that gleam in my headlights. The streets are empty at this hour and most of the houses are dark, but as I turn past the marker for Revolutionary War hero John Davis, I'm proud of these kids and how hard they played tonight. And I'm proud to have worn that Ranger jersey myself.

23

LOUIE THE LOCK MONSTER

IT'S THE FIRST REAL BLIZZARD of the season and my father's presence is heavy in the rooms, almost palpable but still smoky, close by my shoulder. This was his favorite sort of weather, and as I read through the newspaper, watch an old Bruins-Canadiens game on Classic Sports, and play floor hockey with Liam, I can't help thinking of the old man and his love of snow and ice, hockey games on TV, and spiked hot chocolate. Suddenly there's noise in the street and Liam and I rush to the windows with the newspaper spilling onto the floor, to get a glimpse of the big town plow as it rattles by, its yellow light wheeling across the yards.

Unless the roads are cleared, we won't make it to the Lowell Lock Monsters' game tonight. But I'm pretty sure we'll get out, because Methuen has more than its share of yahoos in pickup trucks and be-hatted nimrods of the highway. Whenever there's a snowstorm, a number of these jackbooted, bearded wonders are in evidence, ensconced in their plaid wool jackets and guzzling coffee. Their tires clacking, radios blasting the latest weather reports, their raised plows infuse them with phallic pride.

Two hours later, Liam is shivering with excitement and the subzero temperatures as I hustle him up the stone steps toward the

Tsongas Arena in Lowell, Massachusetts. Hockey fans bundled into heavy coats and ski masks are streaming in from the parking lots, and a giant furry creature with a long tail—"Louie" the Lock Monster—greets us at the double doors. Louie is the team mascot for the Lowell Lock Monsters of the American Hockey League, one step down from the NHL.

Liam glances up at the vast purple creature, waits to be called forward, and then sinks into Louie's arms with a blissful look on his face. For my 5-year-old son, the imaginary is real, and the fuzzy embrace of a nine-foot stuffed animal is worth our voyage across the frozen dark to get here.

Tickets are only $8 each, and armed with our hot dogs and bottled water and peanuts, Liam and I take our seats right behind one of the nets. Lowell's opponents this evening are the Springfield Falcons, and the 6,500-seat arena is filling up with supporters of both clubs. The Tsongas Arena is brand-new, and soon the house lights go down and laser beams and spot lights bedazzle the air, an indoor blimp circles above our heads, and a giant plastic Lock Monster head inflates itself by the players' entrance. Liam is up, stamping his feet and pounding on the glass.

The PA announcer roars his welcome and the fans roar back. Center ice is illuminated and the announcer calls our attention to tonight's special guest, a 6-year-old boy dressed in a Lock Monsters' uniform who's skating around the perimeter of the rink. He's got a nice little stride going, and the fans begin cheering as the Lowell players emerge from the jaws of the inflatable monster.

"Look, Dad," says Liam. "That kid's just like me."

"That's right, Boo. You skate just like he does."

The black-shirted Falcons take the ice and both teams line up for a ceremonial face-off. As the Lock Monsters' young guest clutches the game puck, the PA announcer informs the crowd that the little guy is suffering from a brain tumor. Lately the boy has been receiving chemotherapy, is in remission, and loves hockey in general and the Lock Monsters in particular.

The kid drops the puck in the face-off circle, and the Lowell captain picks it up and hands it back to him. Along the bench and on both sides of the rink, the players clap their sticks against the ice, saluting the boy's courage. Liam is oblivious to the reasons for this tribute and wishes aloud that he was on the ice instead of "that other kid."

Several of the Lock Monsters skate over to the kid and shake his hand. They are large, raw-boned men, and it touches my heart when they bend over, speak to the kid and pat his little helmet. As the boy makes his way toward the rink door, the Springfield captain intercepts him. The Falcon player is 20 years old or so, probably worrying about his career and whether he's going to make it to the NHL. But he leans over and smiles and says something to the little kid with the brain tumor, and I glance over at my own kid, his little hands and the point of his nose pressed against the glass, and my throat tightens up and I have to look away.

Before the game against Andover the atmosphere in the locker room is much more convivial than it was for Billerica. Hearkening back to his profanity the other night, Tim Parker grins and says, "Sorry, my emotions were running wild."

Andover just doesn't have it this year, and Methuen leads 5-1 with ten seconds left in the second period. My old coach, Bill Cullen, who's been in Andover for nine years, decides to pull his goaltender for an extra skater, hoping for a fast goal and some momentum. But Methuen's first line is on the ice and Cagliuso wins the face-off in his own end, knocks the puck to the corner and Fontaine chases after it. He gathers the loose puck along the half-boards and scales it the length of the ice into the open net.

When we come off the ice, assistant superintendent of schools Arthur Nicholson is standing by the door in his blazer and striped tie. "Oooh. That felt good," he says. Everyone in Methuen likes to beat Andover.

As always, Cagliuso and his high-flying wingers are targets for abuse. McCarthy and Fontaine lose their tempers at one point, and the referee sends McCarthy to the penalty box for unsportsmanlike conduct. Robillard immediately benches him for the rest of the game although it's only a ninety-second penalty. Joe's sending a message.

Dave George is throwing his weight around, crashing into Andover players all over the rink. When he comes to the bench, Coach Morin reminds him that the object of the game is to put the puck in the net. "The idea is to go around people, not through them," he says, motioning to Dave Martin. "Coach—have you ever seen anyone literally go *through* the man?" Martin shakes his head, and Morin continues. "David George you are, David Copperfield you are not."

Andover's goalie is having a terrible night, but he has more to deal with than just Methuen's pesky forwards. In between periods, his father lectures the poor kid beneath the grandstand. The goalie is a broad-shouldered six-footer, his dad a pudgy, balding guy about half a foot shorter wearing an Andover baseball cap and ski parka. The guy even stands on tiptoes by the glass and signals to his kid during the game. It gets so bad between the second and third periods that Coach Cullen storms out of locker room and orders his goalie back inside. Coach and father glare at each other. It reminds me that some guys just don't know when to quit.

My father attended just about every competitive hockey game I ever played in. As a kid he may have skated a few times, with heavy rusted blades fixed to his shoes with leather straps, when snow filled the hollows of Glen Forest and the Great War raged across Europe. But he was no athlete, and certainly no hockey player. He developed a passion for the sport, however, sitting up nights to watch the

Bruins on his black-and-white television, tuning into college games, even heading into the city to watch the old Boston Braves of the American Hockey League. My dad's idea of a good time was to attend both nights of the Beanpot Tournament each January, watching Boston University, Boston College, Harvard, and Northeastern play their annual round-robin.

My father never said a word to any of my coaches, except a cordial hello. He never coached me at home or uttered a word of criticism from the bleachers. But I always knew he was there, the oval disks of his glasses shining under the rink lights. All he offered was encouragement, and rides to the rink. That's probably one reason why I love the game so much: it never got tainted by my father's expectations.

The day after beating Andover, Albert Soucy comes into the trainer's room in a rumpled sweatsuit and Kevin MacLennan looks up from taping an ankle. "What's wrong?" he asks.

"Can you do anything about these pants?" Soucy asks. "They're wrinkled."

Right before practice, Dave Gray asks me if I've seen Dan Bonfiglio. When I reply that I haven't, Gray says Bonfiglio is fed up with hockey and thinking about quitting the team. "He scared me," says Gray, with the fright still in his eyes. "But he's not gonna quit."

"Where is he, then?" I ask.

Gray pulls on his practice jersey and shrugs. "He's got a doctor's appointment today. For his heart."

When I mention this to Joe Harb, the muscular young coach shakes his head, laughing at Dave Gray's perspective. "Quitting the team is more important than the kid's heart," he says. "At that age, they all think they're gonna live forever."

Before practice I circle around the rink looking for stray pucks:

in the grandstand, beneath benches, tangled in the extra nets beyond the far glass. It's like an Easter Egg hunt. Soon the players are gathering by the door as the Zamboni machine finishes its circuit. As usual, there's a little tension between the Old School approach of the coaches and the free-spirited teenagers who make up the squad. On the rubber apron, Joe Harb spots the small gold hoops in each of Dave George's ears. "What do you have earrings for, Chin?" he asks. "Are you a fairy?"

"I am," says the affable sophomore.

"Take those out," says Harb.

"I take 'em out for every game and leave 'em in for practice."

Harb snorts at this. "Then your practice habits must be spilling over into the games, because you haven't scored in weeks," he says.

During a sequence where two of Methuen's best offensive players, Eric MacDonald and Kevin McCarthy, bombard Dave Gray with shots, the towheaded goalie makes nine consecutive saves, many of them fabulous. As he flashes out his leg pads and stabs at the flying pucks with his gloves, Robillard says, "That's the way to work, David."

Gray's star is ascending, while his best friend and cohort, last year's all-star Dan Bonfiglio, sits in a doctor's office somewhere waiting to have his heart examined. But today's practice has its lighter moments. Resting on the boards while another line executes a drill, Albert Soucy says, "I think they should have cheerleaders watch our practices. I'd do better if there were cheerleaders out here." The plucky little French Canadian nods his helmet up and down. "Girls with big boobs, too."

24

THE CHRISTIANS AND THE LIONS

I HAVEN'T SEEN DAN BONFIGLIO for a couple days and when he passes by the skate room before our road game with the Chelmsford Lions, I ask him about his doctor's appointment. The easygoing netminder says the latest twist in his saga is that he's developed high blood pressure. His underlying condition, neurocardiogenic syncope, cannot in itself cause death.

Last spring, Bonfiglio fainted during a visit to the school nurse and thought he'd suffered a seizure of some kind. A battery of tests originally turned up nothing, and his abnormality wasn't discovered until the final "tilt table" test, when he passed out again.

"That was lucky," I say.

The goalie shakes his head. "It kinda sucked, actually," he says. During a four-hour operation at Holy Family Hospital, surgeons implanted a tiny, high-tech regulating device into his chest. (The battery is expected to last for twenty years.) Bonfiglio says that the most gratifying aspect of the ordeal was that Dave Gray waited at the hospital until midnight, only going home when he was assured the operation had been a success.

On the bus ride to the Chelmsford Forum, Chris Cagliuso is busy telling a group of sophomores how good the Lions are going to be.

"They got a number 16 who'll be past you before you even see him," says the tri-captain.

When the bus pulls into the sloping lot of the Forum, and the players jump through the rear door like paratroopers and begin unloading their gear, I advise Cagliuso not to lay it on so thick. "You've played at a higher level, you're older, you're mentally tough," I say. "You should help the younger kids get their confidence up. You're scaring the hell out of these guys."

The Rangers are getting dressed in a long narrow room beneath the grandstand. It's cold and dark in here, with NO SMOKING stenciled on the wall every few feet. "Untuck your jersey," Cagliuso says to Albert Soucy. "These guys like to grab you by the pants."

"I like it in," says Soucy.

"Suit yourself. When somebody throws you on your ass, you'll pull it out."

Robillard enters, clapping his hands. "Play with heart, boys, and we'll be in great shape tonight," he says.

Outside the buzzer sounds and the players queue up near the door. "You gotta have faith, boys," says Ryan Fontaine. Sometimes the hardheaded winger can be an annoyance to the coaches and even some of his teammates, but like a good combat soldier, he's valuable to the unit and they love him with all their hearts in these situations.

During the warm-ups, the Chelmsford Lions, Division I state champions as recently as 1995 and North Sectional champs just about every year, conduct themselves at a tempo that amazes the Methuen players. Chelmsford executes every drill at top speed, with a jaunty precision that's far superior to any of the Division II teams Methuen has faced. In their white home uniforms trimmed with burgundy, the Lions resemble a college team. Coming off the ice to allow the Zamboni to make its passes, the faces of the youngest Rangers are blank, almost fearful. It's not a good omen.

Chelmsford scores on their first two shots and collectively, Methuen looks lost, waving at the fast-moving Lion forwards instead of hitting them. Although the Chelmsford goalie looks weak and allows three goals in the first period on half a dozen shots, his teammates pepper Dave Gray and lead 5-3 after just fifteen minutes of play.

"If you didn't come to play, shame on you," says Robillard in the locker room. "Hit somebody, for crissakes."

Cagliuso fires his stick into the bench, and it clatters to the floor. "Five goals in the first period—that's bullshit," he says.

Most of the Rangers slump against the damp cinder block wall, staring at their feet. "You can either feel sorry for yourselves or you can get pissed off and start hitting somebody," says Robillard. "White line—the other lines have each scored. You're supposed to be one of the best lines around. Time to get yours."

Jon Morin pounds his fist into his open palm. "Make it physical," he says. "Make 'em pay."

But Methuen is embarrassed further in the second period. Although the captains and coaches have vowed otherwise, Chelmsford reaches double figures, scoring five painful goals in the span of nine minutes. The Rangers are hemorrhaging everywhere: up front, on defense, in goal. Halfway through the period, Robillard pulls Dave Gray in favor of Dan Bonfiglio. In a telling moment, the two passing goalies nearly crash into each other when they attempt to touch gloves at center ice.

Dave Gray slams his stick onto the bench and sits with his face buried in his hands. I lean over to him and say, "Get your head up, Dave. Be an athlete."

Late in the period, Chelmsford puts on a skating clinic in Methuen's end of the rink, cycling the puck back and forth while the Rangers stand around looking helpless. Some of the Lions are showboating, bouncing on their skates as they elude a half-hearted defense. Mercifully the period ends. Chelmsford leads 10-3.

In the locker room, I pick my way back to the darkest corner and plunk down on the bench next to Chris Martin and Dave George, the local hard guys. "I'd never say this to Coach Robillard, but this game is history," I say to them.

Martin nods at me. "It's over," he says.

"I know what I'd do if I was you. I'd take that little hot dog number 5 and put him through the boards. Simple as that."

Martin and George are grim-faced as the buzzer sounds and they buckle their chinstraps. "We're trying," says Martin.

Passing out of the locker room, Joe Harb says to me, "No fire at all." He waves a hand in front of his face. "If they're winning or losing, same expression."

As I follow the team out toward the ice surface, I realize that the coaches are still in the locker room. Hesitating on the runway, I hear Jon Morin calling and duck back to see what he wants. Joe Robillard, Dave Martin, Harb, and Morin are there in the dark, grinning at me.

"Jay, you got the bench this period," Morin says. "We're going down the street for a couple beers." He's kidding, of course, but my heart races for a moment and I fumble through my pockets for a team roster.

The Chelmsford coach lets up in the third period, playing his youngest forwards. But even these kids are fleet of foot and very skillful. On a couple of occasions, it appears that they're hesitating in front of Methuen's net, holding their shots until they're covered. The Rangers lose 10-4. Chris Martin, Dave George, and Kevin McCarthy all play hard to the finish. Cagliuso injures his left shoulder and Ryan Fontaine can hardly stand on a bruised leg. Others disappear.

"We win together, and we lose together," says Robillard. "And no pointing fingers. I don't want to hear a word on that bus."

Heading into the parking lot, I'm reminded of the bad old days coming to the Forum, and the goalie's dread at facing teams like Chelmsford and Billerica and Tewksbury. This is a tough stretch for Methuen, with no patsies like Westford Academy or Haverhill in sight. And nobody seems that angry about it. When I ask Jon Morin why the kids aren't chewing their sticks and spitting out wood chips at such a humiliating loss, he says, "You're thinking fifteen years ago. This is a different type of kid now."

On the ride home, some of the comedians on the team are writing Joe Robillard's favorite sayings in the condensation on the bus windows:

C'mon. Have some strength.

The players flex their biceps at one another and their teeth flash in the dark. Ducking behind the seats, the two main culprits choke on their laughter and then jump to the next window.

Have some hands.
To who? To who?

Farther back among the seats now, away from the coach, they start impersonating Robillard's low, hoarse manner of speaking during games. Immediately I'm reminded of Coach Parker, in dark glasses and buttoned-up windbreaker, his hands curled into a megaphone and foot up on the dasher, exhorting us to "Skate, skate, skate." We called him Chairman Mao behind his back, because of his getup. But making fun of Bruce Parker was a privilege available only to those who had made the commitment to follow him. That territory was forever off limits to anyone who quit the team or didn't have the nerve to try out.

With his high blood pressure, scant number of appearances, and shaky relief of Dave Gray against Chelmsford, I'm worried about Dan Bonfiglio and go looking for him at school the next morning. A goalie's confidence is based on a fragile constellation of luck and skill and mental preparation, and after sitting on the bench for so long and then giving up goals so quickly, I figure a word or two with the soft-spoken Bonfiglio can't hurt.

The first player I stumble across is Kevin McCarthy, flirting with a pretty girl from the basketball team. McCarthy's one of those quiet, good-natured kids you can't help pulling for. Watching him smile and blush, with the wholesome long-haired girl mirroring his responses, I hope Mac goes to an Ivy League college and writes to his sweetheart twice a week and eventually they marry and produce a nursery full of all-Americans.

"Who's the goalie on your team?" the girl wants to know. When McCarthy replies that one of them is Dan Bonfiglio, she asks, "Doesn't he have a heart problem?"

"I don't think he even has a heart," says McCarthy, deadpan.

It takes a second but the girl laughs, throwing back the sheen of her hair. "No problem, then," she says.

I find Bonfiglio in art class, the moon-eyed senior having his right hand cast in plaster by lovely young Emily. Standing by the door, I watch Bonfiglio peel off the mold, blushing while he thanks Emily for helping him with his project. The buzzer rings, and the class files out.

"Sheesh. You're sickening," I say to Bonfiglio, and he starts laughing. "Get a grip, big guy. Play hard to get."

Later on at practice, Dave Gray thinks this is hilarious. "You're putty in her hands," he says to his best friend, poking him in the stomach. Just then Robillard appears in the locker room to tell the varsity that all they need for the first half of practice is skates, helmets, and sweatsuits. Since they didn't skate against Chelmsford, they'll skate today. Dave Gray goes out and borrows an old, discarded helmet from the skate room.

"That's a nice lid," I tell him. "The bubblehead look."

"Don't make fun of me," he says. "I'm sensitive."

Unburdened by their equipment, the players appear smaller and younger when they take the ice. Especially Dan Bonfiglio, who looks like a waif—some sort of homeless rink urchin who'll skate for his supper.

Halfway through the regular season, Methuen's hockey team is beginning to feel the weight of their schedule. Robillard points out that the players rise each weekday at 6:30 A.M., arrive at school in time for the first bell at 7:30, attend classes until 1:45 P.M., and practice from 2:00 until 4:15. Then they go home, have supper, do their homework, and either go out with friends or work for a few hours at the mall or bagel shop. Some of the players, including defense partners Thom DeZenzo and Chris Martin, are exhibiting symptoms of combat fatigue. In the locker room between halves of the practice, they're expressionless, staring into the middle distance, pale and washed out beneath all the sweaty equipment.

Somehow a purple Boston Latin jersey appears in the second session, and someone drapes it over the crossbar of the net and the players fire pucks at it. "Let 'em have a little fun," says Robillard. "It'll be interesting to see how they respond after getting embarrassed by Chelmsford. Whether the effort will be there."

Dave Gray has a sore shoulder, a banged-up knee from an injury in gym class, and a nasty case of the flu. Dan Bonfiglio will start in goal against Boston Latin, and Robillard notes that he'll need a backup, since Becky Trudel is scheduled to take the SAT exams on Saturday morning. "Be ready to suit up," he jokes, while I consider how much fun that would be. "Just keep the mask on."

Unfortunately for third-string goalie Becky Trudel, confidence in her is low among the other players just as she seems poised to move up to the varsity. Although standing just five feet tall, the shy, dark-haired junior is technically proficient, with a sure and certain knowledge of rink geometry and the stone-faced implacability that are keys to good goaltending.

Lounging against the boards during a shooting drill, Ryan Fontaine shakes his head when a shot from Brian Mueskes finds its way between Trudel's pads and into the net. "She doesn't try," says Fontaine. "She can't move." When reminded that Trudel is the odds-on starting goalie for next year, Fontaine says, "We're gonna be the worst team in Methuen history."

One concern for this season is Chris Cagliuso's health and durability. During a lull in the practice, Cags is doing extra wind sprints to regain leg strength, now that his left thigh is healing. But as he lopes along with his classic stride, he's holding his left shoulder funny. A couple of minutes later, Cagliuso reveals to me that an open ice check in the Chelmsford game has left him with rotator cuff damage—a common injury among baseball players, and one that robs strength from the entire arm.

"I haven't been one hundred percent since the first Boston Latin game," says Cagliuso. He has a dogged expression on his face, and sweat flies out of his cage when he shakes his head. "I'm just gonna try and suck it up for tomorrow."

25
THE AGE OF DISCO

At midseason, I've developed a pretty good rapport with the varsity players, although it's more personal and cordial with some of them than with others. The senior goalies, Dave Gray and Dan Bonfiglio, call me Jay and come over to shoot the breeze whenever they see me in school. Kids that I met last year, like Albert Soucy and Eric MacDonald and the Martin brothers, treat me like a Dutch uncle. The youngest players, the freshmen and sophomores and most of the jayvees, are shy and never say a word unless I speak to them first. And although some of my relationships are still developing—especially with kids I'm trying to help like Ryan Fontaine and Dan Gradzewicz—there's a small number of players who remain aloof.

But when I consider the situation from their perspective, it's no wonder that some of the hockey players have very little to say. If a writer my age had chosen to follow our team through the winter of 1975, that person would have graduated from high school in 1950. Even more significantly, this imaginary scribe would have *been born in 1932,* two years after my father. Such a fossil would have worn a raccoon coat and driven a roadster, I'm afraid.

Before practice one day, Dan Bonfiglio tells me that he was looking at an "old, old athletic program from 1988" and thought he saw my picture there until he checked the names underneath the photo. When I tell him the year I graduated, Bonfiglio stares at me like I'm one of those prehistoric men that gets disgorged from a glacier every few years, a fine specimen of Zinjanthropus. His expression is one of complete surprise, like he has discovered a crude weapon in the wrinkled-up claw that used to be my hand. He wants to know what the 1970s were like, and I tell him it was the golden age of the American family: when we'd all pile into the station wagon to wait in line for gasoline, dressed in leisure suits and platform shoes, blasting the Watergate hearings on our AM radio.

The one thing Bonfiglio and I have in common is stopping pucks. Ice hockey goaltending is a combination of athleticism, technique, courage, self-confidence, and luck, although very few goalies have all five attributes in equal proportion. To succeed, you've got to have at least three of them working at the same time and this season, Dave Gray and Dan Bonfiglio have each surged and regressed in various areas and so have shared the position.

They're best friends. In white helmet and black helmet, respectively, Gray and Bonfiglio are as inseparable as salt and pepper shakers, on and off the ice. Just before practice, Bonfiglio approaches me with a worried look on his face. "Coach Harb screwed me big-time," he says. "Emily's in his class and he asked her whether we're going to the prom together."

This is a "red alert" situation. Emily has a weight-lifting nutcase for a boyfriend, and Dan's move, if he is in fact making one, is supposed to be slow and smooth and patient. I have counseled him in Zen techniques for picking up girls; it's not supposed to look like he's doing it.

Dave Gray is beside Bonfiglio in the locker room, nodding his head. "The cat is out of the bag," he says.

"How do you know?" I ask.

"I was there. Harbie screwed up."

Elbows resting on his knees, Bonfiglio buries his face in his hands. "This sucks," he says. "Coach Harb made it seem like I'm going around saying I'm dating her."

"Well, yeah, but either she likes you or she doesn't," I tell him, drawing on my vast but shaky history in this regard. "So don't worry about it."

Joe Harb is outside the locker room. "Hey, I'm just trying to help the kid out," he says. "Danny's shy. How long is he gonna wait to ask her out? Besides, Dave Gray started it all off. He made a comment first."

When Bonfiglio hears about this, he accuses Gray of sabotaging him. "Shut up, you fucking gypsy," says Gray. "I'm your best friend and you're badmouthing me like this? What's the world coming to?"

It's –1 degree Fahrenheit when I arrive at the rink just after 6 A.M. It's like the good old days, climbing on the bus to drive to some local backwater for a hockey game. Only today it's a trip to the big city for a share of the league title, against Boston Latin.

The players trickle into the rink, yawning and looking to scrounge an energy bar for breakfast. Brian Mueskes, who has bounced back and forth between jayvee and varsity most of the season, is surprised to learn that Ryan "Tibber" Thibodeau has been added to the roster because of his gritty effort against the St. Thomas jayvees.

"Does this mean that Zapanas and English have been devoted from my line?" Mueskes asks.

"That's 'demoted,' you idiot," says James Girouard, polishing his eyeglasses. He may be a bobo, but Girouard knows his verbs. And no regular varsity player can pass up the opportunity to zing a jayvee kid.

The bus arrives and the team mounts the stairs in the frigid darkness. We're headed this morning for Matthews Arena at Northeastern University in Boston. It's no ordinary rink but a real ice palace, with a three-tiered grandstand, banners representing the Hockey East colleges, and large carpeted locker rooms.

Before the game I help Jeremy Abdo tape an extra pad on his elbow, and Dave Martin works on his son Chris's bothersome left skate. "Your dad still tying your skates, Chris?" asks Fontaine.

Joe Harb is pacing up and down. "This is it, boys," he says. "Second place sucks."

"It's better than third," says Chris Martin.

Harb looks at me with surprised eyes. His back to the players, he shakes his head and laughs silently. The Methuen mentality rears up once again.

Chris Cagliuso stands up. "This is the championship right here," he says.

"There's no tomorrow," says Joe Robillard, as the players get up and file toward the tunnel. "Carpe diem."

The coaches walk out to the bench and on the way, Robillard shares an old memory about playing goal here for Boston University. The game had just started and a player from the other team fired a clearing shot from center ice. Robillard knelt down to stop it and the puck hit a bump on the ice and skipped between his legs for a goal. Laughing under his breath, Robillard described how his coach ran along the stick rack and flung all the extra sticks to the ground, he was so angry.

"I concentrated like hell after that," says Robillard. "And we won 4-1."

Methuen's first line swarms Boston Latin's net in the opening minutes, taking three shots from point blank range. None of them go in. The other two lines struggle, and the Rangers go back to the locker room tied 0-0 after one period.

All year long, the coaches have been preaching the value of good, old-fashioned hustle, and driving hard to the net. Early in the second period it pays off when Albert Soucy chases one of Boston Latin's oversized defensemen the length of the ice for a stray puck. They collide and Tim Parker, skiing in Soucy's wake, sweeps the puck into Boston Latin's net for the go-ahead goal.

"Parker! Parker! I could kiss you right now," says Dave Martin, when the beaming forward returns to Methuen's bench.

Just two minutes later, our elation turns to disgust when Ryan Fontaine is pitchforked to the ice in front of the Boston Latin net and he's the one penalized. Dave Martin is livid. Apparently Fontaine cross-checked the opposing player to begin the sequence, and the pitchfork was the retaliation. Still, under these circumstances, both players should be sent off. But Fontaine is led to the sin bin by himself, kicking and swearing.

"That's the first time in history that a ref called the first one and ignored the second," Martin says.

The referee skates over. "The Boston Latin player was merely defending himself," he says.

Martin kicks the door. "Jee-sus. Did our guy have a gun?"

Of course, Boston Latin scores on their power play and we troop back to the locker room tied 1-1 at the end of the second period. "Fifteen minutes of hockey left, boys," says Robillard. "Balls out."

Early in the final period, a Boston Latin winger loses his edge and flies into the boards unprotected. Screams erupt from that corner of the rink. "Call an ambulance. Call an ambulance," the injured player cries. His leg dangling at an awkward angle, the kid rips off his helmet and claws at the ice. His agony permeates the arena, and some of the Methuen parents begin crying. There's a child in pain, and they all know that dreadful feeling.

After several long moments, the sobbing player is helped off the ice and down the tunnel to a medical room. I have seen catastrophic injuries before, and they almost always rob teams of their desire to compete. But which team? Our players lounge against the boards, drinking water from squeeze bottles as the kid's screams fade into echo. The Boston Latin bench is in shock. Their players are all standing, heads turned toward the corner even though their teammate is gone.

Moments later, Boston Latin works the puck down low and scores to take the lead, 2-1. The Rangers press for the equalizer. In the very next sequence, Fontaine, who's playing his guts out, slashes a Boston Latin player from behind. It's a dumb penalty, and time is running out.

In the nearly deserted upper grandstand, a dark-haired guy in a two-toned leather jacket gets up and yells, "Stupid!"

Dave Martin looks over at me. "One guess," he says.

With two minutes to play, Robillard is double-shifting his top line, trying to keep them on the ice as much as possible. But they're pressing too hard, missing their checks, making bad passes. Cagliuso is so frustrated when he returns to the bench that he swings his stick at the rink door and it flies out of his hands to center ice. Seconds later, Tim Parker carries the puck through the middle, gets tangled up in Cagliuso's discarded stick and falls down. It's that kind of game.

We lose 2-1, and will now be playing for second place in the Merrimack Valley/Dual County League. "Yeah, I'm disappointed but I'm happy with the effort," Robillard says to a reporter from the *Boston Herald.*

The players mill around, packing their gear. In his boxer shorts and little round spectacles, James Girouard looks about 9 years old. Jeremy Abdo is beside him, his number 18 sketched in pen on his baseball cap. Sometimes I forget how young these kids really are. On one hand, they're men with well-defined musculature and gold chains who drive Camaros and Mustangs, but they all still live at home and their mothers make their beds and serve them chicken soup when they're sick. Although there was shouting and swearing immediately after the game, most of the players seem indifferent now. They crowd around the soda machine, cadging quarters from one another and playing grab ass.

Abdo emerges from the rink guzzling a can of soda and I hold out my hand like a traffic cop. "Dump that," I say. "Cola is the devil's elixir."

On the bright, cold streets of Boston, we cross lines of traffic in the overloaded school bus, alongside skyscrapers that gleam like towers of gold. "It's like Mr. Parker used to say," Dave Martin tells me. "People from Methuen are happy being mediocre."

26

THE TEAM SHRINK

IN THE MIDST OF A long practice, the players are soaked through with sweat and the coaches are bundled up in long johns and windbreakers against the chill.

While the first unit works on the power play, Dave George takes a breather along the boards. George is a good kid, hardworking and funny. Joe Harb calls him "Chin," after the tough little winger's first varsity shift during freshman year, when he got knocked down at center ice and split his chin wide open. The coaches wanted him to get stitches, but George insisted on patching up the cut with athletic tape and going back out there. "Chin, if ten kids get hurt, you're in there," Coach Harb says to him.

"Who should I hurt first?" asks George, raising his stick.

Harb grins at me. "I like that attitude," he says. When Dave George skates away, Harb adds, "You can't teach a kid to enjoy hitting. It's either in him, or it isn't. Chin's got that toughness, that bite. I like the kid."

Harb and Jon Morin and I've been talking about the attitudes of some of the varsity players. Morin has endorsed my idea of speaking to certain players about aspects of their game—using positive reinforcement as a way to raise their awareness and level of play. I spend so much time in school, observing the players outside of any official duties, that athletic director Brian Urquhart calls me the "team shrink."

I take a special interest in the goalies. Senior tri-captain Dan Bonfiglio, after being selected to the all-league team in his junior year, has been inconsistent so far this season. Although his play is still brilliant at times, in practice Bonfiglio appears listless, affected by his heart condition and lovelorn attitude toward Emily. Today he looks like he's coasting through the workout, and during a water break I ask Bonfiglio if he has any videotapes of his hot streak last year.

"There was something you were doing then that you're not doing now," I say.

The goalie shows more intensity in the second half of practice, even swinging his stick at a couple of teammates who loiter in front of the net, obstructing his view. Afterward, soaked with perspiration, Bonfiglio tells me, "They got pretty pissed about that."

"Are you here to be everybody's pal, or to improve your game?"

"I'm here to kick some ass," he says.

"That's right."

Jarrod Trovato is another player who can use some encouragement. The eager young defenseman is having a tough year. His father, Horace, again suffers from cancer and Jarrod is adrift, needing the camaraderie of the team to get through his troubles but definitely struggling in practice and in the games. Despite all this, Robillard and Morin have noticed a spark in Trovato of late. Against Tewksbury, he kept battling when some of his more high profile teammates packed it in early.

I call Trovato over. "Work hard every drill. Make yourself stand out," I tell him. "There's no law against sprinting back to the line, either." Trovato nods and hustles out to the blue line for the next drill. The kid is improving.

High school kids seem to think that once you get past, say, age

25, you don't work out anymore and you don't have any fun. Tired from their midweek games, the hockey players are restricted to a fifty-minute "dry land" practice after school the next day. This consists of five exercise "stations" in and around the varsity locker room, where Coach Robillard has devised a series of hockey-related plyometric exercises: skate hops, squat thrusts and lunges, Russian twists, hurdle hops, and a dozen more.

On Thursday mornings, I usually skate with a gym class that includes Ranger jayvees Drew Soley and Matt English, and we play torrid games of ball hockey that last about an hour. Then I participate in dry land training after school, for a double workout.

I'm leaning against the cinder block wall of team room number 2, drenched in sweat, waiting for my turn at lateral hops. Chris Cagliuso enters the far door and sees me. "What are you doing this for, Mr. Atkinson?" he asks.

"If I wasn't doing it here, I'd be doing it at home."

Cagliuso is puzzled. "But you're an old man," he says.

Joe Robillard and his colleague Fran Molesso regularly play sports with their charges and, at 48, are fueled by the same antic energy that courses through the hearts and minds of the typical 17-year-old. In the summer they paint houses together, and early in the morning when they start work for the day, Molesso blasts the "Star Spangled Banner" from a portable tape player and they stand at attention with their paintbrushes held over their hearts. I can only wonder what Chris Cagliuso would make of that.

Later that afternoon, I hear that the ice is good over at Lake Cochichewick, which is the municipal water supply for North Andover. At times I feel like just a body, muscles and a heart, and other times it's like, if I shut my eyes for a moment, I'll dematerialize. While I'm circumnavigating the lake, I say, "I am a body," startling the silent woods around me, the only other sound the *wick-a, wick-a* of my blades against the milky shore ice. Then I think, "I am a mind" and that's equally correct; the sound of my skates goes away.

Some of the ice is white and bumpy, but there are long stretches of thick, smooth, black pond ice, the length of three or four hockey rinks consecutively, and I'll shoot the puck as hard as I can and sprint after it until the lactic acid screams in my legs. Or I'll stick-handle in nifty little arcs, feinting imaginary opponents, now-you-see-it-now-you-don't, supplying my own commentary: "Atkinson winds up at center ice, twelve seconds left, he puts on a burst, moves past one man, nine seconds, over the blue line, a fabulous shift through the defense, five-four-three, he draws the goalie—shoots! He scores! Yes, the Rangers win!"

Ice fishermen and their orange flags dot the lake, blowing on their hands, in pairs mostly, wrapped up in parkas and hoods. There are other skaters but not many, fathers and their young sons, and gentle little girls wearing white skates and pink leggings, moving over the ice with peculiar, storklike strides.

I'm about an hour getting around the lake. The surrounding woods are graying like my hair, though it hardly seems cold or late enough. There are an unusual number of deserted homes lakeside, huge mansions with sloping brown lawns, turned-over rowboats and stacked chairs, complete with shrouded outbuildings and empty gravel driveways, like scenes from an old murder, love affairs gone awry.

I race on, past the houses and the long expanse of shoreline and the somber fishermen. The sun's disc is slipping between the trunks of the crowded pines. Sometimes the wind blows at my back; other times, it swings around and comes at me so hard it almost knocks me down. The ice shifts like a giant, brittle skin, booming with pressure, and cracks run ahead of me across the milky ice, spitting tongues of snow. My cheeks burn despite the chill; I'm feverish, body and soul.

In the locker room, Dan Gradzewicz is watching five of his jayvee teammates packing their gear for a trip with the varsity. I motion him over and ask when he's going to be called up.

"I don't know," Gradzewicz says.

"When you're at home, do you think about your game and how to improve it? Do you watch hockey on TV? Do you do sit-ups and push-ups before you go to bed?"

The blond-haired sophomore looks at the crumbling tiles beneath our feet. "I know it's my work ethic, or whatever," he says. "I'm going to start working harder."

I chuck him on the shoulder. "Well, I'm pulling for you, kid."

Athletic director Brian Urquhart witnesses the last segment of my exchange with Dan Gradzewicz. "The biggest variable with high school athletes is right here," he says, pointing at his temple. "Discipline and intensity. At 16 or 17, they can be full-grown but still immature. The mental part of the game is what good coaches spend most of their time on."

Before departing for the Janas in Lowell and our game against Tewksbury, Robillard gathers the team by the rink door. "This is the first time in a while that we've had more talent than Tewks," he says. "But persistence and determination is what wins games. And we've lost three out of four. We need a 'W.' Get in their faces, right from the start, and we can beat them."

An hour later, we arrive at the tiny state rink and the players jam themselves into the locker room. Brian Mueskes doesn't even have a spot on the bench and dresses himself on the floor. In his boxer shorts, he looks like a peewee down there.

"Small locker rooms bring the team closer together," says Dan Bonfiglio. Equipment bags are piled up waist high, and several players are forced to dress in the hallway.

"Good speech, Dan," I tell him.

The goalie shrugs. "Nobody listens to me."

Ray DeZenzo comes to the locker room door with two aspirin for his son, Thom, who has the flu. "If he gets a migraine like I've been having, he won't be able to see," says the concerned father.

"That's okay," says Dave Martin, intercepting him. "He can't see the puck out there anyway."

After Mr. DeZenzo goes out, I call Martin an "equal opportunity ball buster" and he laughs.

"I don't give a shit," he says, downing the aspirin meant for Thom DeZenzo. "With me, you always know what you're getting."

On our way to the bench, I nudge Jon Morin and point to Martin. "Watch for his classic pattern: kiss the referee's ass before the game, scream at him during, and make up afterwards."

Sure enough, one of the referees skates by our bench and immediately Dave Martin goes to work. "How you doin', handsome?" he asks. "Just another day in paradise, right?"

This particular referee is an older gentleman who's been calling games since Joe Robillard was in high school. When he totters away, Martin turns to me and says, "The old buzzard doesn't even know what day it is."

The Tewksbury kids are big, relentless, and more than a little bit nasty. They bang the boards hard, hit after the whistle, and zero right in on Methuen's skill players like Chris Cagliuso and Eric MacDonald. On the bus ride, Jon Morin spent fifteen minutes breaking down Chris Martin's game for me, how he oscillates between huge mistakes and athletic recoveries. With the score tied 1-1 late in the first period, young Martin inadvertently kicks the puck to a Tewksbury forward who goes in alone on Dave Gray and scores.

"That's exactly what I'm talking about," Morin says to me.

We're losing 4-1 after two periods and things are getting ugly.

Under this kind of pressure, the Rangers are an immature team, bitching and moaning at adversity. Cagliuso throws his stick into the bench after a lousy shift, Fontaine is swearing like a sailor on shore leave, and even some of the underclassmen are complaining about one another. Our bench looks like a field hospital. Thom DeZenzo is sitting with his feet splayed and a goofy smile on his face after taking a blow to the head. Ryan Fontaine is smashed into the boards from behind and hobbles off the ice with a wrenched back. Beside him, Dave George has the dry heaves. Anxious mothers line up at the rink door and are repelled by Coach Martin, who tells them that everything is under control. But we're struggling.

Thom DeZenzo is Methuen's most experienced and talented defenseman. But after getting cracked in the head, the senior takes himself out of the game and then seems fine in the locker room, laughing and joking with his pals.

"Thom doesn't look hurt to me," I say.

Looking over there, one of the other coaches also wonders about the severity of DeZenzo's injury. "He's packed it in before," he says.

Methuen gets skunked 7-2. Standing in the corridor outside the visitor's locker room, Robillard is downcast. While a reporter from the local newspaper clicks on his tape recorder and starts asking questions, Methuen's head coach stares at the floor and measures his words. "Why can't we play hard two games in a row?" he asks. "All I know is, I got to go around town and hear 'There's the guy who can't coach.' "

27

SNOW GLASS

LATE IN JANUARY THERE'S A foot of snow on the ground and nightly subzero temperatures have sealed up the top layer so it shines like a mirror in the sun. The snow is stretched tight over the playing fields adjacent to Methuen High, acres of smooth white skin marked by thousands of little pores. Liam calls it "snow glass" and leaving the rink after his hockey practice, he veers off the plowed path to trudge through the drifts. He laughs as he goes along, a tiny hooded figure in a youth hockey jacket, each step sounding like a pane of broken glass.

Tramping along the sidewalk, I call out to Liam, warning him not to get his pants wet—it's cold and we have to warm up the car and hurry somewhere.

It occurs to me that I'm growing old. At one time in my life, I would have stayed at the rink all day and then, heading out, would've seen the vast unbroken plain of snow as an arctic wilderness yearning to be explored. Liam's hat blows off and the north wind cutting across the soccer field whips his hair into a frenzied meringue. The empty goals at either end of the pitch are skeletal, gleaming in the low winter light.

Liam is forty yards distant, his laughter carrying over the open spaces like the tolling of a bell. Starting up the car and going to the bank and post office and all that other middle-aged busy work is suddenly reduced in importance. My son is heading away from me, and I leap over the embankment and go bounding toward the wall of oak trees bordering the horizon. Liam whirls around, giggling at the sight of his old man smashing through the drifts. His feet get tangled up and he falls over, his narrow body wedged into the impression he has made, with his feet sticking straight up. All I have to do is follow the laughter toward my son, and I know I'll get there.

Before the Westford Academy rematch, Chris Cagliuso and Eric MacDonald are dressed in full gear huddling in the corner. The team has lost four of its last five games, and the power play, where their talents are featured, has been impotent lately. Cagliuso says to his younger counterpart, "There's a difference between moving it quick and rushing it."

MacDonald nods his helmet. He has a good pair of hands—earlier this year, he won the most improved player award for the golf team, with an eight handicap.

"Let's play with our heads up, and throw it around," Cagliuso says. He taps his teammate on the shin pads, and Robillard enters the room.

"When we crashed on them last time, they couldn't get the puck out of the zone," says the coach. "Let's squeeze 'em. They can't skate with us."

Outside the room, Ozzy Osborne's "Crazy Train" echoes throughout the MHS rink and the boys line up at the door. I notice Dave George looking at me and he begins nodding and I nod back. There's no expression on his face and a look of absolute determination in his eyes. Dave George is going to war.

The Rangers take the ice, the teams are introduced, and the pep band plays the national anthem. Looking over at Joe Robillard, I think of him and Fran Molesso saluting the flag with their paintbrushes and laugh to myself. Joe's wife, Barbara, an attractive blonde woman in a ski jacket and blue jeans, is attending tonight's game with their 14-year-old son Brad and his friend. Robillard is bustling around the rink, filled with extra pride. He has all the enthusiasm of a man half his age.

Methuen has a 2-1 lead at the end of the first period, but there's a terrible price to pay. While the Rangers are killing a penalty, Chris Cagliuso hangs onto the puck for too long and gets nailed into the end boards and reinjures his left shoulder. Incensed, he throws his gloves and sticks into the bench when he comes off the ice, all doubled over. The crowd falls silent.

During the intermission, trainer Kevin MacLennan examines Cagliuso and reports to Coach Robillard outside the locker room. "It's up like this," says MacLennan, indicating the rise between Cagliuso's shoulder bones by holding his thumb and forefinger a couple inches apart. "It's a bad separation."

"Can't you just pop it back in?" asks Dave Martin.

The trainer shakes his head. "He's done."

Martin rears back and kicks the locker room door. "Shit."

In the second period, Methuen goes ahead 5-1, and the game turns chippy. Ryan Fontaine gets butt-ended in the throat, and when he goes to the bench and shows the welt to Dave George, the Ranger tough guys are fuming. Dave Martin eggs them on, giving Fontaine the number of the Westford Academy player who did it. Fontaine and George hoist their sticks and start yelling at number 10 from the bench.

"Don't incite the lunatics," I say to Martin, and he laughs. The two of us bend down to Fontaine and whack him on the shoulder pads, and Martin says, "Score another goal. That pisses them off more than a cross-check."

In the locker room, Robillard is moved to profanity for the first time all season. "If I see any more cheap shit like that, I don't care who you are—you'll sit," the coach says. "Winners don't play like that."

On the way out for the third period, Jon Morin collars Fontaine and backs him into a corner near the door. "Don't be selfish and go after guys like that," he says.

"But—"

"There are no 'buts.' Don't play for yourself. Play for the other guys. That's what hockey is all about."

Sophomore Jarrod Trovato is rewarded with a regular shift tonight after his yeoman's effort in the loss to Tewksbury. Early in the final period, Methuen is pressuring their opponent's net and the puck floats back to Trovato at the left point. He cocks his stick and sets his feet, intending to unleash a slap shot. But the puck skids beneath his windmilling stick, Trovato falls to his knees, and one of the Grey Ghosts is treated to a breakaway. He races the length of the ice and fires a shot high over Dan Bonfiglio's left shoulder and into the net. Coach Morin pulls Trovato from the ice and the defenseman climbs over the boards and slams his stick against the bench.

Trovato is angry, and that's good. Athletes make mistakes, and sometimes they have to get mad at themselves to improve their performance. But Trovato's reaction is out of proportion to his error. Languishing at the end of the bench, he buries his helmet in his gloves and for several long moments does not even glance at the action in front of him. Paul St. Louis has also been benched and after a while, he throws his arm across Trovato's back and says something into the earhole of his helmet.

Jarrod Trovato is weeping. His shoulders quake and three or four times he removes his glove and sticks his exposed fingers through the cage and wipes away tears. The coaches look away, not wanting to embarrass the kid. What are they going to say? Everyone knows that Trovato's father is ill. But they can't stop the game or tell Westford Academy not to play so hard. For the rest of the team, life goes on.

Trovato is a big, good-looking kid, with short dark hair gelled down on his forehead and braces on his teeth. Since his father's relapse, Trovato has taken on more duties at home and is teaching his dad sign language now that he can't speak. "He's doing good," Trovato has said. "But there's a lot going on."

I was living in Toronto and halfway through a championship rugby season when my father died of a heart attack. He was only 52 years old. All that summer I moped around the house, sleeping late and watching television. It took a phone call from my rugby coach, Cye Beechey, and an invitation to play in Wales to snap me out of my depression. On the tour, we won games in Harrow and Birchgrove, and I fell in love with a raven-haired Welsh girl. But I was 26 years old. Jarrod Trovato is only 16.

Ryan Fontaine keeps a lid on it during the third period and we end up beating Westford Academy 7-4. Afterward Cagliuso appears in the noisy locker room with his left arm in a sling. He's on his way to Holy Family Hospital for an X ray, and several players come over and wish him well. Cagliuso wears a losing expression even though the Rangers have won: an injury to Methuen's star could mean more than just an aborted high school season. A torn rotator cuff or other chronic shoulder ailment could affect Cagliuso's entry into a top prep school and the possibility for a college scholarship. I stop by his locker and wish him luck and he stares at the floor and says "Thank you" in a quiet voice.

Jarrod Trovato is alone in the corner. When I think of the terror that he faces, sitting there untying his skates and stripping off tape, a ball of fear rises in my throat, leaving the taste of bile. The kid doesn't even know what he's up against.

In the background, the guys are yelling and swearing and spitting water at each other. Jon Morin surveys this chaos from his usual place against the wall, arms folded, his dark brow creased and ruminative. "We're still immature," he says. "Lots of sophomores."

I linger there, waiting for him to add something and after a moment, he does. "Time to grow up."

28

THE HALT AND THE LAME

CHRIS CAGLIUSO TURNS UP FOR phys ed on Monday morning with his left arm in a sling and a glum look on his face. He's suffering from a "third or fourth degree" separation of his left shoulder and will be examined by an orthopedic surgeon later in the week. Dressed in tan pants and a blue-and-white-checked shirt, the senior tri-captain says that he'll be out for two or three of the remaining seven regular season games. With his hangdog expression, Cagliuso looks like a puppy that's been struck with a rolled-up newspaper.

His plan to return seems optimistic. In college, I separated my right shoulder and missed six weeks of soccer and wrestling. Methuen's hockey season will be over in less than five weeks.

But I encourage Cagliuso to pursue his rehabilitation and keep in mind that he's a team captain. "Coach Robillard said after the game that the team needs more leadership from the older players," I tell him.

Cagliuso pledges to attend every practice but admits, "It's gonna kill me to miss those league games, especially Andover and Central." The speedy center laughs when I tell him that Dave Martin and I climb the walls before those matchups, wishing we could play. "It's a feeling that never goes away," I say.

"Some guys are gonna have to step up and play better," says Cagliuso. "Guys like Eric [MacDonald] and Albert [Soucy]. We gotta have more from them now."

One player who has improved in recent games is sophomore center James Girouard. With his slight build, spectacles and braces, and childlike face, "Bobo" looks even younger than his 16 years. At practices and during games, Girouard uses an albuterol inhaler to help control his asthma. But he has a fine hockey pedigree. His father, Ray Girouard, 42, played on a state championship team at powerhouse Matignon High in 1975 and has coached James and his brothers, Derek, 14, and Matthew, 10, at just about every level.

James is a stylish player with a good set of hands; the only knock against him is that he's timid in the corners, where the heavy banging occurs. But he's added an edge to his game and is playing with more courage. Against Tewksbury, Girouard's open ice check on the Redmen's biggest player sent both kids sprawling and Bobo's toughness quotient soaring.

Before practice, Girouard comes to the skate room door. Robillard is inside sharpening skates, and sparks fly against his royal blue windbreaker. Fetching a stick from the rack, Girouard waits until Robillard pauses for a moment and then asks, "How long we lose Chris (Cagliuso) for, Coach?"

Robillard frowns at his sharpening machine. "A few weeks, at least."

"That's not good," Girouard says.

"Some guys have to step up," says Robillard over his shoulder. He turns and establishes eye contact with his third line center.

"I know," says Girouard. "I know."

A few minutes later, Joe Robillard calls the team together and issues a warning: "You never know when something like what happened to Chris could happen to you. Any one of you could slide into the boards and break an ankle, even in practice. Career over.

So play with some intensity. Because you never know when it all might end."

Leaning on his stick outside the circle of players, Jarrod Trovato digests this message with a blank look on his face.

Add Dave Gray to Methuen's growing injury list. A new prescription for his contact lenses has caused double vision and a feeling of pressure behind the goalie's left eye. Meeting up with Gray outside the trainer's room, Chris Cagliuso says, "If there's two pucks, stop the one on the left."

"Stop 'em both," I say, "just to be safe."

Gray is reluctant to tell Coach Robillard about his problem. He enters the skate room a few minutes later, intending to say something, but grabs his pads and stick and retreats with a guilty expression on his face. "You have to tell him," I say, intercepting the goalie in the corridor. "That's what Mr. Robillard's here for. To look after his players."

Trainer Kevin MacLennan comes upstairs to the rink, and Robillard hails him from the ice and motions toward the rink door. Cagliuso is standing outside the glass watching the team warm up and Robillard looks over at him and then back to the trainer. "What's your best guess?" he asks MacLennan.

The trainer shakes his head. "It's completely torn," he says, pantomiming Cagliuso's accident. "His left arm was bent, and the other kid came down right on top of his shoulder."

"Think he'll be back?" asks Robillard.

"I doubt it."

Robillard glances at me. "That hurts us. It really does."

On the evening of the Lincoln-Sudbury rematch, Chris Cagliuso drops by the skate room and all the coaches stop what they're doing and look toward the doorway. Methuen's leading scorer reports that the orthopedic surgeon has advised him to take two weeks off before returning for another examination.

"It just seems that people can play with separated shoulders," Cagliuso says.

"Take the rest," says Robillard, who looks relieved. "Two weeks, see the doc again, maybe you're back for the state tournament."

Still thinking aloud, Cagliuso mentions that New England Patriots quarterback Drew Bledsoe played several NFL games with a separated shoulder.

"He's getting forty million dollars to play football—there's no tomorrow for him," I say. "You've got plenty of tomorrows."

It's a long ride to West Concord, Massachusetts. The Valley Sports Arena is a real pit of a rink, with a low girdered ceiling, poor lighting, and a dingy grandstand behind one of the nets that's meant to contain both sets of fans. Dave Martin recalls that he played in a tournament here a few years back, brought in as a ringer by a large computer company. He was told what to say in response to questioning by tournament officials and used a false name. Martin's squad won the championship and he was awarded a beautiful plaque that read "John Smith, Most Valuable Player."

Coach Morin has a more ominous story about this particular rink. For several summers, Morin played on a team that won the league championship every year, including games where they only had seven players and still outskated the competition. Jon Morin is 5' 9", a solid 185 pounds, and during this one game, he was being pestered by a guy half a foot taller and twenty-five pounds heavier. To keep the big fellow off him, he chose an opportune moment and skated up behind the guy and cross-checked him hard in the lower back. Nothing happened. Not only was this guy an immovable object, he got so mad he turned around and began pummeling Morin.

"I was hanging on by my fingernails," Morin says, laughing at the memory. "Just trying to get a little piece of him so he wouldn't kill me."

Morin's eye inflated and his jaw turned purple and swelled up. After the referee ejected both combatants from the game, the big guy found Morin beneath the grandstand and gave him a few more shots for good measure. "I hate this place," says Morin.

Outside the tiny blue crypt of a locker room, we run into Lincoln-Sudbury's coach, an amiable, craggy-faced man who was ejected from the previous game against the Rangers after a questionable call by the referee.

"You gonna behave yourself tonight?" asks Dave Martin.

The other coach winks at me. "Fuck you."

A half hour before the scheduled start, the Zamboni machine is rounding the ice and Robillard asks, "Any chance we can go on early?"

"Depends on the position of the moon," says the Lincoln-Sudbury coach.

Robillard heads into the locker room and goes over tonight's strategy: two-man forecheck, weakside breakout, feed the puck back to the points. Then he reminds the team that they need one more victory to qualify for the state tournament. "Let's get it tonight," Robillard says.

From the drop of the puck, Methuen dominates their opponent but cannot score. Kevin McCarthy, Albert Soucy, Ryan Fontaine, and Jeremy Abdo all have great chances in front of the Lincoln-Sudbury net but are unable to do what they have done all year: find the handle and knock the puck over the goal line.

It's an evening that will hinge on a few mistakes and unfortunately for Methuen, goalie Dan Bonfiglio makes the first one. Eleven minutes into the game Bonfiglio stops a harmless shot near the left post and then, instead of covering the puck, he pokes it back out front and a Lincoln-Sudbury player swoops in and fires a shot into the net. Up in the grandstand, Chris Cagliuso sits between his parents, arms crossed and stone-faced while teenage fans from Lincoln-Sudbury celebrate all around him.

Our kids play their hearts out. But even though the Rangers outshoot the opposition 34-13, the goal stands up and Lincoln-Sudbury pockets a 1-0 upset. As the Warrior fans count down the last ten seconds, a couple of Ranger hotheads display their immaturity. Fontaine skates in front of the grandstand, which is crowded with parents and grandparents as well as high school kids, and tells a vocal group of hecklers to "Shut the fuck up." They rain derision on Fontaine's head and boo the Rangers as they skate toward the rink doors.

Thom DeZenzo rears back and flings his stick over the boards while Joe Harb looks on. "DeZenzo is a baby," says Harb. "He pulled that shit last year."

Inside the crowded locker room, Joe Robillard is disappointed but philosophical. "Every year we have a night like this," he says. "We dominate the other team and can't put the puck in the ocean and we lose. Some night *we'll* get dominated but hang on and scrap and pull out the win. Hopefully in the state tournament."

The saddest moment of the evening comes when we're passing through the gate and I look up to see Chris Cagliuso, dressed in shirt and tie with his game jersey over them, alone in the empty grandstand. Cagliuso has a long face and his left arm is packaged in a sling. He looks pretty small sitting up there, like some jayvee kid who has been injured in practice and forgotten. But his absence is huge.

The players mill around the vending machines and then pass through the lobby and head into the chill of the parking lot. Joe Harb and I escort Ryan Fontaine onto the bus and stand around gazing at the millions of stars that dot the night sky. The coaches climb aboard and through the windshield, I recognize a man dressed in a blue topcoat standing in our path. He has a broad, liver-colored face and two sausages for lips. I nudge Dave Martin and point him out; it's the guy who shoved Brian Urquhart that night in Methuen.

Martin hails the bus driver, Chuck Trudel. "Bump him with the bus, Chucky," he says. "We owe him one."

29
TRIANGLES

IN HIS DRAWING CLASS, Chris Martin is creating a self-portrait that opens into a montage of various photographs and emblems and sports logos that express his passion for aggressive in-line skating and ice hockey. When the teacher asks if Martin wants to add some text, either cutout type from magazines or a short essay, the sophomore says, "No. I don't write. I'll just use pictures." But for anyone who's paying attention, the kid is expressing himself pretty clearly.

Martin's portrait features a remarkable likeness of his face, impassive as always, depicted against a stark black wall. "I want it to look like the ghetto," he says. Of course, Martin has never lived amid inner-city blight. He resides on Dewey Street, in a neat two-story home occupied by the four Martin children—Chris, 15; Dan, 14; Phillip, 12; and Candice, 9—along with their mother, my former classmate, Cathy Martin. Since their divorce proceedings began almost two years ago, Dave Martin and Cathy no longer live together.

What went wrong in the Martin marriage and who might or might not be at fault is none of my business. Dave and Cathy have been friends of mine since we were kids and I'd like it to stay that way. But whereas young Dan sometimes expresses himself with outbursts of weird behavior, his brother Chris is an enigma. Except for moments of hilarity with locker room pals Dave George, Ryan Fontaine, and Thom DeZenzo, Martin is a quiet kid, almost sullen. There's a lot going on behind those blue eyes of his, and a lot he's not saying.

The teacher comes around again and scrutinizes Martin's portfolio. "Choose images that reflect your favorite things, but also the inner 'you,' " she says. "Your wants, your fears, your desires."

Martin has a scrapbook with him that includes pictures of an outing he and his father took to the Hockey Hall of Fame in Toronto, Ontario. In his favorite picture, Martin is standing beside professional hockey's biggest prize, the Stanley Cup. He has a huge smile on his face and his right hand is extended toward the dented old trophy, like he's proud of it. In this photograph, the glum teenager is nowhere in sight, and he's a kid again.

Flipping through tattered copies of *Sports Illustrated,* Martin finds a photo of the University of Maine goalie in full stretch and after cutting the photo out, he remembers an image of planet earth taken from outer space that he saw in another magazine. Using a straight edge, Martin tears out the globe and arranges and rearranges the two illustrations. Finally he superimposes the Black Bears' goalie on top of the world, against the inky backdrop of the cosmos.

"I like this," says Martin, choosing it for no other conscious reason. "It looks cool."

But the idea of a hockey player all alone in the universe hits home with me, and when the buzzer sounds ending the class and the kids all converge on the door, I sit looking at the photo for several moments while Martin cleans up his work space.

In Coach Robillard's final gym class of the day, I participate in a ball hockey game on ice that includes Ranger hockey players Eric MacDonald, Jeremy Abdo, Matt Tetreau, Paul St. Louis, Matt Zapanas, and Albert Soucy. For nearly an hour, we skate back and forth in a game that brings back my swamp hockey days and puts some jump in my legs. The pace is frantic, and Abdo is showing off his stickhandling ability to the girls in the class. He flicks the ball off the near boards, juggles it on the tip of his stick blade while in mid-stride, then snaps it to the ice, threads it between another kid's skates and takes a quick glance ahead.

I dart into open space and for an instant, Abdo's gaze locks on mine and there's a clear alley between us. But Abdo hesitates for an instant, tries another solo move and is broken up by a kid who can barely skate.

"First thought, best thought," I call out, and Abdo grins at me.

Abdo is the flashiest player on our team, but stingy with his passes. It's Tetreau who surprises me. The curly-haired heartthrob of the tenth grade skates well and is smart and generous with his possession. He tries to make everyone else look good.

Hockey is a game of triangles: the equilateral distance any three players must stay from one another to create space and opportunity on offense, or tighten up their defense; as well as the area between an opponent's body and his stick—isosceles, acute, obtuse, or scalene—when you're looking to fire a pass somewhere.

In the midst of some heavy traffic, bodies crisscrossing in every direction, I see a triangle forming with Tetreau up high, me down low, and Abdo in front of the net. Tetreau steals the ball from Zapanas with a poke check, zips it across the ice to me and I throw a soft one-timer out to Abdo, who makes a slick move and backhands the ball into the low corner of the net. This is performance art, something spontaneous and natural that blooms within the span of two seconds and contains an electricity that crackles across the ice. There's no place I'd rather be than the bottom corner of that triangle for that instant. Forget wealth and fame and influence over men; give me some open ice, Tetreau and Abdo for linemates, and stuff all the rest.

Methuen has another opportunity to clinch a berth in the state tournament with their rematch against Haverhill. The question is, will they be able to overcome their offensive funk playing without Chris Cagliuso again? His presence on the ice creates scoring chances for linemates McCarthy and Fontaine and seems to give the younger kids permission to take risks in the other team's end. But for the second straight game, Cagliuso is dressed in street clothes and sitting in the stands.

The Rangers need smart, steady play from their upperclassmen and leadership from their captains. But just minutes into the game, Thom DeZenzo throws a rabbit punch at one of Haverhill's forwards and gets whistled off for roughing.

"What'd I say?" asks Joe Robillard from the bench. "No stupid penalties."

Five seconds into their power play, Haverhill scores to take a 1-0 lead.

Eric MacDonald contributes two pretty goals for Methuen and they head into the locker room tied 2-2 after the first period. It's like a funeral home in there, respectful whispers and muffled coughing. Joe Harb comes in, looks around and says, "A real emotional bunch."

It's the quiet, steady play of Eric MacDonald, who completes his hat trick early in the third period, that boosts the Rangers into the lead. On the white line's next shift, however, stalwart Kevin McCarthy pinches his left arm between the glass and the end boards and returns to the bench wincing in pain. He slams his head against the glass and writhes back and forth. When trainer Kevin MacLennan climbs down from his perch and starts working his way along the crowded bench, McCarthy waves him off.

The jayvees who have dressed but not played are staring at

McCarthy from the corner of the bench. "What the fuck are you looking at?" he asks them, and Matt Zapanas, Ryan Thibodeau, and Brian Bond turn around and resume watching the game.

Haverhill ties the score and then Ryan Fontaine pots a late goal to go ahead 4-3 with six minutes left to play. Flying through center ice, Albert Soucy picks up a loose puck at the Haverhill blue line and drives toward the net, attempting to split the two defensemen who are jitterbugging backward on either side. Soucy is ambushed from the left and right, and just as Robillard has instructed all year, the stout little winger keeps his feet moving and manages to kick the puck to open space.

Brian Mueskes streaks in and fires the puck at the net. The goalie saves, but Tim Parker is there and from an impossible angle slides the puck into the net for a 5-3 lead. The Methuen bench goes crazy. But moments later, Parker is slamming the blade of his stick on the ice and the goal is waved off. Incredibly, Albert Soucy has been penalized for roughing, and since the infraction occurred before the goal was scored, it doesn't count. In addition to erasing Methuen's two-goal lead, this absurd penalty will force the Rangers to play a man down for ninety seconds.

It's one of the oddest calls I've ever seen. Players are never whistled for roughing when they are lugging the puck, and Soucy was also fending off two opponents who outweighed him by a collective hundred pounds.

"You've got to be kidding," says Jon Morin when the referee tries to explain his call. "That's awful. Terrible. It's ridiculous."

There's a sense of doom along the Ranger bench. More than one pair of eyes strays across the rink to where Cagliuso is sitting, a slender figure wearing Methuen's white home jersey. Without his scoring touch and commanding presence, they're like a group of lost little boys.

Halfway through Haverhill's power play there's a dreadful

moment. Someone misses a check in the near corner, the puck goes back to Haverhill's best marksman, and he blasts a shot toward the cage. Dan Bonfiglio is screened by a mass of players. He's in poor position, standing upright in an attempt to see over the screen, and the blurry puck tips off the point of his skate blade and goes careering along the goal line. It tings off the far goalpost and ricochets away from the net and our bench lets out a great collective sigh. The clock runs down and Methuen hangs on to win 4-3; the Rangers are in the state tournament.

"A piece of luck, and we'll take it," says Joe Robillard.

30

WORLD'S END

TWO WEEKS AFTER PURCHASING A "new" used car, Liam and I visit Sheehan's gas station on Lawrence Street, where I bought it. Inside the little office, which is papered with Boston sports heroes like Bill Russell and Bobby Orr and Rocky Marciano, proprietor Bob Sheehan Jr., is juggling three telephones. I pull up to the gas pumps, and Bob waves through the glass and comes outside.

Sheehan is in his midthirties, a wry, crew-cutted man whose gas station is a clearinghouse for what goes on in Methuen. Although he's a big supporter of Central Catholic and a former basketball star there, we're good friends. Bob Sheehan and his dad, Bob Sr., are the only honest used car salesmen in northern New England.

My old car is still on the lot, sporting a sign that says "Like New" and spins around. As Sheehan approaches, I jerk my thumb in the direction of my last vehicle, which I also bought here and traded back. "So much for truth-in-advertising," I tell him.

"I tried to sell it to your brother Jamie, but he didn't believe it either," says Sheehan. He unhinges the hose and begins pumping my gas. "I'll have to shoot myself before I sell that piece of junk," he says, leaning in the window while the numbers ring up on the pump.

"It's a fine automobile. You said so yourself—when you sold it to me."

Sheehan wrinkles up his Irish-looking face. "You never told me the driver's side window wouldn't go up," he says.

"You never asked," I say, snickering at him. "Hey, buyer beware."

The mechanic, Bobby Proctor, comes out with his hands full of grease and asks me if I want a few moments alone with my old car and then he laughs and goes back inside. Directing his gaze over my shoulder, Sheehan breaks into a smile and hails Liam, who's trussed into the car seat. "Hi, buddy. How's it going?" he asks. Bob and his wife Linda have three kids and he knows better than to address a 5-year-old with baby talk or otherwise condescend. "How do you like Dad's new car?"

Liam strokes the nearest bit of upholstery. "I like it. It's smooth," he says. "My dad's old car looks like a taxi."

Sheehan switches off the gas pump and takes my twenty-dollar bill. "Hey, good luck," he says.

"With four bald tires, I'm going to need it," I say, easing into gear.

It's a brilliant, cold day in early February and Liam and I have decided to cancel our various appointments for an afternoon of coasting. Our favorite spot is the idealized landscape of the local golf course, which is arrayed in black and white beneath glassy blue skies. An empty hazelnut tree stands on the expanse of the thirteenth fairway, the sun caught in its branches, and the ground underneath littered with broken shells. Using the tree as an aiming stake, Liam and I trudge toward the largest hill in sight, dragging our thin plastic sled by its cord.

From height of land, I can see as far as World's End in the distance, the trees bundled together along the northern shore and then the great white disk of the pond itself. The ice is over a foot thick now, but the snow is just as deep and unmarked from end to end. Nobody skates there anymore; it's a long walk from the road and there's no concession stand or Zamboni machine or cheerleaders. It seems that kids don't want to suffer any discomfort in pursuit of their pleasure these days. So most of the local ponds go unused.

Liam is wearing his caged helmet, *Methuen Hockey* jacket, and a pair of rubber boots. Below us there's a steep drop of about fifty feet, then a gradual slope that stretches for over a hundred yards before intersecting with a depression in the snow that marks a brook. First we ride in tandem; I'm on the back with Liam tucked between my legs in front. His laughter starts with our first movement and continues downhill, building to a crescendo as we reach top speed. When we fishtail sideways and spill from the sled, his eyes are closed and his voice cracks and then evaporates into breathless mirth. Inside the cage of his helmet, Liam's cheeks are pink with exertion and tears of joy splash his fleece undershirt.

"Let's do it again," he says, when he gets his voice back.

For the next hour and a half, we travel up and down the vales and hillocks of the golf course, sweating in the sunlight even though it's only seventeen degrees. Last year I carried Liam up the hill half the time, but this season he says he can make it on his own. His ascents are slow, due to the length of his legs and his penchant for examining footprints and odd-shaped chunks of frozen snow. Stretched out on the upturned sled, I'm sunbathing in February while my son climbs toward me, the tiny alpinist picking his route along the fall line.

He's pooped and asks if I want to take a ride by myself. Sure, I tell him.

"All aboard," says Liam, and I shift my weight onto the sled and he pushes me off.

The perimeter of the golf course blurs as I hurtle down the slope, Liam's cries echoing behind me. Through some quirk in the terrain, the flimsy sled gets turned around and I'm traveling backward at a high rate of speed. Gravity pulls at my shoulders, hurrying the descent, and high above Liam is watching, his form silhouetted against the huge blue vault of the sky.

The mound of snow is growing from this perspective, thrusting Liam upward, pushing him farther and farther away before I can utter a word. At the bottom of the run, he's out of sight, and I grab the sled and go stumbling back toward him. In every direction, the land is ancient, empty and white.

If nature continues to take its course and my fate follows that of my father's and grandfather's, I often wonder what Liam will retain from this period in his life after I'm gone. Hopefully, his memories will be as beautiful and vivid as they are fragmented, like shards of classical pottery that were lost and then found again. From the vantage point of manhood he'll look back and remember that his favorite companion was an animated aardvark and that he frequented ice rinks and playing fields. All this will seem quaint to my son when he's grown, like his father who said goofy things and trimmed the crust from his cheese sandwiches, and his mother who sang lullabies and danced across the kitchens of his youth. But strewn over his recollections, like the luminous backdrop of those old Greek vases, will be the conviction that he was loved and cared for.

Leaving the golf course, with a rose-and-peach sky occupying the horizon, traffic is light on Howe Street and our bodies are tingling from all the fresh air and exercise. Snug in his car seat, Liam gazes out the window and asks, "Dad, where's heaven?"

I point at the roof. "Up there."

"What about outer space?" my son asks.

"It's past that."

Liam mulls this over. "Is that where you wait for a suitable body?"

"Where did you hear that?" I ask him, craning my neck to see into the backseat.

"On a cartoon."

Liam's queries remind me that raising a child, in some sense, means preparing them for one's own failure, absence, or death. I wonder about Atkinsons I've heard of but never met, Welsh grenadiers and sailors and rakes, and whether at some distant point we'll all be together in the blue-walled ether of paradise, fathers and sons and grandsons alike.

"I feel bad that I'll have to go to heaven someday," Liam says.

I tilt the rearview mirror and meet his eyes. "Why, Boo?"

"Because then I won't live in Methuen anymore."

31

CENTRAL CATHOLIC

JOE ROBILLARD DIVIDES THE KIDS into four teams of three players each, sends Dan Bonfiglio and Dave Gray to opposite ends of the rink, and conducts simultaneous games of full-length three-on-three. With two pucks and a weird set of rules, the tournament fascinates anyone who passes by. Waves of hard-skating kamikazes are buzzing both goalies and intersecting at center ice. It's dangerous out there.

Chris Cagliuso is in skates and sweats, eager to get a workout, but exempting himself from this mayhem. Robillard glides over to the boards and he and his injured star watch the action for a few moments. Cagliuso says that he wants to return for the final home game of the season versus Central Catholic, and Robillard tells him that the state tournament is more important for Cags and for the team. The other thing on Robillard's mind is that Cagliuso needs only two more points to break one hundred for his high school career. This achievement will earn him a spot "on the board," a glass case at the rink that lists the names of Methuen's hockey record holders. Chris's older brother Brett, who starred for the Rangers and then at Holy Cross, is ranked fifth all-time with 104 points.

"When I come back I'm gonna be rarin' to go," Cagliuso says.

Methuen's locker room is raucous an hour before the game

against Central Catholic; the kids are wrestling in the middle of the room, throwing pieces of equipment and swearing at a higher rate than usual. Stuffed into the far corner is Dave Gray, getting dressed while scanning the faces of his teammates.

"This is the last time I'm going to play here," says Gray. "It's sad."

Among the five seniors on the team, Gray and his compatriot, Dan Bonfiglio, seem the most affected by tonight's final appearance on home ice. They dress side by side, as always, but their conversation is minimal and there's a far-off look in their eyes.

"Jay, pay attention to who's singing the national anthem tonight and whose jersey she's wearing," says Bonfiglio.

"Emily?" I ask.

He and Gray are nodding at me and smiling. A moment later, their faces are serious again.

Twenty-five years ago, Mike Lebel and I combined to shut out Central Catholic 7-0. That game was one of our five wins that year, and the beginning of what has grown into an intense hockey rivalry. "If you play for the Methuen Rangers and can't get up for Central, there's something wrong with you," says Cagliuso, who's in street clothes. "We've never beaten Central in my four years here."

Part of the reason for that is the rival school's drawing power. As a private Catholic institution in an era of overcrowded and watered-down public education, Central attracts some of the best prospects from several area communities. And with recent state championships in football, basketball, and track and field, Central Catholic's reputation continues to grow as they siphon off many of Methuen's top athletes.

"Central is an all-star team," Joe Robillard says. "They always have been. To be fair, they should compete in the Catholic Conference."

Thom DeZenzo is pulling his socks over his shin pads, the white game jersey emblazoned with number 15 hanging from the locker beside him. "This is the one team *everybody* cares about," says the senior tri-captain. "Central is the team to beat."

And Methuen seems poised to beat the Red Raiders after a drought of several years. The Rangers are 9-6, compared with Central's 3-11-2, but these matchups are always fraught with high emotion and extremely physical. Anything can happen.

"Best place to be tonight is playing in this game," says Robillard as he enters the crowded, smelly locker room. "From the drop of the puck to the final whistle, let's leave no doubt who the better team is."

By the time the buzzer sounds and the players are ready to pile out of the room, they're jumping around like kangaroos, pummeling each other and cursing in loud angry voices. Joe Harb and I raise our eyebrows at each other—we've been waiting for this kind of emotion all season.

"Let's go-oo-o," says Albert Soucy, banging himself in the cage with the butt of his stick. "Let's beat the shit out of Central."

Jon Morin is standing in the corner by the door, and even he's impressed. "They're pumped," says Morin. "They should be."

Methuen's rink is packed with fans, both sides of the ice and standing room only behind the glass. The pep band is banging away from the far side of the building, and someone in the grandstand has one of those infernal air horns. After one annoying blast, Dave Martin, pacing up and down the bench, growls, "If I find tha horn, I'm gonna shove it—" Jayvee wing Matt Zapanas, who's been asked to dress for the game, is staring at Martin with his mouth open. "Hello, Matthew. How are you this evening?" asks the coach, winking at me.

In their bright red uniforms, Central Catholic warms up right in front of our bench and all the coaches are standing and staring with their arms folded. Methuen's rivalry with Central extends across all generations and all sports. Without any prompting from me, Jon

Morin says, "Nineteen seventy-nine. I scored the winning touchdown against Central. It was our first win in two years. We were six yards out and I ran it left. And it sure felt good."

In a high, nasally voice, the PA announcer calls attention to the Methuen bench and informs the audience that five Ranger athletes will be appearing on home ice for the last time tonight. Tim Parker, Dave Gray, Thom DeZenzo, Chris Cagliuso, and Dan Bonfiglio are all introduced, along with their parents, who come to the rink door for bundles of roses in green translucent paper. When Bonfiglio skates over in his goalie equipment, flips up his mask, and kisses his mother, Jeannine, I feel my throat tighten.

My own mother was never the same after my father died. Although she continued to love us—as kin, as children of her beloved Jimmy, and as grown shadows of the living things that played about her feet when she was young—my mother suffered the next nine years under an abiding sadness, the towel thrown in. When I was 14 and 15, playing youth hockey, I'd have to rise around midnight and wait for my dad to bring the car around. On the kitchen table there would be a little note from my mother, wishing me luck and telling me to take care. She always signed it "From a goalie's mom."

Not long into the game, Eric MacDonald scores a beautiful goal coming down the left wing. He makes an inside move on the Central defender and throws the puck into a tiny space over the goalie's right shoulder. Air horns tear at the silence, and Methuen's pep band launches into a boisterous tune as the young fans clustered along the half boards pound on the glass.

Something flies out of the grandstand and forms a viscous clot on the ice. The referee pinches the tiny octopus between two fingers, skates toward us, and flings it over the glass. "Where'd they get that?" asks Dave Martin. "The sushi bar?"

"The Lobster Den," I tell him. "Pickled calamari. Four-sixteen a pound."

When Albert Soucy scores on a nifty backhand maneuver in front of Central's goal, the rest of the calamari lands on the ice—still contained in the plastic bag. But Central fights back, ties the game in the second period, and just twenty-five seconds later goes ahead 3-2. Two husky Central players glide by the Methuen bench and wave "bye-bye" with their gloved hands. Joe Robillard is livid when the team retreats to the locker room a few minutes later.

"That kind of thing gets me fucking mad," says Methuen's head coach. "Pardon my language. But that gets me boiled up. We need that next goal. We have to have it."

Thom DeZenzo's quick feet and anticipation help Methuen get even when he jumps into the play from his defenseman's position and wrists a twenty-footer into the Central goal. Shortly afterward, hard-charging Ryan Fontaine, while killing a penalty, harasses a Central player in his own end until he coughs up the puck. Fontaine bangs in front of the net and slides a short one-hander beneath Central's goalie for the 4-3 lead.

But Methuen gives up the lead just moments later on a controversial play. Buzzing in the Ranger end, the Central forwards crisscross in front of Dave Gray and one of them appears to knock Gray over when the puck is still some distance from the goal. Half a second later, a Central player fires the puck into the net to tie the score.

The Ranger coaches are screaming at the referee that Gray was interfered with, and that the goal should be waved off. Arms crossed, ignoring the protests while standing only inches from the Methuen bench, the referee sticks to his original decision. No penalty. The goal stands. Teenage Central fans jump on the glass, heckling Ryan Fontaine and some of the other Methuen hotheads. Five minutes later, the game ends in a 4-4 tie.

The kids are disappointed. In the locker room, a sullen Kevin McCarthy takes off his gear, throws on his street clothes, and leaves without a word. There's some locker banging and cursing. But a tie is better than a loss and this is the first point the Rangers have managed against Central Catholic in five years.

The team rooms and adjacent corridors empty out and Joe Robillard waves goodnight with the phone in his hand, calling the score in to the various newspapers. Exiting through the back door of the school, I can hear the echo of my footfalls on the glazed walkway. The parking lot is deserted and quiet, except for the sound of a compressor on the roof of the ice rink.

My car is one of two still in the lot and beyond it, I can make out the dangling legs of a figure stretched out on the loading dock. Dan Bonfiglio is lying there with his balled-up jersey for a pillow, staring at a vast field of stars. We talk for a moment and then I leave him alone, with his thoughts and his memories.

Certainly two of the things Bonfiglio is thinking about are the goals he allowed on consecutive shifts to start the second period, and his as-yet-unrequited pursuit of Emily.

Wearing Bonfiglio's dark blue Ranger jersey and singing in her clear operatic voice, Emily opened the evening's festivities with a warm rendition of the "Star Spangled Banner," but left the rink on the arm of her boyfriend. It's been an emotional night for the 17-year-old Bonfiglio, not all of his feelings happy ones, and as I drive away, I recall a few bad goals I allowed so many years ago, and my adolescent longing for a certain dark-eyed cheerleader who I dated during my senior year. This remembrance sends a bolt through my chest. But thinking of young Bonfiglio and the chances he has left, I'm glad that I've been here to experience all this and how it's provided a sweet reassembly and wringing of my heart.

32
FORGET CAGLIUSO

THE ANNUAL BLUE/WHITE SCRIMMAGE TAKES place on the last jayvee practice day of the season. One tradition that has continued from year to year is Jon Morin and Dave Martin appearing as goalies, allowing their young charges the opportunity to fire pucks at them. After eleven weeks of drills and sprints and locker room push-ups, the jayvees hurry into their equipment, giggling at the prospect of their coaches standing between the pipes.

I've been invited to play in the game and Jon Morin and I are pulling on our gear while some of the varsity players linger after practice to gawk at us. "You guys are looking at Mr. Morin and Mr. Atkinson getting dressed like they're exhibits in a zoo," says Tim Parker to a cluster of his teammates.

"Or a museum," I say.

Jon Morin takes the ice first. During the warm-ups, Becky Trudel is in street clothes by the rink door, watching her coach impersonate a goalie. "Where's Coach Morin's weakness?" I ask her.

Trudel grins. "Everywhere," she says.

I'm playing right wing on a line with sophomore Matt English at center and Paul Sullivan at left wing. We have an abundance of chances around the net in the first few moments of the game and

Morin frustrates us, cackling behind his mask. English and Sullivan are both smooth skaters, and Sully is an intelligent passer so I get a couple of shots right away. Positioned behind the net, Sully threads a short accurate pass between a mass of skates and I'm able to jam a backhand inside the left post for a goal.

"Nice work, Sully," I tell him, as we glide back to center ice for another face-off.

After that, it's mostly the kids whizzing up and down but I have my moments. While attempting to screen Morin and getting my ankles chopped in the process, I step away just as a shot whistles toward us from the point. Morin saves it and I skate in, pick up the rebound and shoot, straight into the goalie's pads. On the second rebound, I gather the puck again and find a seam just beyond Morin's right skate and bang it into the net.

"Aaargh," says Morin, scrambling to keep his balance.

"Gotta work on that stick side, Coach," I tell him, skating away.

On the bench, I lean over and ask "Tibber" Thibodeau what my defensive zone coverage is when I'm on the weak side. The 15-year-old center explains how my responsibility extends from the hash marks on the face-off circle to the slot on the inside. "If the puck's in the far corner, help the defenseman double team the man in front and then release to the boards when we break out, Mr. Atkinson," Tibber says, making a gesture with his gloved hand.

Considering that my body will eventually shut down, and much sooner than I'd prefer, it's a pleasure to curve and stutter and jangle over the ice, sweeping the puck along, left to right, in and out, operating on intuition rather than will. The entire game is an improvisation, and I move from here to there before I know I've done it.

The two-hour session concludes with a penalty shot contest and I have a chance for a clean breakaway against Jon Morin while the jayvees watch from center ice. I recall a goal-scoring tip I received during an alumni game several years ago, from teammate Gary Ruffen: "Put a deke on the goalie about fifteen feet out, then shoot. Because if you're in too close and there's a rebound, you'll overskate it."

Now, taking my penalty shot against Coach Morin, I make the exact same move I made during the 1987 alumni game. The arena is silent as I skate toward the puck and feel its weight on the blade of my stick. Morin is fifty feet away, his eyes riveted on me as I gather speed and bear down on him. I pass my stick blade over the puck while looking at the top right corner of the net, and in the same stride, I fire a shot low to the opposite corner, right along the ice. The puck rings off the far post and slides into the goal, exactly as it did in this same rink, thirteen years ago.

Circling the net, I can't resist a double pump with my arm as the kids shake their heads in wonder. "Wow, Mr. Atkinson scored," says Matt English, a polite kid with an altar boy's face.

Afterward in the skate room I thank Jon Morin for the privilege of playing in the game. "My pleasure," he says. "Except for the two times you beat me."

I hold out some fingers. "Three. But who's counting?"

A short time later I run into athletic director Brian Urquhart in the rink lobby and he asks me how the game went. Counting the alumni game, I now have five goals and three assists for the Rangers, in just two games. "We should do something about that gray hair," says Urquhart, pointing to his temple but meaning mine. "And suit you up. Forget about Cagliuso."

Playing without Cagliuso, the Rangers have won only once in their last three games. Compounding the situation for tonight's game versus Lowell High are the other two regulars missing from the Methuen lineup. Sophomore James Girouard is out with pneumonia and defenseman Chris Martin has been ruled academically ineligible for failing three of his major courses the previous semester.

So when Chris Cagliuso walks into the Methuen High rink at quarter to five in the evening, eyes downcast, carrying his blue game jersey in his hand and dressed in plaid shirt, khakis, and a dark suede jacket, all four coaches track his approach. Cagliuso is returning from his final appointment with the orthopedist, and there's hope among the Ranger staff that he's been cleared to play tonight.

"Another week," says the dark-haired senior, who's been advised to rest his shoulder until the conclusion of the regular season. "I feel like I can play right now. That I can protect it."

Jon Morin talks about using Cagliuso only for special situations, power plays, killing penalties, an occasional shift here and there. But the coaches are grim, standing against the cinder block wall in their Ranger jackets, arms crossed, studying the floor.

"If somebody takes a cheap shot, it's all over," says Dave Martin. "We need you for the tournament, Chris. These games don't mean much now."

But Methuen's seeding for the tournament will be based on number of wins and winning percentage, and Robillard is also concerned about his team's late season slide and its effect on their young psyches. The will to persevere in adverse circumstances isn't an easy lesson for a bunch of 15- and 16-year olds.

The bus ride to the Janas rink is short and silent. As we pass the snow-covered tenements and pizza shops of south Lowell, Morin and Martin and I discuss Chris Martin's academic plight and his hearing with Methuen High principal Ellen Parker, scheduled for tomorrow morning. Since I'm in school every day and have discussed the situation with Mrs. Parker, Morin asks me if I think she'll grant a waiver based on Chris's sleep disorder, which prevents him from getting up on time. Young Martin has been tardy twenty-three times in the past semester, causing him to fail the two courses that alternate during the first "block," or class session, from 7:30 to 8:30 A.M.

"I don't think he's going to get a waiver," I tell Morin and Martin. "Maybe, but I don't think Ellen has ever granted one."

Chris Martin is riding in the back of the bus and when we enter the rink lobby at the Janas, I ask him what he thinks his chances are of obtaining the waiver. He's wearing a black fleece vest over his game jersey and a black baseball cap with an orange Japanese character on the front and a New York Mets insignia on the back.

"I got a ninety-five on my math project makeup, and (the teacher) didn't correct those papers until after the term ended, so I got an F," says Martin.

And then he repeats the mantra that I've heard from kids all year, in the field house, the locker room, the hallways, and cafeteria, whenever their behavior, profane language, or in this case, failure to live up to their responsibilities comes around and bites them on the ass: "It's not my fault."

Inside the locker room, Joe Robillard reminds his team that the Janas is a small rink that contains hardly any neutral zone. "The forecheck is the crash," he says. "Don't hesitate, and don't be late. Or we're gonna be giving up two-on-ones all night."

McCarthy, George, Soucy, Gray, and Bonfiglio, hunched over the benches, stare at the slight figure of Joe Robillard in the center of the room. The coach pauses for a moment, searching for the words to convey the message he's been trying to get across all year. How a team has to play with emotion every time it takes the ice, in order to flatten out the bad bounces, the discrepancies in talent, and the uneven officiating that comes to affect high school hockey.

"Lowell wants to show they can play at our level," says Robillard. "Yeah, we're missing a few guys but that's what being a team is all about." He looks around the room. "Get up. Get your hands in here." The boys surge forward. "One, two, three—"

"Rangers!"

The first period is typical of how things have been going without Cagliuso in the lineup. Pinning Lowell in their own end, Methuen generates a whole barrelful of scoring chances but comes away frustrated. Thom DeZenzo fires a shot that ricochets off both goal-posts, and Brian Mueskes, standing alone in the slot, has the puck on his stick and an open corner but shoots it wide.

"We're not the same without Cags," says Coach Harb, leaning to my ear. "No finishers."

In the second period some of Methuen's best scoring chances are foiled by overeager Rangers crashing into each other—on several occasions, all three forwards are bunched up in one corner and the Lowell defensemen slide the puck around to the opposite corner and break out unmolested. This leads to the first goal, when the Red Raiders find great swaths of open ice and score on their third shot after Dave Gray stops the first two.

Cagliuso comes over to the Ranger bench at the end of the period. "We need to think better, offensively," he says, over the glass. "We're just not recognizing what's going on out there."

Methuen finally breaks through in the late going, when DeZenzo takes the puck end to end for a goal and Shane Wakeen's slapper from the right point sneaks through the goalie's pads. But more breakdowns lead to ugly Lowell goals and Methuen is down 3-2 with eight minutes left to play.

All season long, the refereeing has been uneven and some of the calls in the Lowell game are infuriating. During one sequence, a Lowell forward slashes one of our players and since the Rangers have possession of the puck, the referee signals for a delayed penalty. Inexplicably, the guilty Lowell player falls to the ice and writhes in pain. The puck ends up on Ryan Fontaine's stick, and just as he's about to race in alone on the Lowell goalie, the referee spies the "injured" player a hundred feet away and whistles the play dead.

On our bench, Jon Morin clutches his head and says, "*That* is ridiculous."

But the most confounding event of the night occurs over the final eight seconds. Behind by a goal, Robillard pulls Dave Gray for an extra attacker and with the clock winding down all six Methuen players converge on the Red Raider goal. From our perspective on the bench, the net is obscured by wiggling arms and legs and flailing sticks. Suddenly Kevin McCarthy throws his arms in the air signaling a goal, there's a whistle, and confusion reigns. The clock shows two seconds remaining and although the Rangers are celebrating, the referee is shaking his head and pointing to the nearest face-off dot. No goal.

"I am one hundred percent sure that's a goal," McCarthy will tell me later.

In the midst of all those crashing bodies, McCarthy noticed the puck lying beside the goalie's skate along the goal line. Thrusting himself forward, he used his stick like a pool cue and knocked the puck over the line in plain view of the referee.

"It was six inches over the line, and since there was no whistle yet, Dave [George] poked it all the way to the back," says McCarthy. "Then their guy knocked the net off its moorings and the ref blew the whistle."

We lose 3-2. In the hallway outside the locker room, with our players inside reliving those final seconds in tense, excited voices, Jon Morin and I recall Bruce Parker's twenty-five-year-old advice: you have to play well enough to defeat your opponents *and* the referees. If the Rangers had made the most of their chances, the game wouldn't have been at stake with a few seconds left.

Tim Parker is the last player in the locker room. Hurrying into his jacket and boots, he grabs his equipment bag and slams through the door. Parker hasn't participated in the postmortem of tonight's game, and from beneath the brim of his cap, he says, "I hate losing, but I hate bitching about it even more."

33
THE HATFIELDS AND THE McCOYS

DURING THE LAST BLOCK OF the day, I'm working out with Joe Robillard in the fitness room above the old bus loop. At one end of the narrow, windowed space are two sets of Olympic weights, a brand new Smith machine, and two combination bench/squat racks; farther on, there's a set of adjustable pulleys, four racks of dumbbells, and the creaking wires and plates of a Universal machine. Beyond that are wrestling mats and then half a dozen stationary bicycles, two recumbent bikes, and two computerized treadmills. It's an exercise facility to rival those at local colleges, and Robillard and I chat about the hockey season while taking turns with a set of 30-pound dumbbells.

Tonight there's a spaghetti dinner at Ryan Fontaine's house in east Methuen, and Robillard is explaining the relationship he maintains with his players' parents. Because it backfired earlier in his career, when some parents assumed that cozying up to Robillard would mean more ice time for their kids, he stays away from the families during the season. In fact, during jayvee games, Robillard stands at the far end of the rink, so he can watch his younger players without being lobbied by their fathers.

Robillard says that he's been called aloof and uncaring, but that every year during his remarks at the winter sports banquet, where all the players and their families assemble, he makes his priorities clear. "I tell them that, most of all, I'm here to look after their sons, and that's what I try to do," he says.

That night, sitting at a long table in the Fontaines' skylit, contemporary home, Robillard and Joe Harb and I finish our pasta while members of the team play video games and miniature floor hockey in the family room downstairs. Liam is down there with them, and I can hear the trembling pitch of his voice above gales of teenage laughter. It's a lark for him, a real pageant of sights and sounds amid the smell of homemade tomato sauce, but there's fatherly intention that underpins our evening with the Fontaines. These are some of the most motivated, high-achieving kids at Methuen High and Liam has been granted a junior membership in their fraternity, at least for tonight, and as he goes over his hockey cards with Dan Bonfiglio and banters with towheaded Thom DeZenzo, he's discovering something about masculinity and a larger sense of family that he'll never learn anywhere else.

Kevin McCarthy is at the table with us, sipping a glass of cola, and overcomes his shyness long enough to ask Robillard about college hockey and prep school, two subjects that are on his mind. Robillard says that if Big Mac keeps improving this year and next, he should have no trouble gaining admission to a superior prep school. After the postgraduate year, he'll be able to attend a college or university where he can play hockey and get a good education.

"At a place like Babson, where Coach Morin went, you play hockey and have some fun and really learn something," Robillard tells the earnest McCarthy, who sits across from us, studying the tablecloth. "Because let's face it, a very small number of kids get to play Division I college hockey and very few of those turn pro."

McCarthy nods his head. From downstairs I can hear Liam squealing with laughter and Ryan Fontaine laughing along with him, and it occurs to me that if Kevin McCarthy's mom and dad were here, I know what I would say. I'd tell them that Joe Robillard is looking after their son.

Before practice Chris Cagliuso surprises Robillard by appearing in the corridor outside the skate room dressed in full equipment, minus his shoulder pads and jersey. Bound across his left shoulder with an Ace bandage and strips of athletic tape is a disc of half-inch polyurethane fashioned by trainer Kevin MacLennan. This extra pad and its strapping are meant to hold Cagliuso's inflamed joint tightly in place.

Robillard beams at the sight of his prized forward ready to play again, but he pulls down the corners of his mustache and runs Cagliuso through a battery of questions: How sore is the shoulder? Do you have a full range of motion? Can you take a body check? How much strength do you have?

"Enough to play," Cagliuso says.

Coach and player stand next to the door that separates the warm envelope of the corridor from the chill of the rink, teetering on their skates. Robillard takes off his Ranger baseball cap, scratches his head, and replaces the cap. "I'm only going to use you in special situations," he says. "Power plays, killing penalties—whenever there's extra room on the ice. If there's no problems, I'll throw you out for the odd shift. But there's one thing: stay out of the corners." Realizing the futility of this advice, Robillard amends it. "When you get in there, throw the puck around the boards or out front. Don't hold onto it. That's how you got hurt."

Cagliuso is nodding. With his head angled downward, he says "Yeah, yeah" to every point that Robillard makes—anything to get back on the ice. Especially for the Andover game.

If class struggle can be embodied by an athletic event, Methuen-Andover represents the townies versus the preppies, the old-fashioned savings account pitted against the diversified investment portfolio, and a pork pie from Thwaite's versus a croissant with apricot preserve. The two camps are easily identified: peacoats and work boots on one side, fleece tights, designer skiwear, and furs on the other. Although the economic lines have blurred in recent years, "Me-too-en" against "Ahn-dovah" still means blue-collar grit versus finishing school grace.

Today's game is being played at the old Frost Arena in south Lawrence, the site of my first organized hockey games when I was 13 years old. The decrepit old barn has been renamed in recent years and renovated from top to bottom. Shiny "flex" glass and a raised surface that's as hard and fast as any ice in the valley have replaced the rickety boards and puddles of my youth.

But the Frost still smells the same. Coming in through the lobby there's the familiar odor of Zamboni exhaust and ancient refrigeration coils, layered with the scent of popcorn and sizzling triangles of pizza. As I follow the varsity up the elevated ramp toward the locker rooms, an old Led Zeppelin song booms from the Andover side of the hallway. The Methuen guys are teasing Jeremy Abdo about his narrow chest, and somebody ahead of me kicks open the steel door and we all pile into the dank little room.

"Andover's in there getting jacked and listening to music," I say.

Tim Parker throws down his equipment bag. "And we're talking about Abdo's nipples," he says.

"Only in Methuen," I say.

For some reason, Dan Bonfiglio loves this topic. "Nobody has nipples like Abdo. It looks like he has black Magic Marker around them," says the goalie. "Shane Wakeen has all-American nipples."

"Sorry, fellas, but this is not appropriate conversation for a men's locker room," I say, and the players break up laughing.

Conversation shifts to the topic of Albert Soucy's father, Gerard, who earlier this morning lost the tip of his finger in a snowblower accident. Down the bench from Bonfiglio and Soucy is Chris Cagliuso, half-dressed, bitching about the Andover trainer who stands outside our locker room, waiting to wrap Cagliuso's shoulder.

Soucy looks at me and winks. "If Cagliuso was royalty, he'd be the world's biggest pain in the ass," says the sturdy little winger. "Prince Cags."

The coaches enter the locker room as game time approaches, and Jon Morin wants to know whose bag is obstructing the door. "I'll give you a hint: he's short and friendly and his dad has no middle finger," says Thom DeZenzo, and laughter echoes in the high, tin-ceilinged room.

"My dad is tough," Soucy says. "He didn't even care."

Robillard comes to the center of the room and says that, for Andover, this is a championship game. The "fictitious Golden Warriors," as Soucy calls them, must defeat Methuen to tie for second place in the league, thus qualifying for the state tournament.

Albert Soucy's comment about the Andover mascot reminds me of two-fisted Methuenite Robert Rogers and his Rangers. In his 1760 manual of guerrilla warfare, Major Rogers says that your enemy should be forced to attack, "in the face of constant fire." When hostilities are at hand, he advises his Rangers to "meet them in some narrow pass, or lay in ambush to receive them." Here in the confines of the locker room, the Rangers look like they're making ready for battle.

"There's something my dad used to tell me when I was small: 'whatever you can do, I can do better,' " says Robillard. "We have to have that attitude tonight. If a guy knocks you on your ass, get up and get right back in his face."

Dave Martin goes out and returns a moment later to say the ice is ready. The stands are crowded and the atmosphere is cold and tense and thrilling. Andover circles the near end of the rink, looking big in their gold jerseys and blue helmets. Methuen's warm-up looks tepid, and Robillard has one foot on the bench and the other on the dasher, yelling at his team to skate harder.

Early in the game, Andover scores two quick goals during a nightmarish sequence and the period ends with Methuen down 2-1. Robillard stuffs his team into the locker room and begins dissecting the Rangers' most glaring weakness: lousy movement on their power play.

"We've been on the power play, what, seventy-five times this year? If they shut us off down low, work it up high," says the coach. "Another saying I live by, it's not how you start, it's how you finish."

Dave Martin is bouncing off the walls. Since his son Chris has been ruled ineligible, there's been a marked drop-off in physical play, especially among the Ranger defensemen. Chris isn't very big, but just like his father he's a banger, with good anticipation on the ice and heaps of physical courage. No one has really stepped up during Chris Martin's absence and Methuen's opponents have been allowed more room to maneuver in the offensive zone.

"This is a simple game, but we try to make it complicated," says Dave Martin, his voice rising. "Throw the puck in, chase it, and then bang their defensemen. We're gonna make it like a pinball machine out there." He smacks his fist into his open hand and paces up and down in front of the loaded bench. "Bang, goal! Bang, goal! Knock them into . . . into . . . pulverization."

Ryan Fontaine sits barechested, without his shoulder pads and jersey. His face is contorted and red, and he's clawing at the bench as Martin goes past him. "I want to see these pussies with tears in their eyes after this game," says Fontaine. "Let's make 'em cry."

Methuen scores the only goal of the second period to tie the game up. "After we beat 'em, they're not gonna be too happy," says DeZenzo on his way off the ice.

"First we gotta beat 'em," Dave George says.

Feeling the game in the balance, Robillard hearkens back to the Rangers' best effort of the season. "Remember how we played against Billerica?" the coach asks. "I wish we could bottle that somehow. We have to play like there's no tomorrow. Just like Andover is playing."

Each team scores a goal in the opening minutes of the final period, then Methuen forges ahead with ten minutes left. Andover is frantic, taking huge chances in the neutral zone and pressing hard for the equalizer. A tie won't help them; they need at least two more goals and a victory to enter the state tournament.

With the seconds ticking away, Eric MacDonald intercepts a pass at center ice and darts into the Andover zone. Waiting for a screen of players to develop in front of the net, MacDonald unloads a forty-foot slap shot that slides into the open corner for a 5-3 Methuen lead. Our bench erupts, and next to me Jon Morin lets out a huge "Yeahhh!"

Andover's goalie, a senior and one of their captains, skates over to the bench and throws his stick and gloves against the wall. Flopping over the boards, he kicks his feet against the aluminum outer wall of the rink and the sound echoes throughout the building. The Rangers laugh at this tantrum, and Fontaine flips up his cage and begins to skate toward the Andover bench.

Robillard barks at him: "Ryan. Have some class. Winning or losing, have some class."

Methuen adds a late goal, and the ride home is a brief and jubilant one. While Tim Parker eats a bag of candy in the seat opposite me, bus driver Chuck Trudel tunes the radio to a classic rock station and Parker and I sing along to an old Grass Roots number. "Sha-la-la-la-la-la, live for today, and don't worry 'bout tomorrow, hey, hey . . ."

34
SHOOT-OUT

FRESH OFF THEIR BIG WIN over Andover, the Rangers are scheduled to play Amesbury the next day, in the first round of the season-ending Newburyport tournament. The bus ride from Methuen High is a solemn one, gliding past the gingerbread cottages of West Newbury, alongside tidal pools that are choked with ice and cornfields buried in snow. The tournament is played at the Graf rink in Newburyport, Massachusetts, and the principal topic among the Methuen coaches is the location of the Alden-Merrill cheesecake factory.

"Are their cakes any good?" asks Paul St. Louis, sitting in the row behind us.

In the locker room after the Andover game, some of the Rangers, as part of their celebration, asked the heavyweight St. Louis to "do the bagel." Reluctantly, the shy, bespectacled defenseman stood up, lifted his sweat-soaked T-shirt and made a circle with his hands around the excess flesh surrounding his navel. Ever so briefly, a bagel seemed to emerge from the folds of St. Louis's stomach as the boys roared.

Today, Coach Morin only chuckles. "No cake for you, St. Louis," he says.

Lugging his equipment from the bus, Dan Bonfiglio, who's

scheduled to start in goal against the "Fighting Indians," wants to know if I have exposed my nipples in the past twenty-four hours.

"Yes, but it was a private moment in a strictly heterosexual context and I cannot possibly discuss it with you," I tell him.

Bonfiglio grins. "That's awesome," he says.

The Rangers look a little tired before the game, but they're loose. After all, Amesbury has won only three games all year, while Methuen is headed for the state tournament with double-digit victories. When the game begins, the Rangers look sleepy and slow, like they're skating in oatmeal. Hemming Methuen in their own end, the white-shirted Fighting Indians besiege the Ranger net and pop in an early goal. But talent begins to win out, and Ryan Fontaine contributes two heads-up goals and Methuen leads 2-1 after the first period.

"Good teams come to play every game," says Robillard in the locker room. He speaks in measured tones, looking each player in the eye, always teaching. "We didn't come to play today. Show some heart in this next period or we're going to be in trouble."

Jon Morin pokes his head in the locker room and motions for me to come out. Down the hall, Amesbury's young, first-year coach is halfway through a profanity-laden tirade. In a minute or so, the red-faced coach exits into the corridor, followed by his two assistants. "Was I wrong to say that?" he asks a paunchy fellow wearing a Fighting Indians windbreaker.

Speaking so only I can hear, Jon Morin replies, "Yes." Back in our locker room, Morin says, "The guy's a lunatic. Referees, other coaches, and parents have complained he's dropping f-bombs all over the place, every game." Robillard has overheard just enough of the other coach's rant to form an opinion. "The kids'll stop listening to that after a while," he says.

In the second period, the Rangers take a 3-2 lead but miss a hat full of chances. Albert Soucy's shot nicks the goalpost and bounces wide, and Eric MacDonald snaps off a rocket from fifteen feet that's aimed into the goalie's glove. A few times the puck is lying near the open half of the Amesbury net and the Rangers are too casual to fire it in.

"Hopefully that doesn't come back to haunt us, like it has in other games," Robillard says on the way back to the locker room.

The Rangers slump over the benches, glassy-eyed and spent. They've played seventy-five minutes of varsity hockey in less than twenty-four hours, and even stalwarts like Dave George and Kevin McCarthy are exhausted. While the Amesbury coach rattles and booms from down the hall, Robillard is patient, trying to illuminate what lies ahead.

"We should've had four more goals and buried them," he says. "I don't want to run into you in six or seven years and you wish you did it differently. It's up to you guys. You can be a very good club. I've seen it. But it's all in your attitude."

The Rangers buzz the Amesbury net to open the third period, hungry for that backbreaking fourth goal. Then, on a harmless breakout down the far boards, one of the Fighting Indians takes a shot from long range that eludes Bonfiglio and finds the back of the Methuen net. The Amesbury kids celebrate right in front of our bench, and one by one the Rangers' heads go down. This single moment reveals how immature the team really is: no one gets angry, no one jumps over the boards for the next shift with flames in his eyes. Within minutes, Thom DeZenzo will jam his right shoulder and leave the game, and Chris Cagliuso will argue with the coaches about his decision making during a power play—while the clock is running and he's still on the ice. The Rangers collapse, losing 5-3.

If the bus ride to Newburyport was somber, the trip back to Methuen is downright funereal. Sitting by himself, Robillard writes down the statistics and then gazes out the window, no doubt pondering how his hockey team could be so terrific one day and terrible the next. He says only one thing, just as the bus pulls into Ranger Road.

"We started out 7-2, and we've gone 3-6-1 since then. Shame on us."

Although Methuen has already qualified for the state tournament, in many ways the Rangers' entire year is riding on the regular season finale against the Wilmington Wildcats. Methuen's play of late has been inconsistent and lackadaisical, and Wilmington is a tough, physical club, much like Tewksbury, not very gifted offensively, but relentless and hard skating. The Wildcats are 14-3-3, seeded number 2 in Massachusetts' second division, and a poor effort in this game will no doubt crush the ambitions of the talented but mercurial Rangers. They need a boost.

Robillard has his team dressed in the home whites and crowded into their locker room in Newburyport's Graf arena. "When you put on that sweater, you represent yourself," the coach says. "I would think you'd want people to see you out there and say 'Look at that number 17. He's hustling. He's everywhere.' "

Methuen's number 17 is Chris Cagliuso, who will take a regular shift for the first time in almost four weeks. Third line center James Girouard has also returned, looking pale after his bout with pneumonia but determined to play. The only regular not dressed is Chris Martin, sitting beside Dave George in his street clothes. The gritty defenseman is now officially out for the season, his petition denied by Methuen High's principal Ellen Parker.

Pacing the locker room, Robillard says, "We haven't played three periods of hockey since Boston Latin, and that was January tenth. This isn't youth hockey, where you just pay your money and go out there and fool around. This is high school. Get yourself noticed out there."

When Robillard ducks out of the room to confer with the game officials, some of the younger guys horse around, throwing balls of tape and talking in loud voices. His bad shoulder strapped in tightly, Cagliuso bangs his stick against the matted rubber floor. "This team kicks our ass every year, so I don't know why anybody's laughing," he says, and the room falls silent.

In the opening minutes of the game, the Wildcats swarm all over Methuen, pinning them in the defensive end. Dan Bonfiglio makes several nice stops, keeping it scoreless, and at one point Dave George shows me a nice deep cut on his wrist, from a Wilmington slash.

"Suck it up," I say to him. "If it was easy, everybody'd be doing it."

Finally, Methuen responds to all the body checking with a little chippiness and grit. Twice James Girouard takes a run at Wilmington's captain and the second time, his aggressiveness begins a chain reaction that culminates in a scoring chance for Jeremy Abdo. The rubbery sophomore, closing on a loose puck near the Wilmington net, weaves and wangles through a maze of crashing bodies and feathers a soft little backhand shot between the goalie's feet. Methuen takes a 1-0 lead into the intermission.

Bumping along the corridor to the locker room, some of the players are complaining about the shenanigans that the Wildcats are getting away with, particularly in the neutral zone. "The referees are not calling any of the hacking and holding—they're letting you play," says Morin, his voice rising above the din. "So move the puck along. If you try to stickhandle through the neutral zone, you're gonna get knocked on your ass."

"At least when they hit you, you're hitting them back," says Joe Harb. "Keep it up. One goal isn't going to win this game."

Harb's remark is prophetic. In the second period, Methuen's failure to cash in a few scoring chances combined with inopportune gaffes prevent the Rangers from adding to their lead. First, Albert Soucy uses his speed to break down the left side but then misses the open half of the net. "Alby can't put it in the ocean right now," says Robillard, on the bench.

Just seconds later, Abdo scoops up another loose puck and is frustrated at the last instant by the diving Wildcat goalie. Methuen is awarded a power play shortly thereafter, and only seconds into the man advantage, Thom DeZenzo commits a senseless penalty at center ice and the teams are even again.

"Stupid," Robillard says.

Playing four on four now, Methuen makes a soft clearing attempt and the Wildcats intercept. Throwing the puck at the net, they converge on goalie Dave Gray and knock a rebound over his shoulder for a goal. Less than a minute later, one of their forwards takes a wide-open shot from the right circle and they score again for a 2-1 lead. Hearts sink along the Methuen bench.

But just as he's done all year, Kevin McCarthy ignites another spark in the Rangers. Hustling the length of the ice, McCarthy pressures a Wildcat defenseman, steals the puck, and breaks through the slot at top speed. With one defender hanging over his back and another chopping at his ankles, the hard-charging wing veers toward the Wilmington goal, angles left, and as the goalie thrusts out his stick, tries to throw the puck into the upper reaches of the net. But McCarthy's feet get tangled up in a bundle of sticks and the puck slides out of reach and the buzzer sounds, ending the second period.

The locker room is quiet, but it's not the morgue-like stillness that Joe Harb and I have noted throughout the year. There are some pissed-off faces around the room, and as the players drink from squeeze bottles and adjust their skates and equipment, I look over at Harb and he winks at me. For once, there's a little testosterone in the air.

Ryan Fontaine is sitting in the corner, his head down, strangling the top of his stick. "I liked it better when we were fuckin' winning," says the plug-headed winger. "Losing sucks."

Out in the corridor, Harb pushes me sideways and we chuckle at Fontaine's speech making. "I'm going to war, I want Ryan Fontaine," I say to Harb.

The big guy nods. "Fontaine and McCarthy and Dave George," he says.

All year long, Robillard has been pleading with the Rangers to shoot the puck. No fancy stickhandling or behind the back passes, just plain, old-fashioned blurry rubber. Most of Methuen's goals this season have been ugly: chopped-in rebounds, weird deflections, seeing-eye shots that found a tiny hole and rolled in. But the kids are still trying to make that extra, nifty pass or execute the drag-and-kick maneuver in heavy traffic, and this defiance of the hockey canon has driven Joe Robillard insane.

One kid who listens is Eric MacDonald. And with half the third period gone and the Wildcats playing with even more authority, a seemingly harmless play unfolds in front of the Methuen bench. MacDonald is skating through center ice while the other Rangers are in the midst of a line change. Cutting off a passing lane, he intercepts the puck and skates it toward the Wilmington net. MacDonald is alone: there are two defensemen in front of him, and another Wildcat hacking at the back of his legs. Crossing the blue line, he raises his stick and attempts to unload a slap shot.

At the same instant, Jeremy Abdo comes off the ice clutching his right hand. He throws his glove down to reveal a bright red egg that is already appearing between the bones of his index and middle fingers. Robillard turns for a quick look at Abdo's injury.

MacDonald's shot rises off the ice, accelerates at a fantastic rate, and on its way past the stiffening defenseman, nicks the underside of his stick. This infinitesimal deflection immediately puts a funny action on the puck: it dips, spins, turns sideways, and slows its course through the air. The Wildcats' goalie, heading in one direction, suddenly goes flatfooted and freezes like a statue. MacDonald's shot drops, sinks some more, and then rises a bit and flutters beneath the goalie's left arm and into the net. A fifty-foot butterfly of a goal.

Robillard has missed it but hears the whoop of the crowd and the joyous profanity from his bench. "Who scored? Eric?" he asks. He cups his hands and shouts at MacDonald over the noise. "That's *it.* Shoot the damned puck."

Momentum swings the Rangers' way. After Dave Gray makes a nice save, the Ranger defense swings the puck around the boards to the weak side and Cagliuso and his wings break it out, through center ice, wheeling into the offensive zone. For nearly a minute they keep the puck in Wilmington's end, working it through the two face-off circles, shooting at the net, and recycling their own deflections back to Thom DeZenzo at the point.

With less than two minutes to play, Kevin McCarthy is trying to gain possession at the left post when he is tackled by two Wildcat defenders. Although the referees have called very few penalties tonight, it's such blatant interference that both officials signal immediately. As soon as a Wilmington player touches the loose puck, whistles blow and Methuen gains the man advantage for the final ninety seconds of the game.

Robillard calls a time-out and sends his power play unit over the boards: Cagliuso, MacDonald, and Fontaine up front, with McCarthy and DeZenzo at the points. We pass the water bottles to them, and while the crowd swoons around the perimeter and Kid Rock blasts from the rink loudspeaker, Robillard stands with one foot on the boards, gesturing his team in closer, beneath all the noise.

"Eric, you and Chris work it down low," says Robillard. "Take your time: don't force it. If there's nothing there, send it up high. All we need is one good shot."

The referee blows his whistle and signals a face-off in Wilmington's end. There's 1:24 left in regulation and the score is 2-2. Quickly I add up the tiny X's on my stat sheet and calculate that Wilmington has outshot us 37-12 so far. For the first time all year, the Rangers are in position to defeat one of the Merrimack Valley powerhouses. And they've managed it through a combination of physical play, good goaltending, opportunistic scoring, and plain old good luck: everything they'll need in the state tournament when it begins next Saturday.

Methuen's final power play of the regular season is a study in patience and precision. MacDonald quarterbacks the offense from his usual position along the half boards: sometimes throwing the puck high to DeZenzo, other times slipping it around the curve of the boards to Cagliuso, who's dangerous on the wraparound. The objective is to collapse the box formed by Wilmington's quartet of penalty killers, opening a lane from one side of the rink to the other, giving the off-wing an open net to shoot at. Fontaine is the off-wing. He glides back and forth at the bottom of the left circle, mostly ignored, lurking about fifteen feet away from the Wildcats' goalie. With an uncontested pass, Fontaine can't miss from there.

But Wilmington is a disciplined team. Even with Cagliuso cycling down low, trying to draw two defenders and then bank it to MacDonald for the cross-ice pass to Fontaine, the Wildcats' box only sags for a half-second and then pops back into place. Finally, by sending the puck on a diagonal to McCarthy at the left point, the Rangers crack the box. McCarthy looks to his right at DeZenzo, fakes a pass in that direction, and then slips the puck down low to Fontaine before the defenseman can shift over. Fontaine collects it and bulls straight for the net.

Three defenders converge on him as Fontaine blasts a shot from ten feet out. The goalie flops down and stops the puck, but Cagliuso gathers the rebound on his backhand and swerves around the fallen goalie and the wriggling mass of bodies encircling Fontaine. There are less than fifteen seconds left in the game.

Angled sharply over the ice, the puck clinging along the edge of his stick blade, Cagliuso maneuvers outward and past all the obstructions and then musters himself to throw the puck toward the open side of the net. Just as he releases the shot, the Wilmington goalie executes an unorthodox body roll and collapses into the gap as the puck slides beneath him toward the goal line. His body weight and the force of gravity drop him straight onto the puck and prevent the goal, while Cagliuso maintains his feet and digs at the goalie's chest with his stick, inciting a near-riot as two defensemen crash into him from behind. Time expires from the clock.

Since this is a tournament game, the referee skates over to both benches and reminds the coaches that there will be an overtime "shoot-out." Five players from each team are selected and sent over the boards. Dave Gray remains in one net and the Wildcats' goalie in the other. Alternating between the teams, each of the players is awarded an uncontested penalty shot that begins at center ice. It's hockey distilled to its purest form: shooter versus goalie, dekes and fakes and flying pucks matched against steadfastness and anticipation.

Wilmington goes first. While the remaining snipers sit on the boards, the referee places a puck on the red center dot and blows his whistle. The Wildcat player takes a skating start, collects the puck at high speed, and bears down on the Methuen net. Gray is fifteen feet out, deep in his crouch, intent on the mesmerizing action of the puck. Crossing the blue line, the Wilmington ace fakes back and forth and then darts at the net and snaps a shot off. Gray slides to his right and stops the puck with his leg pad and knocks it away.

0-0.

The Methuen shooters are MacDonald, Fontaine, McCarthy, Girouard, and Cagliuso. MacDonald leads off. Racing through center ice, with complete authority he closes in, fakes left, and scores going to his right. Gray stops the next Wilmington shot and Methuen has the early advantage.

Fontaine's next. He heads straight at the goalie and snaps a low wrist shot at the corner. The goalie saves it. But Dave Gray frustrates the next Wildcat by stacking his pads and sliding out to block yet another steaming drive.

With half the shoot-out remaining, the Rangers lead 1-0. Using the same move that failed in regulation, McCarthy bores in on the Wilmington goalie, shifts to his backhand, and thrusts the puck straight over the goalie's shoulder into the top of the cage. It's a real goal scorer's goal and provokes an "oooh" from both benches and the crowd.

If Gray can stop the next Wilmington attempt, Methuen wins. The Wildcats' tall, rangy forward, who scored the second goal in regulation, carves the puck from the face-off dot and glides toward the Ranger net. Deking to his forehand, the Wilmington player shoots from close range and Gray snaps his right arm downward and appears to trap the puck against his body. But the drive wiggles under his arm and rolls into the net. The Wildcats are still alive.

James Girouard can finish Wilmington off. A little washed out from his illness, the sophomore glides in, tries an inside-out move, and fumbles the puck away. The shoot-out stands at 2-1 for Methuen with one player remaining from each team. Gray looks huge in the Ranger net, nimble on his feet and soaring with confidence. When the final Wilmington shooter tries to fake him out of his crease, the Ranger goalie keeps his eye on the puck, mirrors the other player's footwork, and knocks his shot away. Methuen wins.

"Yeah!" says Robillard, pumping his fist while the bench erupts around him and half the spectators inside the Graf leap up shouting. "We need that. We need that."

The Wilmington coach shuffles over the ice to shake hands with Robillard. "I hope we don't see you again—until the state finals," he says.

Robillard throws his head back, showing all his teeth. "Yeah. See you there."

35

A VIGIL

THE RANGERS' MAIN GOAL this season was to play hockey in March and they've achieved that—in more ways than one. Six varsity players have been selected to the league all-star game: Chris Cagliuso, Thom DeZenzo, Kevin McCarthy, Ryan Fontaine, and both varsity goalies, Dave Gray and Dan Bonfiglio. Under the bright lights of the Chelmsford Forum, the six Rangers, lustrous in their home whites, are introduced alongside the best players from regular season champs Boston Latin, as well as Lincoln-Sudbury, Haverhill, Westford Academy, and Andover.

At one point, Methuen has five players on the ice against the Greater Boston League all-stars: Cagliuso between Fontaine and McCarthy, DeZenzo on defense, and Bonfiglio in goal. Early in the game Cagliuso makes a beautiful wraparound pass, feeding Lincoln-Sudbury's Keith McGilvray for a goal at the left post and the Merrimack Valley all-stars are on their way to a 7-0 laugher.

During a ceremony between periods, Methuen players Cagliuso and DeZenzo are named to the even more select All-Conference team. It's a night for celebration and giving thanks for such a strong season, and the athletic display by the Methuen kids bodes well for the state tournament. But while standing in the packed grandstand, cheering the shutout goaltending appearances by Gray and Bonfiglio, I'm approached by a Ranger parent who informs me that 44-year-old Horace Trovato, Jarrod's father, is gravely ill with a brain tumor at Holy Family Hospital. He's not expected to live more than a few days.

Although we only spoke once, over spaghetti at the DeZenzo's, I feel like I know Mr. Trovato because of Jarrod. He's a quiet, steady kid with more than his share of backbone, so that's what his father must be. Hearing the news about Mr. Trovato's relapse, a lump rises in my throat and I promise to mention him in my prayers.

When practice resumes the following Monday, Thom DeZenzo, who grew up among the Trovato children and considers them a second family, is out of action, keeping vigil at the hospital with Jarrod and his older brother Jason. DeZenzo's absence subtracts from an already weakened defensive corps. Matt Mueskes is out with the flu, Paul St. Louis is getting his wisdom teeth removed, and Chris Martin remains ineligible, despite several late appeals by his parents.

In the corridor outside the skate room, Joe Robillard has been absorbing and synthesizing the grim reports about Mr. Trovato. There's a pall over the rink, the joy of making the playoffs eclipsed by sympathy for a teammate and, for most of these teenagers, fear of the unknown. James Girouard pauses outside the skate room for a moment to tape his stick. "I'm hoping for a miracle," says the baby-faced sophomore.

Robillard nods but doesn't respond. He knows better than to encourage any false hopes in his players. When Girouard departs, Robillard drapes his whistle around his neck and puts on his baseball cap. "It's only going to be a day or two," he says.

Several players take the ice early and the boom of pucks off the boards echoes throughout the lower school. Freshman Drew Soley, a rangy, likable kid, has been called up to bolster the defense. "I haven't skated in a week," he says. "I went away over the vacation."

"You're not supposed to go away during the season," I say to him. "Where's your team spirit? Where's your discipline? Don't be the guy with million-dollar feet and a ten-cent head."

Soley giggles, looking at me through his cage. He skates off.

Nearby, Girouard is fooling with a puck alongside the half boards and Kevin McCarthy glides past. "Hey, Kev, you wanna see my new move?" Girouard asks.

"No."

"Good, because I ain't got one."

Dressed in his gear but without his helmet, Dan Bonfiglio reports that after two blissful dates with Emily she has rejected his offer of a prom date and reunited with her old boyfriend. "I just said, 'Uh, okay.' What could I say?"

"Just play it cool," I tell him, drawing on years of intense training in these matters. "Nothing interests a woman more than polite disinterest."

Bonfiglio starts his warm-up routine and Joe Harb comes on the ice in his blue windbreaker and baseball cap. We've just learned that Methuen's first-round opponent will be the seventh-ranked Danvers Falcons. (Almost all of the top seeds are from our region. If Methuen, ranked number 10, had won more games, we'd be seeded higher and would open up against a lower-ranked team.)

"I'm not so much worried about them as about which team shows up for us," says Harb. "You never know what to expect with our guys. But they give you hope."

Harb skates over to a loose puck and takes a long slap shot that sails half the length of the rink and finds the net. He raises his arms in mock celebration.

"Mr. Harb, that's the first puck you've put in the net for, I don't know how long," says Ryan Fontaine, leaning against the boards.

Harb smiles at him. "I want to play against your line," he says.

"I don't think you're ready for that," Fontaine says. He shakes his head and laughs.

Thom DeZenzo returns to practice the next day. While the players dress, DeZenzo answers a battery of questions from Fontaine, who occupies the locker next to his. The senior defenseman explains that he and Jarrod and Jason Trovato, DeZenzo's defense partner last season, have slept in the Holy Family chapel the last two nights, keeping vigil at Mr. Trovato's bedside.

"We were in there when they took him off life support," says DeZenzo in a subdued tone. "He dropped real bad, in everything, but then he came back. For the past few days, the doctors have been saying that he's gonna die in the next two to three hours."

"So he's being strong, then," says Fontaine, naming the quality that he admires most.

DeZenzo presses his lips together and shakes his head. He doesn't want to spread any rumors of a miracle comeback by their teammate's dad. Across the locker room, Bonfiglio and Gray and Soucy and Cagliuso are engaged in routine banter: bra sizes and bodily functions and who's taking whom to the prom.

Ryan Fontaine sits motionless for a few seconds and then looks at DeZenzo again. "Remember last year, when Jay [Trovato] found out about his dad and was crying? I said something to him that I shouldn't have."

"Like what?"

"I don't know. I don't remember. Something like, don't be a baby, or something. But I didn't know what was going on, then."

DeZenzo doesn't reply at first, bending over to tighten his skate laces. Finally, he straightens up and looks over at Fontaine while pulling on his shoulder pads. "Don't worry about it," he says.

But Fontaine is lost in regret, his expression a mixture of sadness and mortal dread. "I feel real fuckin' bad about that," he says.

Dave Martin has been working twelve-hour days for two weeks, covering a large area as a "trouble man" for the electric company. When he finally returns, in his trademark overalls and decrepit Rangers jacket, the players take a few digs at my old teammate.

"Nice of you to show up for practice once in a while, Coach," says Dave Gray, smiling inside his mask.

Martin whacks Gray with his stick. "If I need any shit from you, I'll squeeze your head," he says. "If you guys weren't so good, we'd be done by now. Instead, I have to coach for free all week."

"Two weeks," I say, indicating the length of the state tournament. "I stand corrected: two weeks," Martin says. Dan Gradzewicz skates by, and Martin hails him. "Hey, chubby, how you doin'? Bet you missed me. Missed me like a bad dream."

It's the last week of practice before the tournament, and the captains are staying on top of their younger teammates. Paul St. Louis is manning the point for the three-on-three drills and he shoots the puck wide on consecutive chances.

"Hey, Paul, get it on net," DeZenzo yells to him. "You're the biggest guy out there."

"It ain't how big you are," says Joe Harb.

Martin nods. "It's what you got here"—pointing to his heart—"and here"—indicating his balls. "That's the whole game, right there."

One guy who has heart and balls and gives his best every time he steps on the ice is unheralded star Kevin McCarthy. Robillard has juggled his lines in search of scoring balance and for the first time all year, McCarthy will not skate with Cagliuso and Fontaine on the premier line. Instead, he'll team up with Eric MacDonald and the slumping Albert Soucy on the Rangers' second, or "blue" line.

Large and square-shouldered in his equipment, McCarthy skates over to me and stops with a tiny hiss from his skate blades. "Mr. Atkinson, did I get dropped to second line to even things up, or because I'm not playing well?" he asks.

I don't want to overstep my bounds, and I know from teaching that you should always be careful what you say to a kid—no matter how much chin stubble he has. "It doesn't mean you're not playing well, Kevin," I tell him. "I think it has more to do with spreading out the scoring. But go talk to Coach Robillard. He'll tell you straight."

McCarthy looks at the patch of ice beneath our feet. "Thanks. I will."

That night, Liam and I enter through the back door of the rink, descend the stairway beside the skate room, and emerge in the Ranger field house. All around us, the grandstand is packed with rowdy young fans. Methuen's opponent for the opening round of the Boys' Division I state basketball tournament is the Beverly Panthers.

Playing at home against a lower seed, the Rangers shake off their early butterflies and pin a huge loss on the outmatched Beverly squad. The atmosphere is big-time: cable television, WCCM Radio 800, and a handful of newspaper reporters and photographers are covering the action. Liam and I sit with Joe Harb and we spot several hockey players in the crowd: Dave Gray, Dan Bonfiglio, Chris Cagliuso, and right after the final buzzer sounds, Kevin McCarthy.

McCarthy is dressed in the standard off-ice uniform of scuffed brogans, cargo pants, plaid cotton shirt, a small gold hoop in each ear, and a black baseball cap pulled low on his forehead. Methuen has prevailed by a score of 80-55, and while the Ranger basketball players and Coach Jim Weymouth form a joyous pig pile in the background, McCarthy ambles over, hands in his pockets.

"How do you like that, Kev?" I ask him, pointing to the Ranger bench while he slaps hands with Liam. "That's going to be you on Saturday."

"Win big?" he asks.

I nod at him over Liam's wide-eyed, angelic face. "Get it in your head starting right now. You deserve to win, and you will win."

36

THE PEP RALLY

IN AN ARTICLE PUBLISHED IN the *Salem News,* the coach of the Danvers Falcons boasts that he has the "nine best forwards in the division" and that Methuen is a "scrappy team that plays physical" but isn't very talented.

This sort of press jockeying is foreign to a guy like Joe Robillard. After reporting the contents of the article to his staff, Robillard says that the Danvers coach is "kind of cocky" but that he plans on ignoring the comments. But Joe Harb sees the posturing as a way to motivate the inconsistent Rangers. Raised with the smashmouth instincts of a football player, Harb can't wait until he has the Methuen forwards gathered at one end of the rink while Robillard is busy working out the goalies at the other end.

"Can you believe this shit?" asks Harb, his eyes bulging from his skull. "Danvers has the nine best forwards in the state?" The husky young coach indicates Chris Cagliuso and Kevin McCarthy and Ryan Fontaine with the heel of his stick. "What does that make you—twelfth? Fifteenth? Sixteenth? That's a bunch of bullshit, is what that is. But you only get to show them once. On Saturday."

Practice is spirited and physical, and during the first drill, mild-mannered Paul St. Louis knocks Cagliuso down twice in the span of a few seconds. "Chris, that ice is slippery," says Dave George, and the other players hoot and catcall. Popping to his feet, Cagliuso goes racing for the puck, gathers it in, and fires a shot past Dave Gray. The captain is back. And with ninety-nine points for his career, he's one shy of the mark necessary for the record board, alongside his brother Brett and other old-timey Methuen stars like Gene Patnode and Ken Hewson and Joe Laperriere.

All season long, Dan Bonfiglio has played conservatively, sitting deep in the net even when loose pucks are lying ten or fifteen feet outside his crease. On a couple of occasions, his style has cost Methuen a goal. Today in practice, however, Bonfiglio takes unreasonable chances and on two nearly identical plays, gets beaten by Shane Wakeen when he ventures more than thirty feet from his net.

The second time it happens, Robillard blows his whistle and stops practice. "You can't make stupid plays like that," says the coach, turning red. "Not this time of year."

Robillard sends Gray in and Bonfiglio glides to the boards, his head angled downward. Dave Martin, who considers "keeping the boys loose" his main job, skates over to the embarrassed goaltender. First he puts a gloved hand on each of Bonfiglio's shoulders, draws his round red face to an inch of the goalie's mask, and serenades him with two off-key verses of "Bicycle Built for Two." Despite himself, Bonfiglio starts grinning and Martin beckons to me.

"Mr. Atkinson, did you see that unbelievably fantastic play Danny just made?" Martin asks with a wink.

"Both of them, coach. He hasn't budged from his crease all year, and now all of a sudden he's Gerry Cheevers."

Martin slaps Bonfiglio in the head and smiles at him. "It's all angles, Danny boy. Angles. You good in math? No? You should go to Catholic school, then. They know math. They got that Guy nailed to the plus sign."

On the day before Methuen's state tournament game, Joe Robillard is standing next to Chris Cagliuso in the field house watching his gym class play "foosketball," a strange combination of football, basketball, and rugby. The action drifts to the far end of the court and Robillard clears his throat. "Mr. Trovato died," he says. "Passed away in the middle of the night."

Cagliuso eyes his coach, looks down at the pale blue floor of the gym, and glances away. "That's sad," he says.

"It's a blessing," says Robillard. "He was suffering."

"And the family suffers along with him," says Cagliuso.

Robillard nods. "They do."

For a few moments, nothing is said; only the cries of the foosketball players are heard and the slap of a volleyball from an adjacent court. Death has entered the world of adolescence, and Cagliuso seems to mull over its significance. "At least Jarrod and Jason are old enough to remember him," he says.

"They will," says Robillard, in a soft voice. "But Mr. Trovato was only in his forties. If you're in your sixties or seventies, you've seen something of life." The 48-year-old gym teacher lets out a breath. "At his age, you should have more time."

In various quarters of Methuen High, the hockey players are contemplating their playoff game while grappling with the news of their teammate's loss. During Mario Pagnoni's Internet class, Dave Gray is wondering whether he or best friend Dan Bonfiglio will start against Danvers. "Sometimes we don't know until we hear our names announced," he says.

"Do you want the call?" I ask him.

Gray looks straight at me. "Yeah. I wanna play."

"Does Dan want to play?"

"We haven't talked about it," the senior says. "He got to start last year. But then he got that penalty and I came in and didn't give up any goals and still got taken out." Gray turns from the computer keyboard and looks at me again. "I didn't think that was fair."

"At least you both got to play."

Gray shrugs. "That won't happen this year."

The most ephemeral and intriguing aspect of hockey is its spontaneity; each rush down the ice blossoms into something different, a new constellation of passes and positioning that happens only once and then melts away, like a snowflake. After you've been playing the game for a while you can sense it coming, the right combination of body English and anticipation, your feet and hands moving together without your head telling them what to do.

On the ice for gym class, I've teamed up with Eric MacDonald and Matt Tetreau against three other varsity players in a width-wise game of ball hockey. It's fast and graceful, and thanks to my linemates' wizardry, we're tied 7-7 and I have two goals. I need one more for the hat trick and there's less than a minute remaining in the class.

Tetreau makes a long rapid pass down the middle of the ice that nicks Matt Zapanas's skate blade and seems headed for Paul St. Louis, who is guarding the other team's goal. St. Louis moves for the deflected pass and using the back of my stick blade, I lunge for it and pop the ball over St. Louis's stick toward the corner of the rink. In the same instant, Eric MacDonald wheels to his left, corrals the bounding ball, and shoots a backhand pass behind St. Louis and across the open net. I dart forward and tap it in for the winning goal just before the buzzer sounds.

Skating off, I feel the surge of endorphins in my chest: tiny, euphoria-producing particles, and with a great explosion they fizz in my bloodstream like a million bubbles, exiting through the back of my lungs. A minute later I walk into the varsity room and Eric MacDonald is sitting there on a bench, untying his skates. "Nice," he says, bumping my knuckles with his fist.

"You just made my day," I tell him and MacDonald laughs, revealing his braces. He thinks I'm kidding.

During the last block of the school day, Methuen High's field house is packed with 1,700 students for the annual winter pep rally. Moments before the hockey team is introduced, three tardy Rangers come skidding through the door like comedians in an old movie: Thom DeZenzo, Chris Martin, and Jarrod Trovato. Seeing Jarrod gives me a pang. I tap him on the shoulder and, pitching my voice beneath the din, speak my condolences into his left ear. Within seconds, Trovato hears a half dozen expressions of sympathy and nods and stares at the floor. But then he walks over and joins the sea of white game jerseys and appears to take comfort there.

Chris Martin is standing near the bleachers and I go over and shake his hand. Although I haven't seen him for a week, various last ditch appeals have failed and he remains ineligible for the state tournament. "How are you, Chris?" I ask him.

Martin looks numb, almost catatonic. His face is expressionless and he stares at the far side of the gym. "I don't know," he says.

"How do you feel about missing the game tomorrow?"

He shrugs. "I've missed so many games I don't care."

"You going to practice today?"

"Why? I can't play."

Clapping him on the arm, I say, "The guys would like to see you."

Again Martin only shrugs.

The hockey team is announced and invited to gather at center court. The throng inside the field house cheers, and one senior behind me in the grandstand yells, "Dave Gray is hung like a horse," and a bunch of kids laugh. Leading the team is Matt Zapanas, dressed in a hooded gray sweatshirt and throwing punches at the air. When Zapanas reaches the exact center of the field house and is joined by his teammates, the tall, shy sophomore drops on his chest for a series of theatrical push-ups while the crowd hoots.

"What's got into Zapanas?" I ask Joe Harb, who's bug-eyed. "He hasn't said two words all year."

"Must be the tournament," says Harb.

The entire team is on the ice for practice five minutes early, and Harb nudges me when Cagliuso goes flying past us, his legs whirring. "Chris can move," says Harb. "Look at him. He's psyched."

Robillard enters through the rink door, blows his whistle and gathers the squad in one corner, beneath the clock. "Take a knee," he says. Tim Parker and Albert Soucy are pinned up against the boards and Robillard motions to them with his gloved hand. "You guys take a knee back there." The coach pauses for a moment while they comply. "You all know about Mr. Trovato. So out of respect for him and his family, please bow your heads."

The players, kneeling around the coaches in a loose semicircle, unbuckle their chinstraps and stare at the milky ice. Making the sign of the cross, Robillard says, "In the Name of the Father, Son, and the Holy Spirit. God, we know that Mr. Trovato is with You now, and we hope that You'll look after him and that he will find peace with You. And that Jarrod and Jay and their mum will find peace."

Robillard crosses himself once more, and most of the players follow suit. "In the Name of the Father, Son, and Holy Spirit."

"Amen!"

Surveying the young caged faces of his team, Joe Robillard says, "We have a big game tomorrow. A big game. But this really puts things in perspective, how precious life really is, and how important your families are. So let's go out there tomorrow and be intense. Let's play hard, and then let it go." He raises his whistle and lets out a shrill blast. "All right. Let's go."

37

THE NINE BEST FORWARDS IN THE STATE

TWO YOUTH HOCKEY COACHES set up a folding table on the ice, in front of the grandstand that's packed with eager parents and grandparents. The trophies are a foot tall, with a base of Italian marble and an iridescent column that sparkles in the rink lights, topped by the figure of a hockey player in midstride. Ranged along the boards, the 5- and 6-year-olds in the Learn to Skate clinic send up a great din of chatter, bumping each other with their caged helmets.

Liam skates away from his teammates and hails me. "Dad, are we getting one of those trophies?" he asks.

"You sure are, Boo. But you have to wait your turn. Go stand in line with the other kids."

My son pivots on his left skate and glides away. Now the other coaches are ready and they begin the procession. One by one the players are beckoned from the line and they slip-slide forward to the table of gleaming hardware. The coaches wait alongside and slap hands with each player as he or she skates past. Liam is about halfway back, with twenty or twenty-five kids ahead of him.

Finally he skates forward and since I'm first in the line of assistant coaches, he stops and hugs my leg. "Go ahead, Boo," I say, when he doesn't move. "High five everybody."

Liam's feet are scrambling and he lurches toward the table, his eyes bright with anticipation. But he has neglected to shake hands with the other coaches and is turned back. For a moment he's facing me again. All his disappointments have been forgotten: the crying jags, frustration over not grasping some of the drills, his inability to skate backward. For twenty-eight weeks, give or take an absence or two, he has persevered through his first athletic season. The grail is within reach.

Liam is spun around again and heads for coach Pat Hoey, who's handing out the trophies. Hoey bends down and asks Liam his name, so he can announce it to the grandstand. My son is shy and mumbles something below earshot. Hoey repeats the question, straightens up, and says in a clear voice, "Larry Atkinson."

The crowd cheers and applauds. Liam gives Coach Hoey a weird look and then takes the trophy and hugs it to his chest. Approaching the rink door he stumbles but catches himself at the last instant. The trophy is safe.

As he climbs through the door I can hear the metallic chirping of his voice: "Look! I got a trophy."

Later on, the day of the state tournament game versus Danvers, Liam and I join the Rangers for a spaghetti dinner at Priscilla's Restaurant on Pleasant Street. Dave Martin arrives a few minutes after us and, while concealing something behind his back, approaches Liam's chair.

My son has just rolled his meatball onto the floor and has tomato sauce on his shirt cuffs and smeared around his lips. Seated all around are Albert Soucy and Jeremy Abdo and Ryan Fontaine and Dan Bonfiglio and the rest, Liam's heroes, and he's as happy as a kid can be.

Martin pats him on the shoulder and using a French Canadian accent, he says, "You like hockey, eh? Here's something for you." From behind his back, Martin produces a dark blue hockey jersey with red and white stripes. "This is the real thing, eh? With the strap on the back to keep it on during a fight. But real players don't fight, eh? They skate."

Liam takes the ream of fabric into his hands like it's a rare and valuable garment, the apparel of kings. His face is aglow, and he's stunned into speechlessness.

"What do you say, Liam?" I ask him.

My son gurgles and sputters. "Thanks!"

Coach Martin helps him pull on the jersey, which hangs down to his knees. The teenagers sitting near us smile at Liam and turn back to their platters of spaghetti. "Come on, Boo. Finish your lunch," I tell him.

He holds his hands in the air. "Take this off, Dad," he says. "I don't want to get sauce on it."

Straight from Priscilla's, we head to the Methuen High field house for the Rangers' boys' basketball game against archrival Central Catholic. The Red Raiders have defeated Methuen in all three regular season contests, and more than 2,000 fans have gathered to see if the Rangers can break the streak and move on to the third round of the state tournament. Joe Harb, Liam, and I are standing in the tiny runway outside the boys' phys ed office, dwarfed by the grandstand on either side and accompanied by athletic director Brian Urquhart.

Urquhart commandeers a chair from the end of the Ranger bench and grants my son the best seat in the house—right in the front row, next to hockey players Matt Foley, Brian Mueskes, and Drew Soley. As the field house shakes with cheers and groans and chants, Liam turns around and looks at Joe Harb and me, smiling and pumping his tiny fist.

"He's enjoying himself," says Harb.

"This is heaven for a 5-year-old," I say.

Methuen is leading 43-31 at halftime when Urquhart ducks out of the field house and returns a moment later with a Methuen High basketball jersey in his hand. "It's against MIAA regulations to wear a hockey jersey to a basketball game," he says, winking at me. "Here, Liam. This is for you."

Liam pulls off the hockey sweater and I help him balance the straps of the basketball jersey on his narrow shoulders. "This is great," he says.

Although Central Catholic shaves Methuen's lead to just three points late in the game, six-foot-two Ranger forward Elvin "The King" Reynoso engineers a key sequence when he rebounds a missed foul shot, makes the hoop, and draws another foul to complete a three-point play. Liam and I know Reynoso from his job at the local pharmacy, where the deep-voiced senior always goes out of his way to be nice to my son.

"Yay, Elvin," says Liam, as the pep band starts up and the fans stamp their feet in the bleachers.

Methuen runs off a skein of unanswered points and wins the game 73-61. To stay ahead of the crowd, Liam and I wave to Harb and Urquhart and exit through the phys ed door. Local good guy Elvin Reynoso is the first of the Rangers to leave the court. He runs past us and into the corridor, leaping and shouting. Reynoso stops short when he sees Liam, rubs my son's head, and asks, "How'd you like the game?"

"I liked it!"

Reynoso explodes with joy, his head nearly touching the ceiling as he bounds toward the varsity locker room. "Yeah! Yeah! Yeah. We did it, baby." He glances around. "Where's my teammates?" The King gulps, laughs, whirls in a tight circle, and sprints back to the gym.

Seconds later, the entire team piles into the corridor and senior forward Chris O'Rourke, another of today's heroes, slaps hands with Liam and stands there palming my son's head while he gives an interview to the *Eagle-Tribune.* This is what I've brought Liam to see: the intimate friendships, the bond of teammates, and the possible results of commitment and sacrifice and dedication to a goal.

Hockey player Matt Tetreau passes in the corridor and I stick out my hand and the curly-haired sophomore shakes it. "Matt, tonight's going to be your night," I tell him.

"That's right," he says.

The Rangers are packed into a dimly lit locker room beneath the grandstand at the Chelmsford Forum. The smell of toilets wafts from the tiny bathroom and above us, the muffled shouts and heavy tread of the fans sound like thunder. Dave Gray is sitting in a darkened corner between two girders, baseball cap pulled low on his forehead and arms crossed. His equipment bag lies unopened at his feet even though game time is only twenty minutes away. Coach Robillard has just informed him that Dan Bonfiglio will start in goal against Danvers.

"How you feelin'?" I ask Gray.

"All right."

"You could still get in. If Dan gets hit in the throat during warmups, you'll play the whole game. So think about that. Get yourself ready."

Gray nods, staring at the floor. He's been a steady performer all season, and his play has often been spectacular. The phlegmatic Bonfiglio struggled early in the year, fearful at times of being struck near his pacemaker with a slap shot. Other times he looked distracted, even lovelorn. So Dave Gray got the call.

Only one goalie can play at a time, and coaches put themselves through all kinds of gyrations trying to guess which of their goaltenders might possess the hot hand. During Friday's practice, Bonfiglio was his old self, throwing his pads at point-blank drives, snatching shots out of the air—a total commitment to the puck. "You can tell Dan wants it," Robillard whispered to me. "He wants to start tomorrow." Joe Robillard has a hunch, and the name of that hunch isn't Dave Gray.

Gray directs a brief look straight into my eyes. "I feel like I've earned it," he says.

"It sucks," I tell him. "Take it from a guy who did his share of sitting, and then some."

Kitty-corner across the room, Bonfiglio is wearing his skates, pads, and blue hockey pants topped by a white dress shirt and striped tie. He's an odd sight, his hair now dyed jet black, looking like Businessman Elvis with half a mind to become a hockey goalie.

"Dave's pissed," says Bonfiglio, taping his stick.

"I would be. So would you."

"You talk to him yet?" Bonfiglio asks.

I nod my head. "He wishes you the best. That your heart stops, and he gets to play."

Bonfiglio giggles at this piece of goalie humor. The two are best buddies and their friendship will no doubt survive.

On the other side of Bonfiglio is Chris Cagliuso, scanning the locker room for a hint of what's to come. "I wonder which team is going to show up for us—the one that played tough against Billerica or those other guys," he says.

"You're the captain. Go around to Abdo and Zapanas and Gradzewicz and tell 'em what you expect," I tell him.

"They don't listen to me," says Cagliuso.

"They'll listen to you tonight," I say. "You're the horse they all want to climb on."

A tournament official calls Robillard outside and while Joe Harb stands guard near the door, a gleeful Dave Martin extracts an ancient, dilapidated piece of paper from his wallet and announces to rookies and veterans alike that he'll now read an inspirational poem entitled "The Creation of a Pussy." Around the room, the players begin clamoring for Martin's time-tested oration and laugh at all the familiar, salty verses.

When he's through, Martin pounds his fist against an open palm and raises his voice. "That's what we're gonna do tonight, gentlemen," he says. "We're gonna slit 'em and slam 'em and screw 'em and smell 'em."

"Smell 'em?" asks Bonfiglio.

"Shut up, Bono. You know what I mean," says Martin, and the boys roar.

Tim Parker is worked up. Usually steady and philosophical before and after games, Parker's eyes are gleaming and the willowy senior pounds the butt of his stick against the concrete floor. "This is what we played all that youth hockey for, guys," says Parker, conjuring up the hours spent together in chilly rinks since they were all toddlers like Liam. "This is what it's all about."

Each Ranger wears a strip of black tape around his left shin, in memory of Mr. Trovato. Then the players converge in the middle of the room, gloved hands on each other's shoulders, sticks raised in exclamation. Cagliuso is the eye of this storm, his cage unbuckled, embracing his teammates.

"This is our game, this is our time, this is our turn," he yells in a hoarse voice.

"Rangers!"

Most hockey players remember their last high school game. In his senior year, Joe Robillard was playing goal for Burlington High versus Marblehead in the 1968 Massachusetts state tournament. "It was one of those nights no one was going to beat me," Robillard recalled. "I was hot."

Late in the game with the score tied 0-0, Robillard signaled that he needed a time-out to fix a piece of his equipment. Nearby in the face-off circle the referee was holding the puck, ready to start play again. "My pad was off to one side and I said to my centerman, 'Danny, I need a minute,' " said Robillard. "Then everyone's going wild and the puck's behind me, in the net. I never even saw it. There was a quick face-off and boom, it was in. We lose 1-0."

Early in March 1975, the Ranger varsity hockey team finished its inaugural season with a record of 5-15-1. Although our team didn't qualify for the state tournament, the coaches had arranged for us to play a postseason game against Bourne High School on Cape Cod. It was a bona fide athletic road trip, and I was thrilled to hear from Coach Parker that I would start in goal.

We gathered on Saturday morning in the clubhouse at Nicholson Stadium to pack our equipment bags and board the bus. In my mind's eye, I can see the young, anxious faces of my teammates and hear the rise and fall of their chatter. I was sitting in a window seat about halfway down, keeping my own counsel as I thought about the game. Already I was aware that the hockey season was a significant time in my life, and I savored the notion of one more bus trip, the locker room, the warm-ups, putting on my jersey for the last time and playing an entire game.

The bus remained in the parking lot for almost an hour. Finally Coach Parker emerged from the clubhouse and mounted the grooved silver steps of the bus, wearing his Ranger windbreaker and smoked glasses. I remember the expression on his face, aggravation mixed with chagrin; he walked halfway down the aisle and stopped beside my seat, announcing that there was trouble with the ice surface in Bourne and the game was cancelled. He said he was sorry.

We groaned and complained and dismounted the bus, going off to do whatever teenage boys did on Saturday mornings in the spring of 1975. But I couldn't help feeling, as I drove away with my crew of Rick Angus and Gary Ruffen and John Sabbagh and Dave Hewson, that I'd been shortchanged one game in my career. And from then on, for twenty-five years now, I've played game after game after game, playing each one as though it were my last.

The grandstand is crowded on all sides and the music from the loudspeakers is overwhelming. The Danvers Falcons share Methuen's colors of royal blue and white, and in their home white jerseys, warming up at the near end, they look impressive. Several of their players are the size of college kids, and Robillard says, "We have to move our feet tonight."

The Rangers certainly move their feet on the first shift, Cagliuso and Parker and Fontaine buzzing in the corners, pinning Danvers in the defensive end for nearly a minute. Fontaine outmuscles both defensemen behind the net and slides the loose puck to Cagliuso, who unleashes a quick forehand shot that the goalie pounces on. It's an auspicious beginning and Coach Martin is leaping on and off the bench, pounding the forwards on the back when they come off.

He grabs Fontaine by the earhole of his helmet. "You're too busy talking trash out there. Talk to your teammates," Martin tells the pugnacious winger. "Tell 'em where you are. Make the game easier."

Five minutes later, Fontaine is back in his usual spot, creating a ruckus in front of the Danvers net. Cagliuso throws a pass out front that Fontaine chops at, roofing it over the goalie's shoulder into the net. We're up 1-0, and the boys are going crazy, hanging over the boards and screaming.

"One goal isn't going to win this game," Robillard tells the young players on his bench. "Let's get to work out there."

Soon after, Danvers ties the game with a power play goal. But a shift later, while attempting to clear the puck out of their zone, the Falcons' defense abandons Cagliuso in front of the net and the puck caroms to him. The high-scoring center throws a head-and-shoulders fake on the goalie, slips to his backhand, and thrusts the puck inside the post for a nifty goal. Cagliuso throws his arms toward the rafters and goes running across the rink on the tips of his skates.

Escaping the first period with a one-goal lead while being outshot by the opposition grows more likely as the clock ticks down. But Danvers finds one of their sharpshooters alone in front of Bonfiglio and with a single sweep of his stick, the score is tied 2-2 when the period ends.

In the locker room, exhausted by his triple shifts, Thom DeZenzo sits in a pool of sweat, his face blanched white in the dimness. Any doubts concerning his toughness and grit are being erased by tonight's effort. "Horace Trovato came to every one of our games in the last five years," DeZenzo says to his teammates. "And this fall he couldn't come anymore, he got so sick. But Horace is up there watching us now. Let's win it for him. Let's win for Horace."

As much as Joe Robillard has tried to spread out his talent, distributing the Ranger firepower over all three lines, when the game is tight he relies on his top players to produce goals. Halfway through the second period, with the score tied, he begins double-shifting the white line, sending them back out every two minutes or so. "If you're a guy not having a good night, forget about it," Robillard tells the players left on his bench. "You're gonna be the hero."

Albert Soucy hangs his head. My son's hero has not had a productive year, and tonight he's struggling with the puck and losing his man on defense. "That's you, Albert," I tell him. "Stick one in, now."

A couple of minutes later, Cagliuso carries the puck from the corner to the middle of the right circle. With a defenseman on his back, he snaps a low forehand shot that rings off the near post and falls dead on the goal line. Barreling in, Fontaine pokes at the puck and jams it into the net just before being knocked flat on his back. He celebrates the goal by waving his arms and legs like he's making a snow angel. Again Methuen seizes the lead, 3-2.

On the ice, Ryan Fontaine is an irritant, an agitator, and an instigator. At 8:47 of the second period, the referee catches Fontaine hooking an opponent with his stick and whistles him off for a ninety-second penalty. During the Falcons' man advantage, Bonfiglio makes three wonderful stops, including a cherry-picking glove save from in close that hushes the crowd. Robillard was right: his two-time all-star is filling the cage tonight.

The Rangers kill off Fontaine's penalty. When his time in the box runs out, the crazy winger bursts over the dasher and catches up with a loose puck near the Danvers blue line. With two defenders in pursuit, Fontaine races toward the Falcons' goal and wrists a shot into the upper portion of the net for a 4-2 lead.

Now the referee is waving off the goal. According to the rule book, when Fontaine exited the penalty box near center ice, he was required to "tag up" in his own end by first retreating over the defensive blue line. Robillard and Martin agree on that. What confounds them is that the referee did not blow the play dead as soon as Fontaine touched the puck. It's almost as if the rule occurred to the ref after the puck went into the net.

Immediately after Fontaine's goal is disallowed, the Falcons score again from a scramble in front and the second period ends, 3-3.

After going with five all year, Robillard is down to three healthy defensemen and two of them, Matt Tetreau and Shane Wakeen, are sophomores with no playoff experience. In the locker room, DeZenzo and Wakeen stare at the wall like zombies; at least one of them has been on the ice at all times.

"Come on," says Cagliuso, looking around the room. His helmet is at his feet and his short dark hair is shiny with sweat. "If you call it quits here, you'll call it quits the rest of your life."

"Fuck them," Fontaine says. He's having a career night, with three points already and no sign of letting up. "I want to hear every one of you guys say 'fuck them.' "

With encouragement from Cagliuso, the Rangers go around the room with Fontaine's mantra. When Matt Tetreau doesn't say it loud enough to suit his captains, Cagliuso rears up and fires his helmet at the sophomore's feet. "Louder, Tetreau," he says. "I want to hear it."

Bonfiglio is sitting next to me, bulky in all his gear. Amid the ruckus, he says, "Freak them" in a low voice, and then laughs. He's having a great game, the black dye from his hair streaking his face. Goalies are different.

Just 1:12 into the third period, Danvers picks off a weak clearing shot in the Ranger zone and converts the miscue into a goal for the 4-3 lead. Immediately their play grows more physical, even desperate, and although some of the body checks appear to be illegal, the Falcons' size and strength begin to wear down Methuen's best players. Cagliuso and Fontaine and MacDonald and DeZenzo and McCarthy are all targets, and one by one they get knocked down in open ice. This, in turn, fuels the catcalls and screams from a large contingent of teenage fans behind the Danvers bench. For long stretches of time, the Rangers don't even muster a shot on goal.

While working the puck behind the Falcons' net, Kevin McCarthy is hammered from behind and his head rebounds off the glass with a sickening thud. A moment later, he comes off the ice on shaky legs, his eyes vacant and staring. "You all right, Mac?" asks Dave Martin, grabbing the forward's gloved hands and looking into McCarthy's eyes like he's a punch-drunk boxer.

"I'm all right, Coach," says the winger. But his jaw is hanging open and his eyes are glassy.

Robillard remains imperturbable although the din is rising around him. He whistles his line changes with increasing frequency, and at one point he leans over to me and says, "Last night in my head I had it 5-4, us, in overtime."

Methuen gets a huge break with just under two minutes to play in the game when a Danvers player is penalized for tripping. Robillard sends Cagliuso, Fontaine, MacDonald, McCarthy, and DeZenzo over the boards and signals for a time-out. People in the crowd are hollering and screaming, and raucous music booms over the PA. Robillard motions Bonfiglio to the bench and leans into the huddle of players.

"Eric and Chris: work it down low. Be patient. Let's get a good shot," Robillard says. He points to his goalie. "Danny, if we don't score right away, watch me when the clock gets under a minute. I'm going to pull you."

The Rangers mash themselves forward, covering Robillard's bare hand with their gloves. "Let's go," the coach says. "You know what to do."

Bonfiglio winks at me. The referee blows the whistle and orders a face-off in the Danvers end. The Rangers control the puck. Cycling in the far corner, Cagliuso and MacDonald take turns setting up along the half boards. They have three options: work a give-and-go between the two of them (the play that led to the first goal), free DeZenzo at the point, or find a lane across ice and slide it to Fontaine in the far circle. Intermittently, Fontaine raises his stick high in the air signaling that he's open, but each time Cagliuso or MacDonald attempts to feed the puck across it gets poked back into the corner and they have to scramble to regain control.

There's under a minute to play in the game. Waving frantically,

Martin calls Bonfiglio off the ice and Robillard sends Dave George over the dasher to replace him. "C'mon, Chin," says Harb. "Get tough in there."

Wild-eyed, his stick trailing behind him, George races through neutral ice toward the middle of the fray. The Falcons sense the open net at the other end of the rink and are desperate to control the puck. But Dave George's presence gives them another body to cover in front and Methuen continues to work the perimeter with six on four.

With 28 seconds to play, his goalie pulled, and down 4-3, Cagliuso tries to walk out of the corner with the puck and squeeze it inside the post. Two Falcons crash into him and he loses possession. The puck squirts away and Eric MacDonald corrals it in front of the Danvers net, slips through traffic, and throws a high backhand shot over a pile of fallen bodies. Everyone in the building is riveted on the puck, as MacDonald's shot hovers like a flying saucer. It appears to hit the net just beneath the crossbar and bounces back out. The Methuen players throw their hands in the air, celebrating the tying goal.

The referees look at each other, at the goal judge beyond the glass—who doesn't switch on his red light—and back at each other. There's no whistle. Play continues.

With the clock ticking down, two of the Falcons break out, chasing the loose puck. Kevin McCarthy pursues, backchecking like a demon. Charging through center ice, he reaches the end boards at the same instant as the Danvers forwards. They collide, and McCarthy falls down. As the puck rolls around the boards, the Falcons' winger kicks McCarthy in the ribs. While lying on the ice, McCarthy slashes the kid across the legs with his stick and the referee sees it and calls a penalty. The remaining Danvers forward collects the loose puck and shoots it into the unguarded Ranger net. There are two seconds left in the game and Danvers is ahead 5-3.

The fans hanging over the glass near the Falcons' bench explode with cheers and insults. Unfortunately, the penalty box is situated directly beneath them and as the referee leads McCarthy over, the Danvers fans begin taunting our player. First the kids in the crowd are yelling at him and McCarthy ignores them. But then something incites the hardworking winger and he opens his cage and stands on the little bench inside the penalty box and starts yelling at them.

"Kevin. Have some class," Robillard shouts across the ice.

McCarthy turns around and appeals with his hands. "They're spitting on me, Coach," he says.

Robillard makes a jerking motion with his thumb, calling McCarthy to our bench. The referee intercepts him on the way out and says, "Get in the box."

"I'm not going back in there," says McCarthy. "They're spitting all over me."

"Get over here, Kevin," Robillard says. The referee says something else but McCarthy can't hear him with all the noise and skates away, toward our bench. Tears are running down his face and the upper half of his jersey is dotted with spit. On the ice in front of us, Fontaine has his helmet under his arm and is looking over at the taunters with his eyes bulging. I nudge Robillard's arm.

"Fontaine looks like he's ready to pop," I say.

"Ryan. *Ryan.* Get over here," says Robillard. "Get on the bench."

The game ends. The Falcons form a jubilant pile on top of their goalie. He's made a total of seven saves. At the other end, Bonfiglio has stopped twenty-seven shots. He bangs through the side door and joins the rest of the Methuen players stumping toward the locker room. Bonfiglio is crying and just inside the dank, shadowy room Dave Gray embraces him. Within days, Bonfiglio's left arm will swell up and turn purple and he'll be rushed to the hospital where doctors discover a large blood clot near his pacemaker. After dissolving the clot with blood-thinning drugs, the doctors tell the "good son" that he can never play hockey again.

By the door a tournament official is congratulating Joe Robillard. "You can always count on Methuen to play hard and play with class," the man says.

Shortly after tonight's game, the Rangers will win the James F. Mulloy Ice Hockey Team Sportsmanship Award handed out by the Massachusetts Interscholastic Athletic Association and the Massachusetts State Hockey Coaches' Association. In a sense, this award will allow Chris Cagliuso to reach one of his preseason goals: the plaque is presented to Methuen's tri-captains at the FleetCenter in Boston prior to the state championship game.

When the official departs, Robillard looks around the locker room and sighs. "I don't know what I'm doing wrong," the coach says. "I'm a good Catholic."

The Methuen players shed their equipment and Robillard keeps it brief. He surveys the ring of solemn young faces and says, "You left it on the ice. Danvers beat us, that's all. They had some good forwards." For a moment, the coach struggles with his emotion. "I appreciate your efforts for me this year. You younger guys, work hard this summer and make yourselves better hockey players."

Chris Cagliuso goes around the room, shaking hands, joking with his close friends on the team. His career is just beginning and he's relaxed, almost beatific. Next year, Cagliuso will attend Phillips Exeter Academy and then move on to college hockey. And since he has figured in all three goals tonight, he finishes his career at Methuen High with 102 points. Cagliuso's place on the board in Methuen High's rink is now guaranteed, right below his older brother Brett.

Tim Parker has just played his last varsity hockey game. Although he's toyed with the idea of enrolling at tiny Daniel Webster College in order to continue playing the sport, he's decided to attend the University of Massachusetts Lowell, where he'll study engineering. The River Hawks boast a Division I program, and with his ten career points, "Bobo" Parker won't be playing there.

He packs his equipment slowly, the last player to leave the bowels of Chelmsford Forum. Parker zips up his bag and looks around the darkened room, a faint smile on his face. Then he stands up, slinging the awkward bundle over his shoulder. Referring to his departed teammates, he says, "I guess I'll see these guys in the over-30 league."

38
REQUIEM

SUDDENLY WINTER IS OVER. Gliding along East Street toward St. Monica's Church, I ease my car into the cortege of mourners for Horace Trovato's funeral. From St. Basil's seminary to Pollard's Funeral Home, the storm drains are running in a chorus. Green cardboard leprechauns and glossy shamrocks adorn the windows of neighboring homes, and although the grass of the churchyard is brown and withered, tightly rolled buds have appeared on the oak trees and only small patches of snow remain in the shadows.

The new St. Monica's is the size of a cathedral, smelling of new wood and incense, and a large congregation has gathered beneath its laminated big top. Dressed in a gray suit, black turtleneck, and cowboy boots, Dave Martin is alone in one of the pews adjoining the main aisle. I nod to some acquaintances and take the seat next to him. Within minutes, Coach Robillard and the varsity hockey team join Martin and me. The players are nearly identical in their khaki pants, pressed white shirts, sneakers, and ties, as they genuflect and cross themselves and enter the pews until two entire rows are filled up. The sound of organ music swells the air.

Six pallbearers roll Mr. Trovato's coffin into the church, where it's covered with a snow-white pall and left before the altar. Father Dave Keene, a young, dark-haired priest who's new to Methuen, opens the Mass and the assembly lapses into the familiar, comforting rote of standing, kneeling, sitting, and reciting prayers. Across the nave of the church, Jarrod Trovato and his mother, Joan, and older brother Jason gaze over the bier at Father Keene, their faces contorted with grief. From the choir bay, a female soloist performs "Ave Maria," her soprano rising toward the vaulted ceiling of the church.

Attending Mass is the peg that secures my week, but the Catholic funeral service bends outward to include more arcane rituals than that of the daily liturgy. Assisted by a lector, Father Keene circles the coffin with a brass censer on a chain, praying in Latin and dispensing incense that settles over the pall like dust. I'm somewhat acquainted with these mysteries, but the hockey players are gripping the edge of the pew and staring. Even the oldest among them are reduced once again to children, and the baby-faced contingent, Brian Mueskes and Ryan Thibodeau and Dan Martin, are wide-eyed at the prospects of eternity.

As a young man I saw my share of it, unfair death, sudden death, and lingering ones. And as I grow older there's more, the generation ahead of me, some of my friends, my peers. But in the tomblike silence of St. Monica's there's a message in all this, and if I allow the scene to rush away and just listen, I can hear it. I can hear what Horace Trovato is telling me. *Go down swinging.*

Finally Jarrod Trovato rises from the first pew and mounts the altar, crossing toward the illuminated lectern. In his navy blue blazer and tie and wire-rimmed spectacles, he looks like a young scholar, far beyond his sixteenth year. Standing before the congregation, solemn and clear-eyed, Jarrod removes a small piece of paper from his breast pocket and unfolds it with sure fingers. "My father gave all the love that he possibly could, and I always did my very best to return that love," he says. "I may not have shown it at times, when I was angry or maybe even depressed about something, but deep down, I knew and he knew that we loved each other more than anything and no one could take that away from us. When you lose someone, you never completely lose them. They will always be with you in your heart and in your thoughts. I feel this way about my father, because he was a great, kind, and loving person, and no one could ever be a better father than him."

Sitting to my right, Dave Martin squirms and reddens and coughs into his closed fist. On the other side, Joe Robillard stares at the floor, pinching the bridge of his nose. Several hockey players are crying now, their faces wet, Adam's apples sliding up and down. Jarrod returns to his mother's side and the Mass concludes with the long lines of communion. Shuffling my feet, hands folded, I approach Father Keene amid the file of young hockey players, all of them polished up and smelling of soap.

Matt Zapanas is right in front of me and I hear his "Amen" and then it's my turn and the host disintegrates on my tongue.

We go blinking into the sunlight. On the paved path, Dave Martin clutches my arm and says he'll see me tonight at the rink, our usual Monday night game. The hockey players glide past, splitting into twos and threes as they head for their cars. Several of them stop to shake hands, telling me it's been fun, that it was a good season. Chris Cagliuso pats me on the back and says that if I play my cards right, there might be a Springsteen ticket for me next month. Then he walks away, his image flickering like an old newsreel as the light holds him briefly between the trees.

The lot empties out. For a minute I chat with Cathy Martin about her sons; she's worried that Chris and Dan will falter in school without the discipline of hockey season. Joe Robillard comes over and shakes hands, saying that there's open ice this afternoon and I'm welcome to skate. In fact, I'm free to take part in gym class every day, if I want to. But we both have a sense that something has ended.

Twelve hours later, I arrive at the rink with my gear and dress in the varsity room. One of the guys takes out a small flat stone and begins working on his skate blade. "I lost my edge last week," he says.

"I lost my edge about twenty years ago," says Dennis Dube.

Dube calls me "Guy" and uses a French Canadian accent whenever we play hockey together. During the warm-up, he steps in front of a rising slap shot and the puck hits him above the thigh pad, leaving a round red welt. He limps to the bench, slams the door shut, and takes a seat.

Dube says, rubbing his leg, "Many year we play this game, Guy."

I spit through an aperture in my cage. "Many a fine year."

There's a fast group on the ice tonight and my legs feel good and my vision and awareness seem heightened somehow. On my first shift, the puck comes out from the corner and I score on a one-timer from the slot. Next shift: off the right post and in. Boom, off the crossbar and in. A while later, I dash out from the corner and tip in a slap shot from the right point. Then it's a doorstep rebound, a backhander up high, and through the goalie's pads "five hole." Everything I touch goes into the net.

My teammates leave me alone between shifts, at the far end of the bench. I'm in a trance, staring at the ice. Mike Alianiello heaves himself over the dasher and because we've known each other for thirty years, he sits beside me for a moment. "You're having a banner night," he says.

All I do is nod. In other sports, they call it "being in the zone," but here it's a simple case of puck luck. Sometimes when you're a kid, on a frozen pond or an old rink somewhere, you fall into long streaks of exaggerated ability. The puck slows down and you see where it's going before anyone else does, and every little move you

make has a saintly glow. Eventually the nimbus of light surrounding you recedes and you're ordinary again. But you don't care, because tomorrow you'll come out and play and see what happens. Besides the elasticity in your joints and an abundance of time, most of all you have hope when you're young. There's always another day, another game.

Not so at 42. I know this is a rare occurrence and between shifts I'm numb, trying to stay in that magic place. Late in the game, I score on a forehand drive from the right circle and a rebound over the goalie's shoulder. I miss two chances to score a hat trick on a single shift, but cruise toward the end of the evening with nine goals.

Nine.

Once, playing youth hockey, my best friend Rick Angus scored a goal just five seconds into the game. The teams returned to center ice, the referee dropped the puck and Rick did it again, just ten seconds later. After his third goal, all in less than a minute, Rick appealed to the coach to take him out of the game—it was getting ridiculous.

My night passes swiftly, although I don't want it to end. For these minutes I'm happy, which means I'm temporarily in my life without wanting anything. And over the course of the year, these minutes have added up to hours and I survey just how happy I've been. My son has discovered the game for himself, and I've expended a great deal of energy on this particular sheet of ice.

Sometime after eleven o'clock, the Zamboni machine backs out from its cubby beyond the glass, and its loud beeping resounds throughout the rink. One of my teammates sends a pass through center ice that springs me for a long breakaway. In the background, the shouts of the other players and the clap of their sticks on the ice grow dull and distant. It's so late in the hour that a few players exit the rink before I even get near the beleaguered goalie.

I have a second to think about it and decide to use Gary Ruffen's famous inside-out move—it hasn't failed me all season. I close to fifteen feet and fake a shot to the glove side and then slide a bullet along the ice to the stick-side corner. Just as I begin celebrating, the goalie recovers and flashes out the tip of his right skate and knocks the puck aside. A couple of guys over near the locker room hoot at my last, failed bid, and for an instant my hands tighten on my stick and I jab at the air with the blade. But it's been a great night, and now I have an incentive to come back next year.

AFTERWORD

"CRAZY TRAIN"

BENEATH AN ARMADA OF CLOUDS, I'm driving north, through the cold gray towns and leafless valleys of New Hampshire. November gloom has descended over the landscape, and even six-year-old Liam knows that hockey is in the air. He sits in the back-seat, reading the signs on white clapboard churches and asking where we are headed, whom we are going to see. Chris, I tell him. We're going to see Chris Cagliuso.

A year after their final season, the seniors from Methuen High's 1999–2000 hockey team have moved on to new challenges. Thom DeZenzo and Dave Gray are roommates at the University of Massachusetts Dartmouth. Tim Parker is enrolled at UMass Lowell, along with another Methuen kid named Dan Bonfiglio. Although he never struck up a relationship with Miss Emily, Bonfiglio occasionally receives phone calls from Utah, where his former crush is attending college. Of the five former Rangers, only Cagliuso is still playing hockey. Tonight, he'll suit up for Phillips Exeter Academy, one of the best prep school teams in the country.

The Phillips Exeter roster is loaded with talent. Six-foot three-inch Eddie Caron, recently named the Old Spice athlete of the month by *Sports Illustrated,* is committed to the University of New Hampshire. Caron's linemate, Tom Cavanagh, will play for Harvard next year. (His father, Joe Cavanagh, was a three-time all-American for the Crimson back in the early 1970s.) On his new team, Chris Cagliuso is not the star. But he's still fast and sure-handed, one of Coach Dana Barbin's penalty killers and the left wing on Exeter's third line.

Inside the concrete bunker of the rink, Ozzy Osborne's "Crazy Train" is blaring on the PA and it's strange to see Cagliuso in the maroon and white of Exeter. But he's wearing his old number 17 and during warm-ups it's easy to spot him: the hips canted back, left shoulder drooping, his stick held across his knees like a rapier. Liam and I run into Mr. and Mrs. Cagliuso, and they invite us to sit with them. Jane Cagliuso is a serene, fresh-faced woman, and she smiles when Chris nods in our direction and raises the blade of his stick. "That's as much emotion as you're going to get from Chris," she says. "I hope he plays well."

He does and Exeter wins 7-6, but Chris Cagliuso's role is grittier than the one he played in Methuen. While Tom Cavanagh scores six times, drawing gasps from the crowd, number 17 helps to kill penalties and hustles on the backcheck. Late in the third period, Cagliuso races past the defense and cuts in front and his mother tightens her elbows and throws her hands up like two flags. At the last instant the goalie slides out and knocks the puck away, and Jane Cagliuso says, "Oh." Her hands come down. "Nice try, Chris."

The game illustrates that there's another level of hockey above Chris Cagliuso's, where the players are bigger and faster and heading for the NHL. Afterward, Chris meets his Mom and Dad on the concourse. His hair is damp and he's wearing a RANGER FOOTBALL T-shirt and carrying a pullover embroidered with *Methuen Hockey.* Dressed in team jackets, various college scouts are hovering around the Exeter players and their families. Lately Cagliuso has narrowed his choices to half a dozen schools, including Holy Cross, where his brother Brett played. Although hockey is important, Chris's priority is a good education.

Liam has made fast friends with another little kid and they dart over the concourse with sawed-off hockey sticks. Mounted on the wall are photographs of Exeter teams dating back to 1912. In the early years, Exeter carried only six or seven players. Goalies were outfitted with narrow calfskin pads more suited for cricket than ice hockey, and team managers wore overcoats and homburg hats. In these old tintypes, the eyes of the players are eerie and dilated, like Civil War soldiers. Soon Chris Cagliuso will appear on this wall, among the dashing Exeter stars of the 1920s, the depleted squads of World War II, and the shaggy, gap-toothed behemoths of the 1970s.

Right now he cares little for history. "I hate the food here," Cagliuso says. "Let's get some pizza."

A few hours later, Liam is wearing his pajamas, which are figured with tiny wrenches and hammers and toolboxes. One thing I've tried to teach him is that prayers are a gift you bestow on other people. Liam snaps off the bedside light and asks God to look after his family and teachers and classmates. My son is reduced to a tiny voice in the darkness when he says: "God bless Chris Cagliuso."

Methuen's Santa parade resembles one of the those Soviet extravaganzas from the Cold War: ranks of State Police, Marine Corps and Air Force color guards, SWAT teams, Revolutionary War re-enactors, and other boot-wearing paramilitaries. As yet another piece of hardware drifts past, Liam is trembling with excitement and I shake my head at what has happened to Christmas. Nothing says the birth of our Savior quite like the Police Tactical Command Unit.

After the parade, Liam and I head off for a little shopping. Compared with the drama of its construction, "the Loop" on Pleasant Valley Street is both a curiosity and a disappointment. Methuen's new retail complex is a melange of "superstores" and chain restaurants, with broad, concrete walkways and old-fashioned streetlights.

An inflated peak, like the work of a drunken cartoonist, tops the 18-screen Cineplex. The Loop is supposed to provide a "hometown" feeling, but there's an infuriating generality to the place. This Main Street could be anywhere.

Nearby at Mann Orchards, bright yellow mums line the driveway and hundreds of pumpkins squat outside the farm store. The store is bustling with shoppers, and the robust smell of the apple harvest fills the air. Inside the kitchen, skeins of pie dough run along a conveyor belt, where they are flattened by a roller and cut into one-foot circles. Proprietor Bill Fitzgerald stands to one side, ladling blueberries into a large, stainless steel mixer. We shake hands, and I ask Bill what he thinks of his corporate neighbors across the street.

Fitzgerald adds a generous amount of sugar to the blueberries and washes the mixture down with a sanitized garden hose. "Those buildings aren't meant to last forever," he says. Fitzgerald throws a switch, chopping the fruit into blueberry goo. "Nowadays, developers make their money in the first few years."

As frost gathers on Bill Fitzgerald's pumpkins, things in Methuen are changing. Pleasant Valley Street is clogged with traffic, the Masses at Saint Monica's are standing room only, and while out running I pass two large homes on Baremeadow Street that weren't there last year. Just a few months ago Peter Miville sold the 1859 House, and my old teammate Dennis Dube has relocated to Michigan and is trying out his routine on the ladies there.

"Thirty years from now, the Loop will be gone," I tell Bill Fitzgerald. "Just like the old mall."

In Mrs. Crane's English class, Ryan Fontaine is listening to Mozart and reading a paperback novel. Joe Robillard says that Ryan has matured over the summer, and as one of the hockey team captains, is setting an example for the younger players. Fontaine has a

B average in English and earned a 95 on his most recent test. His hair is buzzed short and he's wearing a maroon pullover and cargo pants, with two silver hoops in each ear. Next week, Ryan will deliver a presentation on the book he's reading. A class handout states that people remember only 10 percent of what they hear and 15 percent of what they see, but 90 percent of what they teach to others. Here in his senior year, Ryan Fontaine is trying to prove that he's a student leader, despite a few rough edges.

An hour later, Fontaine and fifty-two other players show up for the Rangers' first hockey practice of the season. Methuen High's rink has been outfitted with new boards, a fresh coat of paint, and reconfigured locker rooms. This year I coached freshmen soccer alongside Dave Gordon and will be watching hockey from the stands. But Liam and I can't resist coming by for the tryouts and we eavesdrop while Joe Robillard addresses his team outside the locker room. "We got a lot of guys on the bubble," the coach says. "You better impress me, because time is running out."

Becky Trudel is there, with an equipment bag slung over her shoulder. "How you feeling?" I ask her. "Like the number one goalie?"

"Some things I gotta work on." She's wearing an oversize gray sweater with black stripes, two silver studs in her left ear.

"Who else is there?" I ask. "[Dustin] Aziz? The sophomore?"

Trudel glances over at the boys standing beneath the clock and nods her head.

"Time to get competitive," I tell her. "This is your year. He's got two more." Trudel nods again.

In the corridor outside the skate room, co-captain Kevin McCarthy chats about his line's scoring potential, and James Girouard, taller and wider but still wearing his spectacles, asks me for an energy bar. Dave George is leaning against the wall, his arms crossed and a disgusted look on his face. The hard-nosed winger failed English and has just learned that he's ineligible. He can practice with the team, but won't be allowed to appear in any games until the new marking period ends in February.

"Chin, you should be ashamed of yourself," I say, shocked by the news.

He stares at the floor. "I know."

Paul St. Louis walks past in his skates and practice jersey, looking as big as an NFL lineman. Rushing to change out of his shirt and tie, Jon Morin hectors one of the freshmen, and says, "Here we go again." (Recently married, Joe Harb decided to coach football this year and skip hockey, focusing on his snowplowing business.) After hellos and a handshake, Albert Soucy tells me that he was in pain most of last season. In the summer he underwent arthroscopic surgery on his left knee and has been fitted with a special brace that allows the kneecap to track properly. "It feels a lot better," he says, flexing it. Dan Gradzewicz, Matt English, Brian Mueskes, and Matt Zapanas stop by for equipment and Joe Robillard checks their names on the varsity roster: they're all moving up.

On the rink apron, Al Soucy and James Girouard are waiting for the Zamboni to finish its circuit. Soucy looks down the grandstand, spots Liam, and removes his helmet. Using his stick as a cane, he walks toward him over the runner. Soucy reaches down to shake Liam's hand. "How's hockey going?"

"Good," Liam says.

"What number are you wearing this year?" asks Soucy, winking at me.

Liam glances up at his hero. "Sixteen," he says.

Al Soucy wears number sixteen. "That's the way to go, Liam," he says.

The Zamboni disappears through the far wall of the rink, blasting its horn. Soucy unlatches the door, and he and Girouard buckle on their helmets. "Got any pucks?" asks Girouard. "I need a puck."

Soucy hops onto the ice. "First guy on," he says. "Just like last year."

Girouard raises his stick. "Hey, Mr. Bobo," he says. "Watch this."

He rises up on his toes and runs toward the open door, hitting the ice without breaking stride. "Woo-oo," he says. "Feels good."

In the next few minutes, the Rangers emerge from the locker room and take the ice: Matt Tetreau spinning his stick like a baton. Dan Martin and his brother Chris, both academically eligible and wearing Maine hockey jerseys. Drew "Ten Cent Head" Soley. Eric MacDonald, in his mismatched socks. Freshman prospect Corey O'Connor. Brian Bond. Matt Foley. Freckle-faced Jake Cowdrey, whom I coached in soccer. Matt Mueskes, with a little green shamrock on his helmet. Central Catholic transfer Marc Boucher.

Liam sidles over to Jeremy Abdo and Shane Wakeen, who are sitting on the bottom row of the grandstand tightening their skates. My son watches and listens, studying the two players. When they stalk away, Liam imitates their banter by saying, "What's up?" and spitting on the tiles.

Jarrod Trovato comes out adjusting his elbow pads. Nine months after his father's death, the dark-haired junior is even quieter than usual but he smiles at Liam before hurdling the dasher.

Wearing his old lineman's overalls, Dave Martin is the last one out of the locker room. He grins at me and asks, "If we evolved from apes and monkeys, how come there's still apes and monkeys?" Then Martin slams through the door onto the ice, jiggling the piece of rope that closes the latch.

EPILOGUE

"THE PETER PUCK LEAGUE"

January 2002

AT FIVE A.M. ON SUNDAY MORNING Baremeadow Street is dark and empty as Liam and I drive toward the Methuen High rink, gliding along with an old Rolling Stones ballad on the radio. A huge white moon hangs above Nimmo's field and Liam rustles in his jersey and equipment, latched into the backseat.

"It's still night," he says. Liam is seven and in his third year of youth hockey. "I'm not asleep."

We arrive at the high school just as the other kids come trooping in. There's apple-cheeked Connor Donahue and Zachary Spartz and Shane Pouliot and Erek Croteau with his front tooth missing, rubbing their eyes beneath the rink lights and yawning at one another. By quarter to six we're on the ice and the rafters echo with high-pitched laughter and the trilling of the coaches' whistles.

"Peter Puck" is an intramural league for very young players who aren't ready for the rough and tumble of Mites but have grasped the fundamentals we teach in the Learn to Skate clinic. Liam's team, which doesn't even have a name (the kids argue over the relative fierceness of the Mighty Sharks versus the Rink Rats), is decked out in yellow "pennies" worn over their blue Ranger jerseys. Today they're going to play in their first hockey game.

We stretch the kids out and divide them into lines and assign each of the goalies—in full gear, borrowed from the Mite division. The game begins and the kids putter up and down at varying speeds, swatting at the puck as it goes whizzing by. Everyone in the rink is smiling, even the sleepy parents swathed in their overcoats and drinking coffee up in the grandstand.

I don't really notice the first actual shift in Liam's career, since I'm too busy making up rhymes with Tyler Elliott and high-fiving Shane Pouliot and practicing my "face wash" on Dale Armstrong. I skate past a row of eager faces hovering along the dasher and ask the musical question from a popular cartoon series "Who lives in a pineapple under the sea?" and the kids on the bench sing out in unison, "SpongeBob Squarepants!" and everybody laughs. I'm the Dave Martin of Peter Puck, riding my stick like a witch's broom and telling the kids to eat a roll of tape if they're hungry. But then I spot Liam being herded through the door and I reach out and tap gloves with him.

"How was it?" I ask. "Did you have fun?"

Liam scoots along the bench, nodding his cage. "Oh yeah, baby," he says, talking around his mouthpiece. Sitting alongside, Liam's pal Erek Croteau tells him to spell "I-cup" and they erupt in laughter when Liam says, "I-see-you-pee."

It goes like that for an hour and then we're off, crowded into the warm stench of the locker room and the kids are dancing around in their hockey socks and T-shirts, ululating like wolf pups. On the far side of the room, two of the Yameen triplets, Dylan and Nick, strip off jerseys and pads to reveal their pajamas underneath, decorated with tiny zoo animals.

Connor Donahue's father, Mark, a big rugged guy who grew up

in Somerville, Massachusetts, laughs when he sees the Yameens. "That's old-time hockey," he says and we trade stories about midnight wake up calls and sleeping in our equipment. For a few moments I rhapsodize about the smell of brewing coffee and my dad hustling my equipment down the back stairs and the stars gleaming overhead.

"All right," says Coach Donahue, giving me a shove. "Don't get carried away."

On our way out we pass by the Methuen Ranger honor roll, a small glass case where Chris Cagliuso's 102 career points are enshrined in magnetic letters. These days Cagliuso is studying Economics and playing varsity hockey at Hamilton College in upstate New York while Ryan Fontaine is working toward an electrician's license. Tim "Bobo" Parker is entertaining his professors at U Mass-Lowell, classmate Dan Bonfiglio plays guitar in a band called "Fame's Revenge" and part-time student Kevin McCarthy skates for an elite amateur team sponsored by the Lowell Lock Monsters.

The wheel of Methuen hockey keeps turning. A dozen new faces populate the Ranger bench this year and Eric Macdonald and Matt Tetreau, no longer shy sophomores, are the team captains. Senior Jarrod Trovato anchors the defense, and Jeremy Abdo is on the top line. Dave Martin's youngest son, Phillip, who I remember as a squeaky-voiced twelve-year-old, is a freshman now and playing for the jayvees. And my son and his buddies are becoming fixtures at the rink, hailed by Zamboni driver Paul Trussell and Coach Robillard and Jim MacDonald, who's apt to slip Liam a buck when I'm not looking.

In the lobby, Erek Croteau says, "It's getting light out!" and he and Liam and Connor Donahue sprint to the double doors. They raise their sticks at the sun rising over Methuen, and their fathers and I amble along behind, laughing.

ACKNOWLEDGMENTS

I HAVE LONG DREAMED of revisiting the love of hockey I felt as a kid but until I met my agent Neal Bascomb and the fellow who would become my editor, Pete Fornatale of Crown, that did not seem possible. But Neal and Pete's unabridged enthusiasm for a book on this subject made one of my fondest wishes come true. If you see either of these gentlemen in a public house, please stand him to a pint and charge it to my account.

I am also very grateful to Methuen's varsity hockey coach, Joe Robillard. When I first described my project to Joe, he embraced the idea and extended all sorts of perquisites and privileges. He and the other Methuen hockey coaches, Jon Morin, Dave Martin, and Joe Harb, along with athletic director Brian Urquhart and his secretary, Lisa Alaimo, accommodated all my requests and made my return to Methuen High a genuine pleasure. School superintendent Dr. Charles P. Littlefield, assistant superintendent Arthur Nicholson, town solicitor Maurice J. Lariviere, and my old friends, town accountant Tom Kelly and city council chairman Bill Manzi, hastened the official approval of my project and made arrangements with the publishers, which helped a great deal. During the year, I made my headquarters in Methuen High's athletic department, and I'd like to thank Karen McLaughlin, Karen Bergeron, Mimi Hyde,

Kevin Pezanowski, Fran Molesso, Joe Robillard, and Larry Klimas for their hospitality.

Methuen High principal Ellen Parker and secretary Ellen Sicard provided me with insight, logistical support, and loads of encouragement over the course of writing this book. The faculty, staff, coaches and alumni of Methuen High assisted in a number of ways; I especially thank Lynne and Walter Cheney, Robyn Reitano, Anne Marie Desroches, Sarah "Queen of the Birthdays" Field, Dan Herlihy, Doug Hallbauer, Mario Pagnoni, Paul Trussell, Don Dufresne, Roger Fuller, Bud Jennings, Judy Hiller, Anne Eckman, Marilyn Dufton, Donald Smith, James Healey, Dave Whiting, Elaine Crane, Stephen Francis, Officer Jim Mellor, Peter Salemi, Dee Gabryjelski, Tom Hey, Jim Weymouth, Bill Cullen, Dave and Robin Gordon, Patricia Borucki, Tim Kelly, Jean Matthes, Roger Lenfest, my former writing teacher Andrew Melnicki, Glen Gearin, Mike Drouin, and Jane Obshatkin. All the kids at Methuen High were great, and I offer a special thank you to the members of the varsity and junior varsity hockey teams and their families. You are the heart of this story.

I am very grateful to the Fitzgerald family of Mann Orchards in Methuen for their cheerful support, and the unlimited access they provided to the journals and other writings of Charles W. Mann. Historian Mike Hughes, a teacher at Methuen High, contributed invaluable materials and insight into the history of the town, as did the legendary Ernest Mack and Dr. Pete Ford, history professor at Merrimack College in North Andover. I'd also like to thank computer guru David Driscoll, research librarian Debbie Friedman, Dr. James Donohoe, Jane Fletcher, Veronica Gadbois, Dr. Clifford Lewis, Dr. Melissa Pennell, and Pam Kenyon at the University of Massachusetts Lowell. Literary agent Peter McGuigan of Sanford Greenburger Associates and publicist Karen Sheehan contributed valuable advice. Writers Paul Marion of Lowell and Steve Whipple of parts unknown offered their pond hockey memories and several helpful suggestions.

I'd also like to thank Sid Harris and Skip Otto for information and statistics regarding Methuen Youth Hockey. And I'm grateful to my dentist Dr. Brian Mangano; my accountant and C. F. P., Frank Posluszny and Bob Needham, respectively; my attorneys Randy Reis, Fred Nagle, and Linda Harvey; and the girl who cuts my hair, Rachel Demers, for their low-priced psychiatry. You're keeping me in business.

Perhaps most valuably, this book rekindled friendships with my old high school teammates Rick "Stick" Angus, Dave "Nigh" Frasca, "Captain Ken" Schelling, Curt "Heavy Lunch" Goulet, John "Truck" Kiessling, Gary Ruffen, Rich "Dust" Zacharias, Ronnie "Nose" DiCenso, Bob "Face" Daigle, John Sabbagh, Mike "Hibner" Weinhold, Frank "Coma" Mistal, Henry "Blind Baby" Marrone, Art Soucy, Dave "Mole" April, Mark "Gull" Seagel, Bruce Richards, Gerard and Gerald "The Twins" Comtois, Dave "Mon Ami" Hewson, Jeff "Homer" Edwards, and Steve "Skinner" Longtin. See you guys at the rink.

Last, I thank my dear friends and family for their memories, encouragement, and support: Glenn and Marianne Gallant, Jeff Ness, Sean and Deirdre Sullivan, Lawrence Berry, Arthur and Natalie Wermers, Scott and Mary Leonhart, John and Jackie and Jessica and Nick Atkinson, Jack Maynard, Patricia Foxx, Eric Shaw, Jill Atkinson, James Atkinson Jr., Patrick and Deanna Bower, John and Jodie and Matthew and Katelyn Berry, my late parents, James and Lois, and my beloved son, Liam.

ALSO BY Jay Atkinson

A year in the life of a rookie private investigator and the story of a legendary incorruptible cop and genuine American hero.

Legends of Winter Hill
1-4000-5075-8
$24.00 hardcover
(Canada: $34.00)

"Collaring the reader from the start, *Legends of Winter Hill* pushes hard and fast, propelling larger-than-life characters across the page, never loosening its grip, never going soft."

—*Boston Herald*

Available from Crown Publishers wherever books are sold
CROWNPUBLISHING.COM